What Doesn't Kill Us:
My Battle with Anxiety

L. A. Nicholson

This work is a memoir.
Some names of people and places have been changed to protect
the privacy of the individuals.

ISBN: 1-4663-3440-1
ISBN-13: 9781466334403

In Memory of Gwen Tyrie

Table of Contents

Chapter 1
Before and After

Until that Saturday morning, I never knew what people meant when they said an event "divided time". But for years afterwards, I would think of everything in my life as Before and After that phone call.

My sister's voice on the answering machine said very calmly, "We have an emergency". For an agonizingly long time after that I couldn't reach anyone, not my mother, my father, or my sister, Sara. I finally got through to my dad at my sister's house.

My father told me later that he would never forget the sound I made after he told me the news. I learned the origin of another cliche then, as my knees gave way beneath me. My husband came running in, caught me, and caught the phone as I held it out, saying, "Mom's dead. Mom's dead". John took over the conversation in horror, as I got up and ran to the bedroom, where I flung myself across the bed and only thought for an instant before letting myself wail dramatically, "Mom, Mom—no!"

Our four-year-old son was unfortunately left to his own devices as John grabbed me in his arms and said, "I know, I know". In a rage I sputtered, "Somebody killed my mother, and I want a chance at him!"

That was the last time I would feel that particular emotion. The kid who hit my mother was immersed in his own crisis even as I railed at him. He was a 20-year-old from a small mountain community, driving a flatbed truck early on a mild January day, when he was blinded by the sun coming around a curve and suddenly realized he had hit something.

My mother, a 61-year-old third grade teacher, wife, mother, and grandmother of four, was doing her Saturday morning run, facing traffic as she was supposed to. Somehow she failed to hear the truck or realize she would have had to jump into the ditch to avoid its oversized, passenger-side mirror.

The impact fractured her skull, and as far as we know, her death was more or less immediate and almost certainly painless. No one could have retained consciousness after such a blow. The arm of the mirror dented in the door of the truck.

The local sheriff was quoted in the paper as saying that he had never seen a human being as broken up as the driver when he arrived on the scene. That never failed to make me think, bitterly, "except my mother", and yet at the same time, I appreciate that the young man was holding my mother in his arms as she died, just beginning to take in the way in which his life had changed.

In our home in Atlanta, there was a flurry of agonized phone calls; a careful, tearful explanation to my son, and then I found myself, amazingly, packing up for the drive to my hometown. One hour earlier, my mother had been a beautiful, vivacious, kind and funny human being, and now I was choosing what to wear to her funeral. Meanwhile, my friends were lighting up the phone lines sharing the news, discussing what to do, and figuring out who could drive up to see me in the North Carolina mountains. The ones who had experienced tragedy were calling me, while the others sat or moved through their days in a state of shock, wondering what to do. All of them had known my mother, and they knew what we had lost.

I didn't call my stepfather just then; my mind reeled at the thought of facing his pain. Henry had never been an easy person to get to know, and in his individual, quirky way, he loved my mother like I have never seen a man love a woman, before or since. However, I steeled myself to call him once we got there, and for some reason I felt the need to go to their house on the day she died, even though we would be staying with my sister.

Before we left Atlanta, John fixed himself a sandwich, and I was sitting on the kitchen counter talking in a stream-of-consciousness kind of way. At one point I noticed he was crying, and I felt both surprised and guilty, as I had thought only of my own grief, and his role of comforting me. "Oh!" I said, "You're sad, too!" and I ran over to hold him.

The six-hour trip to Blue River seemed like an eternity. We stopped at a breakfast-style restaurant partway, and I ordered toast, bacon and tea—comfort food. The mentally handicapped busboy looked at me with a grin and asked, "Are you makin' a bacon sandwich?" and I broke into my first smile since the news, feeling some strange connection with him as I said, "Yes, I am!"

But I was still amazed when I arrived at my sister's house and the first thing she said after our hug was, "I hope you're hungry!" The house was full of people, her three boys, a family friend, my father—red-eyed, Scotch in hand—and food was already pouring in. I couldn't believe she was talking about such earthly things on our first contact since becoming motherless, but single moms of three and newly minted family matriarchs are practical by necessity. I myself was on an anti-depressant, not for emotional issues but chronic headaches, but I still believe it helped me enormously through the ordeal. Yet my sister, sans pharmaceutical help, was holding up better than I.

The next six days are an oddly warm memory for me, a time in my life when all the daily trivia, and even non-trivial aspects of life, like working and running a home, were suspended to simply be with people who loved my mom. Of course we had to make arrangements: meet with the pastors, order the flowers, rent the candelabras (although the folks who ran the company wouldn't hear of us paying for them), but mostly we visited with the steady stream of folks who came to "sit with us". We answered dozens of condolence calls, took our combined four sons on nature walks, held each other and cried. The influx of food became a joke—although with seven of us in the house, including four growing boys, we consumed it steadily. Our running joke became trying to steer people away from lasagna and toward brownies when they called to ask what they could bring!

I remember two phone calls distinctly. My big, gruff brother-in-law Doug, with whom I have never been close, called on behalf of himself and his wife. He automatically asked how I was and then berated himself: "How ya doin', what a stupid question, I know how you're doin', duh." Later in the conversation he said, "We're both just so sorry," and I thought, Perfect. How hard is that? Why was it impossible for so many people to say?

The other call was from my dear friend Scott, whom my mother always not-so-secretly wished I had married! Not sure who had answered, he started out bravely, "This is Scott Bryson". But as soon as he realized it was me, his voice dissolved into an anguished, "Oh Laura Anne!" I appreciated it so much. His anguish was for me and for my mom, and for himself, because he loved her, too.

We set the memorial service for Wednesday evening, when the droves of children and adults that my mother had taught in her 24 years at Shining Rock School, could attend. The thrice-weekly Blue River paper and the once-a-week *Shining Rocket* both gave her death front-page coverage, with a beautiful color picture that broke our hearts all over again. Her school kicked into gear, with fellow teachers and administrators arranging meetings and counseling for her students and their parents, and a friend of my mother's coming out of retirement to take over her class for the rest of the year.

I saw my mother's husband on the night of her death; I simply called and said, "Can I come over—just me?" and didn't give him much choice. On my arrival her two little dogs greeted me with confused and needy affection that eclipsed the awkward moment with the raw new widower. I tried to be calm, soothing, and efficient, offering to make tea or fix food, but Henry refused everything, and we ended up sitting in the cozy living room by the fire, talking in a shell-shocked way about how many hours she had been dead (I said, "It seems like three years"), how her bedroom slippers were still where she'd left them before her run, that there was chili in the crockpot that she had made.

I learned from this horrible event that some people simply have a gift for handling such situations, and most of us who have never experienced such trauma do not. A mere six weeks before that day, my dear friend's young nephew died in a motorcross accident and I...sent a card. I am so ashamed of that now, but I simply didn't know how to react, how horrible it was, whether she would want to talk. And people *are* different in their reactions to unexpected loss, but from now on I will be the first one to call, the first to show up with— brownies, and the bereaved can tell me to go away if they like. I lost friends over the fact that a few people, who knew what happened, never acknowledged my mother's death to me.

Another odd thing is the American compulsion not to cry. I, too, hate tearing up at peanut butter commercials, but if you can't cry when your mother has died on the side of a road, when can you? If you can't sob at her funeral, you will never have a reason to cry. I found myself longing for the traditions of other cultures, of women "keening" at a wake, of draping the door of our home with black, of wearing black clothes myself. I wanted everybody to KNOW. I didn't want them to think I was the same person I had been before. For weeks afterward I approached the other mommies at my son's play group feeling like a grim reminder of everyone's mortality.

The memorial service became something we were looking forward to, a goal we were working toward, almost a production which, when done well, would be our tribute to Gwen.

We also knew it would be a treat to see everyone, because, let's face it, it takes something like a death to make everyone drop what they are doing and make it a priority to show up. No soccer game, no job deadline, no final exam was going to eclipse *this* obligation.

On that evening, people gathered at my sister's home, where she was making gallons of tea and setting out the many edibles that had collected in the house. My mom's brother and his family drove up, as well as two of my close friends, and my in-laws. John's parents greeted and hugged me like they would have at any encounter, which caused me to say to Agnes, rather pointedly, *"You'll* have to be my mother now". She immediately teared up, which actually helped; after all, this was not any encounter, this was the tragic end of a life. Pretending it hadn't happened was not acceptable—crying was.

My girlfriends Lisa and Joni and I were in my sister's room at one point, and Lisa lent me a lipliner, which we all agreed brightened my look considerably. Although Joni is one of my oldest and dearest friends, we didn't really discuss anything except who was riding with whom, whether they would stay over, etc. In spite of my defense of crying, I did not want to start the evening with a breakdown.

When we arrived at the church, there were already so many people that my husband called his parents and said, "You'd better hurry if you want a parking space. This is like Princess Di's funeral!"

The influence my mother had had on the community was be-coming clear to me. There were so many people that the attendance was the first news story on the local radio station the next day. And so many of them were children. The church choir, which she had been a member of, was rehearsing in the sanctuary ahead of the service, and the altar was filled with flowers. My sister knew everyone, and was reminding or telling me who they all were as we waited to be seated.

Sort of like a wedding, I thought, as we the family entered last, to take the seats of "honor" at the front of the church. My son and my sister's youngest, who was six, had been left home with a sitter (who wouldn't hear of being paid), but her two older boys, ages 11 and 13, sat with us. My father and his wife, although invited by Henry in a fit of magnanimity to sit with the family, were in the back, visibly shaken, as were my dad's brother and his wife.

The music was beautiful, of course—music meant so much to my mother that she had been specifying selections for her service for as long as I can remember. Two ministers, neither of whom I knew, spoke, but it was the one who quoted Hebrews 12 that I remember: "Wherefore, seeing we also are compassed about with so great a cloud of witnesses…let us run with patience the race that is set before us." I do not consider myself religious in any traditional sense, but I am from a family of runners, and I loved the minister's image of a stadium full of fans—the people who loved us who preceded us in death, cheering us on as we run our race. The idea that, whether it's a beautiful day or one with howling winds and sleet, whether we are relaxed or grimac-ing when we cross that line, finishing is still a triumph. We didn't DNF (with apologies to non-runners), and we are finally released from the pain of that turned ankle, those scorching lungs.

Then came the part of the service where others were invited to speak about the deceased. Henry, although generally a very private person, went first. He had told us he wanted to do it for her, and he had prepared notes. He shared more than I expected, and held up very well but for a few moments when he had to pause and collect himself. At the end, although he seemed composed, he nodded to my husband, who had been forewarned that he might need help making it down the altar steps. Not for physical reasons—Henry is one of those runners—but rather because he could not see through his tears.

Following Henry, my mother's cousin spoke, then some colleagues, and next up to the podium strode Drew, my 11-year-old nephew. We have always told Drew he could "make a lawyer" because of his gift with words, but let's just say that after the service I asked the sixth-grader if he would please speak at my service, too!

And then the children—loads of them, little ones from her current class and lanky middle schoolers who had since moved on. They had been coming up prior to the start of the proceedings laying single roses on the floor beneath the showy floral wreaths, and now they shared their memories of her. Their stories and musings brought many smiles, but a few broke down, and that was the hardest part of all. My husband had been teary through the entire thing, but I only cried then, and recovered.

We left the sanctuary to the strains of "Amazing Grace", my sister and I singing gustily and smiling at each other. Later she said to me, "I remember feeling like I was being borne out of the church on a groundswell of love and beautiful music, but when I look at the video it wasn't like that at all. It was just a bunch of stricken-looking people making their way toward the door."

Mom's friends in the choir had prepared all kinds of food for the reception, and we were to stand in a receiving line. But individual members of the family were quickly mobbed, and Henry and I wound up being the official "receivers", while my sister had her own line across the room. The outpouring of love for my mother had adrenaline running through my veins, and I have always been able to work a room. For the better part of two hours Henry and I hugged, shook hands, introduced, remembered, teared up and yes laughed, as people determinedly waited to pay their respects. Lisa and Joni were two of the last, and Lisa said, "Your lipstick is holding up marvelously!" cracking me up with both the humor and the relief of finally being able to Turn it Off. The great hall was finally emptying, and it was nearly ten o'clock. I was too tired to even eat, and we still had to clean up the room and haul out the leftover food.

As we loaded things into the car I finally noticed it was freezing (this was, after all, January at 3300 feet elevation). Once we were back at the house I poured myself a beer, sank gratefully into the sofa, and simply digested it all with Sara and John. I had said to Henry as we left, "Well, we're done with the hard part" and he had replied, "No, we're just beginning the hard part".

Boy, was he right.

Chapter 2
Before That

The phone call bringing news of my mother's death made certain the end of a very happy stage of my life. A few years before, I had remarked to a coworker, Pamela, that things were so perfect, I was just waiting for something awful to happen. Pamela, a beautiful Indian-American woman with a sunny disposition, had responded, "I wouldn't worry about that, Laura Anne. Something awful always happens sooner or later. Just enjoy it while you can!"

Like most young couples, John and I had started out our married life in a small apartment and moved around several times (Chapel Hill to Baltimore, Baltimore to Atlanta) before settling into long-term jobs. We met in the Triangle area of North Carolina, working in the same biotechnology lab. With my degree in botany, I was in the plant tissue culture group, and during the course of our subsequent moves I worked in a retail nursery, did some temporary office jobs, and was the assistant curator for tropical plants at the Atlanta Botanical Garden before hitting my career zenith as the PR Manager for the ABG. This was probably the perfect job for me.

I'd had no public relations training, but the Garden's Marketing Manager took a chance on me and trained me from the ground up. I brought a wealth of horticultural knowledge that was unusual and beneficial to the position, and my boss honed my writing and communication skills until I was fit for the work. I loved the combination of plants, writing, and talking with the media, and thrived during those three and a half years. I also picked up some media contacts that enabled me to freelance a bit during my stay-at-home mom phase.

As it happened, John and I bought our first house, in 1994, just a few months after I landed the PR job. We had suffered through five landlords (one mean, one crazy) in six years, and we were thrilled to finally have our own place. We fenced in the yard and adopted our dog Molson that same year, and I also traded in my 1983 Honda Civic for a '92 Accord. During the previous four years, I had worked in the ABG Conservatory, wearing jeans and a work shirt every day, so I loved wearing office clothes and having clean fingernails for a change. I used to drive home in my "new" car, press the remote button for my own garage, and walk in to greet my handsome husband and faithful dog, thinking, *Oh yeah, I'm all that!*

John, who was working for an engineering firm only two miles away, concurred. He assembled a glider for our backyard patio, and we began sitting on it having a drink after work in the evenings, watching Molson chase butterflies and saying to each other, we have arrived!

To my dismay, part of my job at the Botanical Garden was being interviewed by local TV stations about various events there. These usually came down to pre-recorded sound bites about the Daffodil Show, or the new vegetable garden, but once we hit the front page of the Atlanta paper. About a dozen of the poison dart frogs from the tropical conservatory were stolen, and the media swarmed to the story. I did four network affiliate interviews that day, and a live interview on WCNN radio, in which the reporter demanded to know if the public's safety was at risk! (I had to bite my tongue to not reply, "only if they eat one!")

At home, John and I fell into very traditional roles. I love to cook and garden, and though I have no design ability at all, I fussed with our modest furniture and few decorative items to make our home cozy and inviting. John mowed the lawn, cleaned the gutters and changed the oil in the cars. Each evening, I would prepare dinner with my husband acting as "chore boy", chopping onions or grating carrots at my direction, and afterwards I would assist him with the cleanup. On weekends we got together with numerous friends, and took Molson to the unofficial doggie play area of Piedmont Park in Midtown.

I never thought of us as yuppies, but perhaps we were. Or DINKs (double income no kids). I just knew that life was good and I was spectacularly lucky. John and I were fond of comparing other people's marriages to ours, poorly; we were the happiest couple we knew! In fact our friends liked to say we made them want to throw up, still holding hands and touching all the time after eight, ten, twelve years of marriage. It was just easy for us. We were super-compatible: irreverent smart alecks who could live happily on not much money. We had the same priorities, with the exception of running; that was John's "second job", as he put it, and I was only the support crew, having burned out on running years before. (The way I put it when I quit was, "We're both always tired, there's too much dirty laundry, and I am sick of eating dinner at 9 o'clock. One of us has to quit, and it's obviously not gonna be you!")

When it became clear that as a couple we were infertile, it didn't take long for John to convince me we should adopt internationally. He has an adopted brother and sister, and going international meant there would be no issues with birth parents changing their mind. In addition, it meant a spectacular adventure for us!

It's hard to believe now, but this was during the days before everyone was on the Internet, and we collected information about different agencies by snail-mailing our requests to the ones that advertised in Adoptive Families magazine. Once we had received all the brochures, we went out for a large Italian meal, ordered a pitcher of beer, and spent the evening comparing different country programs: China, Vietnam, Russia, Ukraine. By the end of the evening, we had decided on both the country and the agency we would use.

(This sort of systematic selection process appealed to both of us. When we chose our wedding china, John announced going in, "You choose three patterns without telling me what they are, and I'll choose three. Then we'll see if there's any overlap." As it turned out, there was exactly one mutual choice, and that was it. No muss, no fuss!)

It ended up taking exactly nine months to adopt Leo Nikita, from the decision to bringing him home. It was a stressful nine months, involving an exhaustive home study, references from friends, banks and employers, the accumulation of mountains of documents from birth certificates to a Russian business visa, and, worst of all, the wait to go get our son. We had "Nikita" (his birth name) identified, with two photos and a brief video clip, before the holidays, but we couldn't travel until February. I only had one minor breakdown one evening when we were going to bed, and I said to John, "I just hope he's okay. I hope they're kind to him, and he has enough to eat, and he's in a clean diaper. I hope he's not scared in the dark at night!"

As it turned out, seven-month-old Baby Nikita had never worn a diaper in his life until we met him—a fact that became uncomfortably clear when the nurse at the Russian hospital where he lived, handed him to me for the first time. He must have been excited to meet his mama, because he let loose all over one of the two pairs of pants I had brought on the trip!

John and I and, for a while, little Nikita, stayed with a wonderful Russian family in a high-rise, concrete block apartment building in the frozen city of Yekaterinburg during the adoption. The family included an ancient great-grandmother who never understood that we didn't speak Russian, a matronly grandmother who took great care of us, and a beautiful 12-year-old granddaughter who often served as translator. When Masha wasn't around, John and I communicated with Nina, the grandma, in our pidgin Russian and her pidgin English, while frequently pointing to entries in our respective Russian-English dictionaries.

Going to Russia to adopt our son was the trip of a lifetime. From the snow-blanketed Moscow airport in the early hours of a frigid February morning, to the bright orange caviar with bread and butter Nina served us for breakfast, to being handed our child for the first time, nothing will ever compare to it for me. Although some Russians disapprove of adopting babies out to Americans, everyone we encountered was encouraging to us, with one exception. While we were waiting for our flight back to Moscow from the Yekaterinburg airport, a middle-aged woman saw the three of us and realized what was going on. She began to babble to us in Russian, and then to wail and cry, becoming more and more dramatic until she was covering her face with her hands and rocking back and forth. Everyone at the gate looked uncomfortable but no one said anything to her, until the Polizia came and took her away. She was not allowed on our flight.

We were met at the Atlanta airport by John's parents, Agnes and Rob—who walked right across the security line to envelope us in his arms. We were so thrilled to be home, and to hand off the baby to his brand-new grandma as we collected our bags. On the train on the way back to the terminal, my normally-reserved mother-in-law turned to the stranger sitting beside her and announced, "This is my grandson."

As a stay-at-home mom, my life was even better than before. I was living my dream, caring for my beautiful, easy baby, meeting all the neighborhood mommies, and still regularly going to the Garden, where little Nikita and I were met with gushes of enthusiasm. I annoyed all my friends by remarking how easy this parenting thing was—why did everybody make such a big deal? Of course my baby, bless his heart, had spent his first seven months in a Russian hospital, where crying was probably useless for getting attention. He went to sleep on his own, woke up and amused himself until I came in, and ate whatever I fed him until it was gone. I had to learn to stop at a reasonable amount of cereal, because otherwise he would eat until he spit up massively afterward. He was growing, of course, at a tremendous rate, after being underweight in the hospital. The nurses had told us he was "the most beautiful boy in the hospital" and that he "never showed any displeasure".

John loved having a stay-at-home wife, too. When he kissed me good-bye in the morning, as I sat in a rocker in my robe and slippers, giving Nikita his bottle, I would just beam at him, and he would beam back. At first, he called me twice a day, for a "morning check-in" and an "afternoon check-in". And since I did all the housework during the week, on weekends we could do whatever we liked, around Nikita's schedule of course. I usually cut out at least once Saturday or Sunday to go to a bookstore or meet a friend for coffee.

My friend Joni had been a stay-at-home mom for years by the time I got around to it, and I had always envied her. The first time she came over with her kids for a play date, I was ecstatic. Here we were, in the middle of a weekday morning, in my sunny home, with our kids crawling or running around at our feet while we sipped tea and talked diaper rash! I had always joked (somewhat caustically) about the "Mommy Club" that I hadn't been allowed membership in, and I was finally there.

Of course this simple time couldn't go on forever; babies grow up and learn to talk back, and have to be potty-trained and go to preschool where they may hit someone's little darling or grab someone

else's toy. I worried (something I was excellent at) whenever my neighborhood play group didn't go well, or the preschool teacher told me
of any incident involving my son. I'm sure I stressed more than any
of the other mommies over what I called Play Group Politics. In retrospect, our little bunch seems so benevolent and wonderful, and everyone involved sympathetic and kind. I guess since I had left workplace
stress, I had to fill in with some other type!

When Leo was four, this sort of stress was growing within me,
as was concern about my newly-divorced sister and her three boys.
John's layoff came on January 2, 2002. He was given two weeks' notice
and two weeks' severance pay. He had two days of work left on the
day I got the Phone Call that changed everything.

Chapter 3
Athens

There was little relief from grief for the next two months. John had been laid off, I was a stay-at-home mom, and Leo—who went by his first name now—only attended preschool three mornings a week. I ran the household and cared for Leo, taking him to play group or the preschool programs at the library. John trained, logging many, many miles; and looked for work on the computer. This was still the immediate aftermath of September 11, and there was an odd subdued quality to almost everything, particularly for our family. Like so many couples, John and I held each other all night every night. Like so many people, we ate comfort food: macaroni and cheese, mashed potatoes and layer cake. Leo toddled on, meeting life head-first as he always had.

My dear friend Lisa got married four weeks to the day after Mom's death. I was hosting a shower for her at my house that weekend, so she was one of the first people I called after receiving the news. Lisa had called back and offered to keep our dogs, even though she is not much of a "dog person" and her intended was even less so. At Lisa's wedding, I wore a knockout black dress and drank entirely too much at the reception. I remember feeling terribly wise compared to everyone else there, and also picking at the dregs of the wedding cake straight from its plate with my fork.

After a couple of months I began to feel a little less stunned. One day I actually turned on the car radio, finally not finding it intolerably trivial. During that time I had halved my dose of anti-depressant medicine because I felt like I couldn't cry enough, but now I felt a small step closer to overcoming autopilot.

In March things got interesting again. John accepted a job offer from the University of Georgia and we prepared to move to nearby Athens. I welcomed the change, thinking the fresh situation would somehow blow the cobwebs from my mind. I had been just surviving for the past two months, simply plodding through my days, and now it was time to move forward again. Of course I was sad about leaving my neighborhood mommy friends and my former coworkers at the Atlanta Botanical Garden, but I have always liked variety and found moves exciting. The small college town would be a huge change from Atlanta, and I felt more secure about Leo going to public school there.

Truthfully, after our two years in Athens ended, I looked back at Leo's school as one of the only positive things to come out of our time there. The rest wasn't negative, just…neutral. And lonely. I hadn't foreseen how lost I would feel without anyone around me who knew my mother.

Athens, Georgia has a certain genteel quality, with stately homes and trees arching over the roads, with children who say "ma'am" and "sir" and accents that would melt butter. It was a gentle place to live, and we were happy as we could be considering our losses. The house we bought turned out to be a big white elephant, but at the time of its purchase we were jazzed. It was in a great older section of town, close to everything, and sat on nearly an acre of varied and interesting gardens. A large hodgepodge that had started in the sixties as a cottage, it needed lots of paint and TLC.

John built and I painted a white picket fence, so the dogs had a big yard to run in, and Leo had an old iron swing set with red-painted wooden seats, as well as trees to climb and lots of space for soccer, a kiddie pool, etc. I fell into the gardening gratefully, with its many challenges and possibilities, as Leo turned five and no longer needed my constant attention. I walked for miles in the neighborhood, substituted at the preschool, did freelance writing jobs when I could get them, and worked on the house.

One of my favorite places was our covered back porch, where Leo and I would sit and watch thunderstorms, and he would beg to strip to his underwear and dance in the rain. Before we dismantled the ramp to the back door, we raced matchbox cars down it, sometimes with caterpillar "drivers" whom Leo was confident enjoyed the thrill ride. We had a dining set on the porch, and all summer John would come home for lunch and the three of us would eat there, with Leo allowed to take his popsicle and climb his favorite tree afterward. It was the lifestyle of a 1950's middle-class family: comfortable, orderly, and traditional.

I dreaded Mother's Day that year, and decided to visit Sara so that Leo and I could be with our counterparts in loss. I knew Sara and I would have to focus on being mothers, rather than being motherless for the first time.

Our boys rose to the occasion. On Mother's Day morning, muffled shouts and "confused alarms of struggle and flight" emanated from my sister's kitchen as she and I, per orders, sat up together in her bed. Our four boys, or some combination thereof, were working on the obligatory breakfast. Seeing as how their ages ranged from five to 14, it was going to be interesting. A furtive trip to the bathroom revealed that in fact, the 14-year-old was still abed, leaving the 11-year-old in charge.

And then a literal alarm—the smoke detector. Sara and I looked at each other like moms in a Disney movie. But before we could react, Drew stuck his head in the door. "Everything's okay! Do NOT get out of bed!" he ordered. I was amazed his mom agreed to this, but it was, after all, her house.

That breakfast will go down in history, for many reasons. The menu included bacon (the piece de resistance), and a carbohydrate fest of bagels, toast, and doughnuts. All four boys were up now, and the two littlest came in bearing their contribution: a bowl of dried apricots and Cheez-Itz. For many years afterward, Sara's kitchen floor bore the scar from where Drew had set the frying pan in order to attend to a bacon-grease burn on his foot. The mark probably didn't amuse Sara day in and day out, but it always made me smile as I remembered a Mother's Day that could have been miserable, saved by our children. There weren't the kind of niceties—linen napkins, hot coffee, single roses—that other mothers might have been getting that day, but after all our kids were operating without benefit of fathers, or sisters (okay, call me sexist!), or any kitchen experience whatsoever!

***

In August, our Atlanta house sold after four months on the market. It was a huge relief, and John and I celebrated by taking our second vacation in Oregon—our dream state. Oregon was where we had taken our first vacation as a couple after becoming parents, three years before.

The oppressive Georgia heat finally gave way to fall, and one day about lunchtime John called me from work.

"You're not gonna believe this," he began. "I just got laid off."

I stood in my kitchen, at a loss for words as my mind took this in. He sounded almost jocular, maybe the only way his ego could take giving me the news. It was November, with Thanksgiving coming, just as Christmas had been eminent the year before when his previous company let him go.

After you've gotten a call that your mother is dead, there aren't many other things that are going to freak you out. I felt myself funnel into autopilot again, and got the details. The severance "package" was negligble, as it had been before; we would rely on Unemployment again. I went into brave little woman mode by evening, and went to work at the preschool the next day.

John, who had a remarkable penchant to stabilize at Happy, started doing contract work for both his previous employers right away. In addtion, he became the stay-at-home parent, while I found various things to do, or, as a friend of ours facing a layoff once said, to our delight, "something to do that someone will pay me some amount of money for!"

I hosted Thanksgiving that year, for my sister, whose boys were with their dad, and my dad, whose wife was with her people. For the World's Greatest Family, as we called ourselves when I was growing up, the four of us had come to a surprising state of affairs. My parents had divorced after 23 years of marriage and my sister's divorce after 16 years had been finalized the same week my mother died and John's job ended. As the four adults and one child posed for holiday photos in our cavernous great room, I thought, this is what we're down to. Five people. That's the best we can do.

I love hosting Thanksgiving and always have, so I am no longer intimidated by large, slimy bird carcasses or even making gravy. But as I worked, Sara gave me a sympathetic look and asked, "Stressed?"

"No," I answered honestly, "just sad." It was the first major holiday without our mother.

There were many blessings in my life: a wonderful husband, a healthy child, our own house, my big garden, our terrific dogs, Molson and Guinness…. and I was shouting distance (so to speak) from friends and family. But the thing that was missing, in that aftermath of Mom's death, was joy. I just didn't feel it. I wanted it.

My paternal grandfather is always quoted in our family as saying, "That little Laurie Anne, she's a go-getter!" It's not always true, but I do try to fix things (sort of like a man), so I tackled the joy problem. For the first time in my life I sought psychological counseling. It made sense. I mean, that's why they're there!

I contacted a local psychology clinic that charged fees based on a sliding scale. It was reasonable, so I made an appointment.

Since those days I have become very used to counseling offices, to glass windows reading "Do not open" that protect the receptionist from us unstable folk, and even signs saying "No concealed handguns" or "Warning: You May Be Exposed to Tuberculosis", but at the time I felt more than a little odd. I looked around at the other people in the waiting room and wondered what their problems were. Were they alcoholics? Wife beaters? Manic depressives? They looked so normal! The office, on the other hand, went right along with the stereotypes—especially the very muted lighting. Everyone seemed to speak in hushed tones, too.

After my name was called, I found myself in another dimly lit room, in a soft chair facing an earnest-looking young woman. She looked over the answers I'd written on their interminable survey.

"How many drinks do you have per week?"

"Maybe five, tops?"

"Do you ever find yourself unable to go to work because of alcohol?"

"Uh…no."

"Do you ever drink in the morning? Are your friends concerned about your drinking? Do you feel you could give it up at any time?"

My God! what would these folks do with some of John's friends? (not that they'd EVER appear here!) I imagined the conversation:

"How many drinks per week?"

"Oh, three beers a night, maybe four or five on weekends, what's that add up to?"

And then the truly disturbing questions. "Have you ever wanted to hurt yourself or anyone else? Ever TRIED to hurt yourself or anyone else? Were you ever beaten by your parents or your husband? Have you been sexually molested?"

I'm a smart aleck, but I was finding it hard to seize on any comic material here. And when I did, I never got a laugh. I felt more and more certain this wasn't for me as the hour progressed.

The sliding scale was pretty kind to me, considering that our income consisted of John's unemployment check. We hit the bottom of the scale at $28 an hour. But even that sounded like too much when the therapist asked me if I would mind being *videotaped* during our sessions for educational purposes. Now, mind you, the therapist wasn't videotaped, only the thera-pee. Face and all! In our little town! Nothing like anonymity. I did not agree (maybe I would have if the sessions had been free!)

The clinic would assign me to someone after reviewing my answers to their questions and my initial visit, I was told. When the lucky winner telephoned me several days later, if my mind had not already been made up, her call would have decided it. "Um, I think you all are set up for people a lot more *disturbed* than I am!" I told her, and I laughed when I said it. She didn't like hearing that, of course. What would happen to me if I did not avail myself of their services? And so she asked me what I planned to do instead. "Well, I've found a grief group, and I think that will help," I replied.

"Well, it might help with your mother's death, but what about all the other stuff?"

Boy, I thought, why don't they *train* these people? Could it be that the trainers don't get it either? Do only people who have lived loss understand it?

"'All the other stuff' can be resolved," I explained patiently. "You can get a new job; you can't get a new *mother*."

Chapter 4
A Decision

They say it is women who talk about feelings, but my father is the exception to the rule. Okay he's not the exception to all the rules. His ego is…healthy. At 73, he's still a jock. He loves to fly-fish, hates to apologize, and is correct nearly one hundred percent of the time.

However, he is sentimental to the core, and it was he who suggested that we all get together on the anniversary of Mom's death for a dinner in her honor. Of course my sister was the lucky hostess.

I drove to North Carolina alone, since John was on a job deadline, and Leo stayed with Daddy since reflection was not his strong suit, at age five. Sara's boys, Ben, age 14, 11-year-old Drew, and Mason, age six, had just returned from a visit with their father "down the mountain" in Durham. They brought tales of the intestinal bug that had slammed them there:

"I threw up six times!"

"I threw up nine!"

"Dry heaves don't count!"

Fortunately all were well for the occasion, and Sara, who is an accomplished and inventive cook, served us a feast. It had been a tough year, and it was good to come back together and share warm-fuzzies. My dad has always honored his late relatives, but I think he felt even more driven to do so now because he and Mom had divorced 18 years prior to her death. There could be no closure with her, for him now. But he could keep her memory alive and respected.

Sara and I, who share the bond of having suffered the same tragic loss, had taken to referring to Mom's death as The Anvil. As in, the one that fell on your head. We started noticing it happening to other people. When a running friend, a lovely woman with a husband and baby daughter, was hit by a van and killed in front of her husband the following year, my email to my sister was titled, "The Anvil fell on someone else". Through agonizing pain and injustice, you learn to help others through the same. Now I try to offer bereaved friends and relatives help such as errand-running and child care (everybody else is bringing food!) And I come back a few weeks later, when everyone else has gone away. Our culture allots us about a month of mourning, after which we are expected to be pretty much back to normal. But "normal" has changed forever. Or, as I said to John once, after Mom died, "I've just realized that 'everything' will never be okay again".

But that anniversary was a turning point for me, one I never expected. It was as if my heart had been in the grip of a vise, and someone turned the handle just a half turn to the left. I wrote in my journal that my grief "still defined me", but it eased just a little after that first year. Sara commented that I must have purged myself somehow the day after our dinner, by throwing up 12 times.

***

And so a new year had begun. In scanning the want ads for my husband one morning, I saw one that piqued MY interest.

> *Wanted: People to rate 8th grade standardized writing tests on a scale of one to five. Payment is by the piece. Paid training provided.*

"I saw that, too," John said, but he didn't seem too interested. He had picked up quite a bit of work, and was able to make his own schedule. This consisted of getting up about 7:00, taking care of the dogs, having coffee while reading the paper, then warming up and going for a long run. About 11:00, he would be showered and settled at the computer in our pretty guest room, a sandwich at his elbow, checking the stock market and getting down to work. He would work until 5:30 or 6:00 and then call it a day, open a beer, and feed the dogs. (Looking back, it's a good thing we had dogs.)

I, on the other hand, had very little freelance work, so I went to apply for the rating job. I was not surprised to be hired, given my writing and editing background, but I was surprised that it seemed to take me longer than most trainees to get the job down. I wanted to take too long on each five-paragraph piece, and initially I was only making four or five dollars an hour.

The perk of the job was the unintended laughs. I couldn't hold them in, and never understood why my coworkers in the room didn't periodically giggle as I did. The subject of the students' essays was "leisure time", a wide-open field. I learned a great deal about the generation coming up behind me, and had to get hip to their slang. Was "off de chain" good? or bad, as in a killer dog? Was "crunk" simply an illegible version of drunk? And when, exactly, was "back in the day"?

Illicitly, I copied down some of the funnier sentences, and amused my family with them in the evenings. Leo liked them, or maybe just the idea of them, so much that he would ask me if I brought home any "senators" each day.

How can I stop people from taking durgs their are over alot of people who have die from durgs.

School, Movies and going to the mall the lord have give them to me to do and have fun.

Sometimes sitting, on my bed, in my room, at home. After a vaction to the beach, I can almost feel the warm sincere air, and hear the rapid waves crash upon a grainlike textured surface, we humans call sand.

* * *

Meanwhile, Leo continued in his new preschool, where he did much better and was much happier than he'd been at our preschool in Atlanta. My theory was that these Southern ladies would jerk a knot in his tail, figuratively speaking, if he sassed them or wasn't a little gentleman! And since Leo was a child who needed the odd knot in his tail, he responded well, and I almost never got the humorless notes home recounting various infractions (from hitting to "using his pointer finger as a gun—it just upsets me so much!") that I used to receive from the Atlanta school.

It all worked, in a treading-water kind of way, but after a while we began questioning exactly what we were doing in Athens, Ga. It was almost like we had landed there by default—it had been John's only job offer, and manageably close to where we were. There wasn't really anything there we had been seeking, such as mountains, or snow, or cooler weather, like both of us preferred. We hadn't known anyone in town. John's contract work could be done from anywhere. In short, there was really no reason for us to stay.

But, where would we go?

The choices were limited. We both wanted mountains, but my hometown was just too small, too familiar; going there would be too much like declaring defeat. John's family's home of Raleigh held no appeal for either of us. Asheville was appealing, and certainly on the short list. And then there was our wildcard: Brake, Oregon, our favorite vacation spot. It was 2,000 miles away, completely different from anything we were used to, being a northwestern town in the "high desert", but we thought it was paradise. Snow-capped mountains were visible from the Safeway parking lot, summers were sunny and dry, winters exciting with snow and all the winter sports, and it was a short drive to everything from redwood forests to out-and-out deserts with sand dunes. In spite of the aridity, the charming downtown had a river running through it, which provided for some grass and Ponderosa pines in its immediate vicinity. It was, for us, the town with everything.

Except family, friends, or a remotely familiar lifestyle—details, we thought.

And so, in March, we bit the bullet and put another house on the market, shocking all of our loved ones with the news. L.A. and John were at it again. The couple who had gotten engaged 37 days after their first date, and married six months later. The couple who had skipped fertility treatments or even testing and flown to Russia in February to bring home someone else's baby. Now we were moving to the other side of the country, with a child, two dogs, a cat—and not a job between us. But hey, we had thought it out rationally, mulled it over for some time, even made a list of the pros and cons. (Pros included things like "lots of fresh salmon, and really great coffee!") We were hardly jumping into anything!

The realtor we chose priced our house at $265,000—$40,000 more than we had paid for it 12 months before. We were giddy with delight, and as the initial wave of buyer interest broke over us, we congratulated ourselves on our business acumen. After all, we had nearly doubled our money turning the Atlanta house over in less than seven years.

But if we thought it took a long time to sell *that* house, we were in for our comeuppance. After the initial response to a new listing, there was very little action all that spring and summer. We quickly lowered the price, and then lowered it again. It was frustrating to have made the decision to take this huge leap, and then to be unable to do it while we had the initial momentum. I was, at this point, *so* ready to go. The last thing we needed was to start Leo in kindergarten in Georgia, only to yank him across the country before he'd even adjusted. Honestly, it had never occurred to me that by listing our house in March, we would not have sold it by fall. Silly me.

Chapter 5
To Hear the Gods Laugh, Make Plans

I couldn't believe it. Actual good news in the mail. With 13 elementary schools in the county, and our first choice the smallest one, we had, by sheer luck, won the lottery. Bartow was a quaint K-5 in our neighborhood. I couldn't back this up, but I always had a feeling that the Old Money in Athens who *didn't* send their kids to private schools, got them into Bartow. But perhaps I'm being cynical.

As I had feared he might, Leo spent the summer—after days playing in the yard, going swimming, vacation bible school and beach trips—fretting at bedtime about starting "big boy school". One night he broke my heart by saying, "Please don't send me to big boy school, Mommy. I've learned a lot already!"

But passages happen, whether we're ready for them or not, and so I walked him into school on the first day and sent him off on the next big phase of his life. Actually, I learned to love parking in the church lot next door and walking him in by the hand, watching the adorable parade of children arriving on foot and by bike, accompanied by their parents, baby siblings and sometimes the family dog.

Leo was immune to the scene's charms, however, being a hyperactive six-year-old boy who had never spent more than four hours at a time in preschool. His teacher was sincere but lacking in humor, and did not seem to tolerate active boys well. Once he realized he was going to be stuck there seven hours a day, five days a week for eternity (from his perspective), every drop-off became a trauma. After a couple of months, to Mom's relief, he began to settle down, and sometimes was even able to retain all his "behavior carrots" on the bulletin board (when this happened, we celebrated with Slushies!)

I was pleased to see Leo develop a friendship with a boy in his class, Wyatt, who often stayed at the playground with his sister and mom after school. Wyatt soon began to ask his mother if Leo could come home with them, and she usually said yes. Given Leo's often volatile relationships with other kids, and my general wimpiness, I was hesitant to invite Wyatt home with us—although it was Leo I would worry about, and not his friend. My boy had a good heart, but was rather lacking in impulse control.

But my mother raised me right, so eventually of course I reciprocated. I fixed the boys my signature snack—a bowl of peanut butter mixed with chocolate syrup, and pretzel logs to dip in it. It was a pleasant day, and I set up a lawn chair by our swingset and brought out a book (really, I was hovering). Our playset had a trapeze bar, and Leo loved to do tricks on it. On this particular afternoon, I nixed sailing off the bar into the kiddie pool, so they were just pushing each other as high as they could go. The lawn sloped down away from the swingset, so by the time they let go at the top of the arc, they had a long way to fall.

They say that 90% of the things we worry about don't happen, but this must've been the tenth day. I looked up at the sound of whimpering and saw the two boys in a heap on the ground, with Wyatt holding his arm.

"What happened?"

"He fell off the bar, Mom."

Poor little Wyatt was sitting on a rock, holding his arm and making little moaning sounds on every exhale. On the inhale he would seem calm, but then his mouth would form an "o" again, and that soft little cry would ensue.

"Honey, let me see it—" Wyatt held forth his arm.

No, it couldn't be. There was no mark, but his forearm was noticeably curved inward. "Let me see your other arm," I directed, fighting the rising panic in my chest. Sure enough, that one was straight as an arrow. I ran to call his mom.

What a trooper! She hadn't been gone 20 minutes and already I was calling to tell her that her son's arm was bent in an unnatural way. "Oh, so you think it's broken?" Janice asked, almost matter-of-factly. "I…I don't…maybe," I answered lamely.

While Janice drove over, I set Wyatt up on the couch with a bag of ice. The whole time, my mind was racing. How had this happened? How could it have happened on Leo's very first home playdate in kindergarten?? What could I do to make it up to the family? Were they the kind of people who would sue? Why did everything happen to me? How did my mother get killed, my sister divorced, my husband laid off twice, and someone else's child break his arm in my yard, all in the space of 15 months?

And it was broken, all right. Both bones in his little forearm. Did I mention it was his writing arm? And for six weeks afterward I walked Leo into his classroom and said good morning to the little boy in the cast.

Clearly, I needed something else to do other than to worry about my only child. And of course, we could always use some money. We were now buying private insurance policies for three people—need I say more?

I had worked for Manpower in Baltimore the first year we were married, so I turned to the local branch now. I liked the variety and flexibility of "temping". The office was close by and pleasant, and when I walked in I clicked with the women who worked there right off the bat. The downside of it all was that before I knew it, they wanted me full-time to work in-house.

John and I discussed it, and finally decided that I should accept the offer. He was still home and able to pick Leo up after school (since the first day riding the bus reduced him to tears), and Leo would be able to stay for a while and play on the school playground with his friends—provided he had kept enough behavior carrots!

Once this routine had begun, I teased John about gossiping with the other mommies at the schoolyard picnic table while the children played. "Get any good recipes?" I asked him. "Tips for getting your whites their whitest?"

"Daddy doesn't sit with the other mommies," Leo put in. "He just stands over by a tree and cries!" (already the wise guy, our little one!)

And bless Janice Stenson's heart forever, she was still inviting Leo home with Wyatt, and asking if Wyatt could come home with him!

I began to enjoy my work at Manpower, dressing professionally, leaving all that lunch-packing business behind as I justified Leo buying his lunch since I was working so hard! Not for me the pressure to bake cupcakes or volunteer at the science fair—I was a busy woman! And truly, Manpower ran like a clock, an efficiency I enjoyed, and my colleagues and I had a lot of laughs when we weren't tearing our hair out over an employee's failure to show up for his assignment, or a customer's demand for 10 people within the hour. I found it rewarding giving work to our reliable and deserving employees, and got a little power trip out of picking and choosing from among them when assignments came in. There was another side to that, though. My most depressing day on the job was the one in which all three of us spent the afternoon calling long-time employees to tell them their assignment had ended, just before Christmas. How well I knew *that* feeling!

And so winter came, and showings of our house dwindled to almost zero. John never seemed to find any permanent job possibilities in his endless hours online. Leo was weary of Big Boy School, and the tenor of my office had changed with a large new account that was difficult to manage from off-site. In the weeks before Christmas, I decided we all needed something to look forward to. At 40, I wanted to go to Disney World.

John, a "child of privilege", as I always called him, had visited Mickey several times, but I had never been, and now that we felt Leo was old enough to not desperately need a nap in the middle of the day, we decided to take the plunge and plan a trip for March.

Just before Christmas, Leo got the flu. He was so not himself, for so many days, it broke my heart. As a still relatively-new mom, I worried excessively whenever he was ill, especially because it was so rare. One day, I called him to the table with John and me and gave him a gift to open early. It was one of those Bionicle-Power-Ranger-Bust-'em-up kind of action figures that he normally loved. I showed him all the moveable parts, trying to pique his interest. Then, in a phrase so uncharacteristic I nearly panicked, Leo said, "I think I'll go lie down" and he left the toy at the table.

He had already been to the pediatrician, but by now he hadn't eaten well in five days, and I took him back a second time. "I can't cure the flu," she told me patiently, but her examination revealed bronchitis and an ear infection, and she ended up writing two prescriptions.

Of course he was on the mend soon after that. Most children are resilient, but from what I've seen, boys from Russian orphanages are practically made of Kevlar. Unfortunately, I was not. I succumbed to the bug just in time to preclude the "over the river and through the woods" trip to Blue River, and figured the sad three of us would be on our own for Christmas. But since Sara didn't have her boys, she and my father came through and brought Christmas down to Athens in the form of a Honda loaded with gifts. Another tiny holiday gathering. I remember sitting on the sofa on Christmas Day, in my robe, surrounded by wrapping paper, and feeling depressed because I was too tired to clean it up, and because my sister, unlike me, wasn't anal enough to mind it.

***

After our company left, in keeping with the general karma, the southern temperatures plunged uncharacteristically to single digits. In our big, drafty house, with all of us home all day over the holidays, we burned all of our wood and even some we scavenged from the side of the road to keep off the chill. I called and called, but could never find anyone to deliver us a load.

My headaches were terrible that winter, and in hopes that that was one thing I could change, I visited a doctor and asked about switching medications. She prescribed a tricyclic anti-depressant, a change from the SSRI I was taking. I had no trouble making the switch, but noticed that while my headaches decreased in frequency, the ones I still got were of the slam-bang No-I-Won't-Respond-to-Excedrin variety, almost crippling. Meanwhile, I had a "vision disturbance" which began one day while I was vacuuming—it became harder and harder to see the dirt, and then the floor itself. The middle of my field of vision became slowly obscured as if under water. I sat down to ride it out, thankful I wasn't driving or on a (paying) job. Gradually my vision cleared. The whole thing had taken about 45 minutes. I was determined to stay on the medication, and the vision-blurring didn't happen again, but since the headaches never substantially improved, eventually I stopped. For the first time in four years, I was medication-free.

I have a home video from about this time, in which I am deter-
minedly sunny. In it, I focus on an unenthusiastic John and say, "John
Nicholson! You've just placed second in your age group in the Bartow
Boogie 5K! What are you gonna do now?" followed by "Leo Nicholson!
You've just kept all your behavior carrots!" and finally a shot of me with
John declaring, "Laura Anne Nicholson! You've just placed six people
in jobs at Manpower! What are you gonna do now?"

The final shot of course is me, dressed and made up cute, spin-
ning in glee and effusing, "I'm going to DISNEY WORLD!!!!!"

Chapter 6
The Leap

When it actually happened, it was hard to take in. Our (new) realtor called to tell us we had an offer on the house. In 13 months, this had been the only one.

We would wind up selling the house for $5K less than we paid for it (ouch) but we could finally pursue our dream. And just as it had been hard NOT to move on with our plans when we first listed our home, it was a little rough making the leap overnight to "Let's buy a house across the country and move there—now!"

We had to be out in six weeks. OMG, as the kids say. John's folks, who really hadn't believed us when we declared our intent, were called upon to house/child/pet sit while we flew to Oregon to buy a place. We had been corresponding by email with a realtor in Brake, so we had that ball rolling. I told my girls at Manpower what the schedule was, and off John and I flew.

Although very excited, I started feeling a little sick about this time. Anxious-sick. Of course the circumstances were enough to make anyone nervous, but just four months prior I had stopped taking the medication I had been on for several years. Even though I had taken it for headaches, there had been mental side-effects, which in my case were unsought benefits, especially when my mother died. I believe as we headed to Oregon I was extra jittery because of the cessation of medicine that had smoothed over my emotions for quite some time, whether that had been the intent or not.

We stayed in our favorite hotel in Brake, the Sunriser. In addition to very nice rooms, a good location and excellent service, the Sunriser had a killer continental breakfast. Every day for the five days we were there, I made my own waffle and downed several cups of that West Coast coffee, fueling up for a long day of house-hunting. It was a luxurious childless stay for the two of us, and an almost incomprehensibly exciting time in our lives. But after our agent had taken us to a dozen or so surprisingly similar homes (new-ish, in good shape and on absolutely tiny lots) and we had put in an offer on one, I felt a definite edge of anxiety during everything we did. Which included celebrating our 15th anniversary with a delicious and very expensive dinner, and renting bikes for a ride along the river, with a stop at one of those primo coffee shops with seating on the riverbank.

John was in heaven. He couldn't believe it was really happening. The house we had bid on would be the nicest we had ever owned, and Brake was an outdoor enthusiast's paradise. I looked forward to settling in and being able to enjoy it with him, once it had all become reality and my butterflies had calmed down.

We returned to Georgia in triumph, with a contract on a house and many pictures and videos of our place. Rob and Agnes were excited for us in a dazed sort of way, and Leo didn't know quite what to think. He wasn't going to miss his school, but he was a creature of habit and not sure about a new house. He did giggle when he saw Daddy's video of his room and walk-in closet in the new place, with the narration "Leo COULD move into his closet, and just live there!"

In the hectic weeks that followed, I held a yard sale, packed feverishly, gave stunned friends and family members the lowdown, and made the inevitable calls to utility companies, banks and movers making the necessary arrangements. John almost jokingly requested a TripTik from Triple A, but they came through gamely with the 2,547 mile trip directions ("Take I-80 W passing through WYOMING, then crossing into UTAH—- 828.1 miles"). Though I maintained our couple bravado in the face of doomsayers, sending out an email with our new contact information with the subject line "Go West, Middle-Aged Couple!" I began to have trouble finishing my meals. John made good-natured fun of me, but I wonder if he was beginning to feel ever-so-slightly alarmed about the reality of our dream.

June 14, 2004. With our possessions headed across the country ahead of us, along with those of about four other families in a behemoth truck, John, Leo and I, dogs Molson and Guinness, and Eliza the cat in a carrier, left West Lake Drive in John's 1996 Subaru Outback and my '92 Honda Accord. On the back of the Honda I had written

"Oregon or Bust" and John had the more specific and grammatically correct "Brake or Burst!" on the back of the Subaru. We made the short drive to Atlanta to spend the night with Lisa and her husband before launching the cross-country sojourn. Lisa was pregnant for the first time at age 40. I don't recall what we did that night, but I remember thinking that I would never see her baby, and lying awake for hours, fretting about falling asleep at the wheel the next day. John awoke around midnight and I said to him, frantically, "I can't sleep at ALL!"

When John and I were on our way to Russia to adopt Leo, I remember the feeling of being swept along by an unstoppable current, and deciding to just to enjoy the ride! This time, the current was also unstoppable, but the feeling was of dread. Of course, there wasn't any turning back now. If there had been, at this point, I would have.

Chapter 7
Falling off a Cliff

I had never seen America. I had lived my entire life, save a short stint in England, in various locations in the Southeast. I had traveled to Canada, Mexico and Russia, visited New York City, New England, the Pacific Northwest, the midwest, and Anaheim, California. But I had never experienced the enormity of The West. I had never seen the vastness that is Wyoming. Seen a view so wide that there could be a thunderstorm in one direction, sunshine in another, and a tiny distant train stitching its way across yet another corner of the landscape, with a doll-sized puff of smoke issuing out of it. I had certainly never seen a sign on a highway reading "Drinking water, 1/4 mile on left" or one that said "Next rest stop, 144 miles". There was so much we wanted to take in, but the necessity of catching up with our belongings forced us to fly right past it all. In St. Louis, I photographed the "arch" from the car, and sighed over missing out on their famed Botanical Garden with its distinguished Climatron glasshouse. In Ogden, Utah, we stopped at a rest stop with views so spectacular we asked each other why we hadn't just moved there and saved ourselves some mileage.

My 13-year-old car purred like a kitten the whole way, and we talked between cars on the walkie-talkies we had bought for the trip. Neither John nor I had a cell phone, and the walkies were a real novelty to us. Leo especially loved operating them, to report wildlife sightings to his dad, or more often, just to be silly. We had only one casualty, which happened the second day. Leo closed the car door on his thumb and the blood welled up immediately. I ordered him to stick it in his mouth and hustled him into the gas station for help. They didn't have a first aid kit or even bandages, and at one point there was so much blood the attendant asked if I wanted an ambulance. But eventually the bleeding stopped, as we sat on the floor holding his thumb above his heart and applying pressure with paper towels. I purchased

BandAids and first aid cream and for the rest of the trip changed dressings twice a day. I'm happy to report that his thumb bears no scars, but the injury did kill the possibility of playing with his new Game Boy for the rest of the trip.

The drive took six days, of scenery and boredom, fast food and dog walks, motel swimming pools and Continental breakfasts. We stopped for the last time only 110 miles from Brake, preferring to be well-rested when we arrived at our new home and faced the enormous task of settling in. That night, my low-level anxiety ratcheted up a notch. Leo accidentally upset John's can of beer on the motel bed, and after cleaning it up and dealing with John's ire, I remember worrying excessively over whether we'd be "caught" and charged for cleaning the carpet. Normally, of course, I would have just told the desk clerk what happened at checkout, apologized, and offered to pay any costs.

At any rate, I drank my coffee as usual the next morning, and we took off for our new hometown. I felt we should honk or cheer or something as we passed the Brake city limit, but John didn't acknowledge it, so I didn't either. After nearly a week of travel, it was both overwhelming and strangely anti-climactic to arrive.

We stopped at our realtor's office to pick up the keys. I didn't seem to remember any of the streets, or have any idea where in town our house was—nothing looked familiar. I simply followed John, my heart pounding as we pulled into our new cul-de-sac and then our own driveway. I did not feel like a proud new homeowner and resident. I felt like an interloper, someone who had no right to be there. I looked furtively around for neighbors, but everyone was inside during the heat of the afternoon.

To compound my feeling of illegitimacy, our key didn't work at first. As John struggled with the lock, a neighbor appeared and greeted us. I trotted nervously over to her and introduced myself, tittering that our key wasn't working. Finally, the lock gave way. I was relieved to abandon the stranger, and scurry inside the house.

And now what?

Our furniture turned out to be rather further away than we expected, so we had two days knocking around an empty house (days that could have been spent at the Missouri Botanical Garden!) We camped out in our living room, all of us plus the three pets, and prepared the most rudimentary food, like tea and eggs, with the kitchen kit we had packed. There were of course phone calls and arrangements to be made, but we spent some of that time exploring our new town and neighborhood.

We talked further with the woman I had met on our arrival. Lilly was a sturdy and outspoken young person with a home day-care agency across the cul-de-sac from us. What was noticeable was that her charges ranged from infants to kids really old enough to be babysitters themselves. "How many kids do you keep?" I asked, but she was vague in her answer.

She wasn't vague at all, though, about the neighbors, and started dishing about them right away. The ones whose house was about 12 feet from ours had an eight-year-old, she told me, whom she didn't like having around her house. "He's just really physically aggressive, plays too rough" she told me, and went on to add that it was probably his mother's fault, seeing as how she cared for him so little that he had gotten off the bus one day and come home to find no one there. "What could I do?" she shrugged, "I let him in".

This conversation, on Day One, heaped dry leaves, pine needles and lighter fluid on the small burning flame of my anxiety. Children Leo would have problems with, or who would be bad influences on him, were my worst-case scenario. Since he was a toddler I had worried about him inadvertently causing harm, either to himself, other children, or property. He simply acted first, and thought later, and his actions tended to be on a larger scale than those of most kids his age. At 18 months, he pulled a dresser over on himself by climbing the drawers. At 20 months, he climbed the sofa arm, snapped the bulb of a wall lamp off at the base, and was playing with the shards of broken glass when I found him. If a group of children were building something and he wanted to do something else, he might just walk through the middle of the construction project to "convince" them to come play with him. His preschool teacher told me she would "vault over chairs" to intervene between him and another child whom he might have unintentionally antagonized.

Of course he was now nearly seven, but I still had concerns about his judgment.

I felt something almost physical as Lilly told me these things, almost a flush at the base of my head or a skin-creeping on the back of my neck. I have since read about "brain burn"—an actual permanent change in brain chemistry caused by extreme anxiety—but I have no idea if such a thing actually happened to me. And I can't remember when I crossed the line between just being jittery and being pathologically anxious, but I'm certain it was a matter of a very few days after our arrival. I can almost follow the deterioration of my state of mind in caffeine consumption. I love tea and coffee and drink them daily, but once we had arrived in Brake, I was so jittery that I never had another cup of coffee until the following Christmas, and I probably had three cups of tea, total, while we lived in Oregon.

I have been an avid journal-writer since the age of 14, but I made no entries while we lived in Brake. Once I got to the point where I was unable to eat a normal amount or sleep more than an hour or two a night, I honestly don't remember if I still thought I might "adjust" and feel better, or if I knew I had fallen off an emotional cliff. I just kept trying everything I could think of to feel better, as we drifted along in our unstructured days.

We did have a plan, of course. John would seek contract work or a full-time job, and continue to work for the companies that he had contracted with before. Leo would enroll in first grade at the neighborhood school in September, and once he was in school I would get a job. I began scanning the local paper and working on my resume as soon as we had unpacked. But no work came in for John, and since we had arrived June 21st, Leo still had a lot of summer left. We got up at a reasonable hour and had three regular meals a day, but it was certainly the most unscheduled routine we had ever had as a family.

Leo wasted no time in meeting the local kids. The "aggressive" child next door, Dylan, was out of state with his father—so I had six weeks to worry about meeting him—but the house across the street was a gold mine of playmates, and there were other boys his age in the neighborhood as well. He met A.J., another seven-year-old, as our furniture was being unloaded. Eddie, at the impressive age of eleven, was just up the street. Leo might have been nervous about leaving Georgia, but once we landed in Oregon he never looked back.

I often ask myself if things would have been different there had we simply bought a house in another neighborhood. The foreignness of central Oregon in general was a big part of my problem, but the neighbors, and Leo's interactions with them, were an even bigger issue. I am a Southern girl, raised by a lovely Southern lady, who taught me not to wear white shoes before Easter or after Labor Day, and I'm pretty sure Lilly had never heard that rule. EVERYTHING was different in Brake. The grocery stores were different, the prices scary-high for unemployed people who had just taken a gigantic financial leap of faith, and I never could find the things I wanted in them. I would wander around and around the store, lamenting the absence of products I loved, and trying to find the pinto beans. The network news came on at a different hour, because of the three-hour time difference, and I had no idea how to garden in sand. It never rained! It got cold every night. And not a single neighbor baked us cookies as a welcome gift!

I'm a child of divorce; I lived with my husband before marriage, but I never expected to land in a neighborhood where there was not one traditional family besides my own. There were single people living alone, single people (Lilly) with foster children, couples living together with children that belonged to one of them, or in the case of AJ, a grandmother raising her grandson because the mother had her hands full with his unstable teenage brother.

And what a lady AJ's grandmother was! I first met her when she came swooping into the cul-de-sac in a convertible with the top down, a large, white-haired woman with a cigarette hanging out of her mouth and a voice like a Mafia boss. The sight of Grandma in the convertible would become familiar, as she was averse to walking the three blocks between our houses. She made the trip in her car instead, roaring AJ's name, the few times she required him home.

Eddie's parents, on the other hand, remained invisible for the entire summer, despite the few hundred feet between our houses and the enormous amounts of time our sons spent with each other. The most I ever knew about them was what I learned when Eddie showed me his enormous beer-bottle cap collection, and told me his father and a friend had drunk all of it on the 4th of July.

Rounding out the cul-de-sac were a 60-something single man, who once invited Leo into his house "just to talk"; and Dylan's mother and her boyfriend, a muscle-bound former football player who liked to tell Leo that soccer "sucked", and describe the latest wild game he had bagged—in one instance, a moose. Moose Slayer, as we called him, was actually quite friendly even though John met him our first night in Brake by complaining to him about his sprinkler hitting our bedroom windows!

The kid, Dylan, actually turned out to be one of my favorite neighbors, which just shows you what the competition was like. He was good-natured, athletic, and had at least one actual chore: cleaning up the dog poop in his 1/6th of an acre yard. AJ, on the other hand, was clearly a child headed for trouble, although I had flashes of insight into the more sensitive aspects of his nature, such as his love of plants, which I found heartwarming. The only one with social graces was Eddie. I liked his respectful tone, but John was convinced he was the worst of the lot, and that it was all a snow job. It was John who nicknamed him "Eddie Haskell".

Unlike in Athens, Leo received quite a few social invitations here. Dylan's mom had Leo over for burgers once, although we never saw the inside of their house. "Grandma" invited him up to cook out several times, and it was after one of these functions that I nixed going to AJ's house.

"There was a fire, Mom. The flames from the grill were like, four feet high, and the neighbors were yelling to call 911."

"Where was AJ's Grandma?"

"Inside watching television. It was okay, though, we put it out with a fire extinguisher."

On Leo's seventh birthday, I wasn't sure what to do. We'd been in Brake only two weeks, and many of the children he played with, at Lilly's day care, weren't allowed to go in other people's houses. Eventually I set up a card table on the driveway just outside our garage, and invited a few of them over for cake. I was feeling overly guilty for not hosting a bash at Chuck E. Cheese's—something that had never bothered me before!—so we probably went overboard with the gifts. We took Leo to pick out a new bicycle, and also to a pet store for two gerbils and their accoutrements. In the evening we had a family celebration with gifts from the relatives far, far away.

In spite of my misery, Leo probably had what he would consider the greatest summer of his childhood. He was so busy playing outdoors that he virtually never turned on the TV. Daylight lasted til ten o'clock, and the sun was always shining when he woke up. There were kids everywhere. In addition (and mostly in an attempt to get him away from those kids), I signed him up for soccer camp, vacation bible school, and swim lessons. But he was happiest when having unstructured time with the neighborhood posse. I didn't stay outside and hover but did check on them frequently. I often had to break up a crabapple fight or stop someone from throwing rocks. Once I caught AJ swinging his skateboard around like a hammer thrower and then letting it rip across the cul-de-sac, which was full of children. Another time I came out to sounds of distress from Leo, to find Dylan threatening to throw him in his dad's cement mixer. ("I was just kiddin' around," Dylan shrugged. "I've been in there.") Invariably, no matter how many children were out, I was the only grownup present.

And of course, they got into trouble. Lilly informed me one day that the kids had popped her "$35 wading pool" by jumping their scooters over it. I could tell she wanted money but was disinclined to offer any since there was no way to know who the actual perpetrators were. Another day I stopped by AJ's to pick up Leo on my way to clothes shop for him at the mall, and found him with his chin split open and only a BandAid over it.

"What happened?" I cried.

"Rocks!" rasped Grandma, lurching toward the door. "They were playing baseball with rocks! I alus tell 'em, ya play baseball with rocks, somebody's gonna get hurt!"

Turned out AJ had been the one to clean Leo up and apply the BandAid. Where was Grandma?

"Watching her soap operas", Leo said.

One evening as I was fixing supper, Leo came running in the house, yelling, "Mom! A man just gave me $5 for telling him who broke his truck!"

"What??" I grabbed the bill and strode out into the street, looking for the stranger, but he had gone. "Leo, never, NEVER accept money from a stranger! And never take money for giving someone information!" What kind of place were we living?

That night I was an emotional wreck and John urged me to "take your anxiety medicine and go to bed", which I did. I was almost asleep when someone pounded on our door. I listened as John answered and had a conversation with two other men. I could tell it was getting heated, and jumped up to grab my robe and defend my man, but by the time I got to the living room, the visitors had left.

Even John looked bothered this time.

"That was Lilly's brother and some other guy."

"What did he want?"

"He asked if we have a little boy that rides a blue and red bike. I said yes, and he said Leo broke the glass in his camper cover that was sitting in Lilly's driveway."

Just then there was a crash, followed by the sound of tires peeling off. We hurried outside to see what had happened.

"It's my brother," said Lilly, standing in her yard close to tears. "He's a hothead and a jerk. He just pushed my car into my garage door with his truck."

Well, THAT was a night. Turns out Hothead was determined to make someone pay for his broken glass, which was probably caused by the desert sun and soaring temperatures, and had tried to get the money from Lilly. She clearly sent him to us, although she skirted that part of the story in her telling. John said the brother was holding a big piece of metal off the camper cover and was accompanied by a friend, who "was actually trying to calm him down". John had refused to pay on the grounds that "there are a million kids around here and there's no way to know who did it", which was when the conversation had gotten heated.

"I'm getting a restraining order", Lilly said. "I'm gonna put a big "No Trespassing" sign in my yard." I wondered how this would affect her day care business, but by now I had pretty much concluded that I was living in the Wild West, and sure enough, the number of kids over there never lessened.

* * *

The main reason we had moved to Central Oregon was its great outdoor beauty and recreational opportunities, and we tried to take advantage of them. One of the most beautiful places in the world, in my opinion, is Smith Rock Canyon. So we loaded up the dogs one day and drove over. The canyon is so enormous that I felt dizzy on the hike down. Leo scrambled over the rocks and climbed into tiny caves while the dogs splashed in the river and John and I took in the incredible colors of the sandstone and the ruggedness of the vegetation. The entire Eastern seaboard simply has nothing like this, and in spite of my emotional condition I could appreciate its grandeur.

Another day we drove to a state park high up in the mountains to take a walk around a small lake. Imagine our surprise when we found the stone picnic tables swallowed, in July, by drifting snow. The snow was wet, dirty and old, and the temperature mild, but by its sheer volume it wasn't going anywhere anytime soon. It did beg the question exactly when the tables COULD be used in a calendar year. The area around the lake was a bog of melted snow, and we ended up slogging our way around the far side, losing shoes and laughing over Leo's outraged cries of protest as we made our way back.

On the 4th of July we took advantage of Brake's small-town charm to attend the downtown festival. The weather was perfect and Duck Park stunning as always. There were clever events like a rubber duckie race on the river, and shooting plastic fish out over the river with a giant slingshot, for a prize if you landed one in floating hula hoops. I remember how handsome John looked with his black hair and his red golf shirt, wearing a snazzy pair of reflector shades he had won in a recent 5K. But I never got out my camera—I never took a picture the entire time we lived in Brake. Somehow I knew looking at them would just bring back how bad I was feeling at the time.

Sitting on the courthouse steps waiting for the parade to start that day, we met a young family much like ours, except that their child was a girl. They were also new to Oregon, and the mom and I exchanged phone numbers. John and I were excited—potential friends! While Leo had them out the wazoo, we hadn't really connected with anyone yet. John was constantly on the lookout for people to run with, something we thought would be no problem to find in a town as obsessed with fitness as Brake is. However, it seemed the sports of favor among the lean, tanned townspeople were mountain biking and skiing. In the weeks that followed, I contacted the mom of that family repeatedly, but somehow nothing ever panned out and we didn't see them again.

I suggested trying the Unitarian Universalist Fellowship. Not being terribly religious, we thought their worldview might jive best with ours. It turned out that the small congregation didn't even hold services in summer! but they did have an outdoor potluck coming up, so we went to that. There we met more lean, tanned people and made little if any connection.

Several times we went to the riverside farmers' market. It was filled with young, healthy-looking families scanning the abundance of summer berries: strawberries, blueberries, raspberries and the large blackberries unique to Oregon known as marionberries (as former residents of the D.C. area, we found this name hilarious.) You could buy a gorgeous mixed four-pack of quart baskets of these at many stalls for $10. Each time I looked at them and yearned, but I would never spend the money, as I was sure we were going down financially in the world's most expensive small town.

One day we took a picnic to Duck Park. As ever, it was sunny, the river sparkled, the ducks swam along peacefully, and Leo was happy playing along the edges of the lake. As John and I finished our sandwiches, he gave me a wicked grin. "Don't we feel sorry for everyone who isn't us?" he asked. I stared at him. I had never felt such a large disconnect from my husband in our 15 years together. But of course on the surface, everything was lovely. It was only inside that I was falling apart.

Chapter 8
Fighting for Control

Among the many actions I took to make myself feel better were daily walks. I frequently hiked up The Butte, an odd protrusion in the middle of town that was very popular with walkers for its view and the steady climb. A sign at the bottom of the trail told of a recent cougar sighting on the butte, and gave instructions on how to react should you encounter the big cat ("If you are wearing a coat, open it to make yourself appear as large as possible. Do not run away.") Funny, but in spite of my overwhelming anxiety, I was not in the least worried about being mauled by a cougar. A wild animal attack is very straightforward: you follow your instinct and fight for your life. Pathological anxiety is a constant fear and dread of irrational things or things you can't even name. It's the fear that you're doing everything wrong. Sometimes it is simply the fear of more anxiety.

When I didn't drive to The Butte, I walked around our neighborhood. Occasionally in the evenings John, Leo and the dogs would join me for a family parade. John had met a nice man with a son near Leo's age and we were on Friend Patrol on these walks, hoping to meet them and introduce our families. I was always hoping to find Leo some friends I would approve of, that would take him away from the cul-de-sac gang. I never succeeded.

There was a view of Mount Bachelor, in its snow-capped grandeur, just a couple of blocks from our house, and I always looked at it in wonder, thinking how surreal it was that I owned property here. I knew it must be terribly exciting and thrilling and that the folks back home wouldn't believe it, but somehow the thrill stopped at my eyes, never reaching my heart or my soul.

On one of these walks I met a very friendly neighbor about our age. He told me his wife was inside resting, and that their newborn was going to be released from the hospital in a few days. In spite of the new arrival, Sandy and Rita were evidently on more rigorous Friend Patrol than even John and I, for by the end of our conversation Sandy had invited us to dinner! I of course insisted he check with his wife, but within a few hours he had called our house to make it official. They had us over before Baby Kieran was even sent home. Sandy and Rita were really the only friends we made in Brake, and in the weeks to come I would find she was the only one to whom I could begin to confess my inner turmoil.

Far from being "all in my head", my anxiety had undeniable physical symptoms. The one that bothered me most was a tingling sensation in my arms and legs. This was later explained to me as adrenalin coursing through my system, preparing me for the fight or flight which rarely ensued to make use of it. My heart beat heavily, sometimes pounding, and I struggled with shortness of breath. Although my stomach was not actively upset, I had little appetite and often left food on my plate—a definite new development for someone who, in college, had the nickname Endless Void for the amount I could consume without putting on weight.

My energy level was very low, and although I could walk or hike, I was easily fazed by the thought of any task that involved concentrating. If I realized I needed to food-shop, I would feel completely overwhelmed at the thought of facing the Safeway again and coming away with what I needed. Whenever all of us left the house, I would worry that someone would hurt or set loose our dogs, or vandalize our house. It seemed, somehow, obvious to me that the neighborhood kids would want to do that and would capitalize on the opportunity we provided by leaving our property unguarded. I also had a definite feeling that we were losing control of the house: we unavoidably tracked in sticky sap dripped from the Ponderosa pine in our front yard, and it stuck to the carpet and linoleum and was almost impossible to remove. The kids had broken some of the lights bordering our driveway, and I didn't even know when it had happened, let alone who was responsible. There were systems in the house that we never learned to use, including an intercom, a sprinkler system in the yard, and a hot tub we never filled. I would stand at the doorway of darkened rooms and flip switch after switch, repeatedly, because I could never seem to learn which ones worked which lights.

I felt, always, eyes on me through the windows of our house. There weren't any, of course, but our yard was tiny and the neighbors close, and the house had lots of glass. The only places I felt secure were the most interior: Leo's bathroom, where there were no windows, or the shower stall in ours. I always looked forward to sitting in Leo's bathroom with him while he took a tub, washing off the brown desert dust that coated him every day. Here I could pretend we were in one of our Georgia homes, where a person could actually relax. The memory of how different I had felt everywhere else I had lived was astounding.

In fact, I would have changed places with anyone I saw in Oregon. They all belonged, they had relatives here, friends, jobs; they were *from* Oregon, or at least some neighboring state, or they had a history here. I, on the other hand, was from another planet, a whole different species, from everyone else here. They were all having a normal experience, living their lives without fear or insomnia or skulking around their own homes. I was just a freak.

To me, you see, this was Oregon sickness. It was caused, clearly, by an emotionally wrenching cross-country move, and it would not have occurred had we not moved. This was actually only partially true. My anxiety was stress-induced, and the stress was the move, but that was only the crowning stress on top of my mother's death, infertility, my sister's divorce, international adoption, John's two layoffs, and parenting concerns. John had made the same move, and he was fine. Heck, people move to Oregon all the time, and as far as I can tell not many of them wind up in mental hospitals as a result.

From my perspective six years later, and having been through much more since then, one of the key factors to my illness was having stopped my anti-depressant four months prior to the move. I don't think under any circumstances I would have been happy in Brake, but unhappy and pathologically anxious are light-years apart.

By this I do not mean to say I believe the medication withdrawal *caused* my anxiety; since this episode, I have witnessed a relative who had never taken anti-depressants experience severe anxiety, and I have taken more interest in my grandfather's diagnosis as a manic depressive back in the 70's. I believe I have a genetic propensity toward anxiety induced by severe stress. I often thought of it, at the time, as a thermostat that had broken in my brain. Whereas most people experience extreme anxiety at some points in their lives, the needle swings back to stable after awhile—ten minutes, half a day, a week or a month. My needle was stuck on adrenalin surge. The result was complete misery.

I tried everything. I went, for the second time in my life, to a counselor. Although she was sympathetic and provided some insights, I couldn't justify the cost of the sessions for the help I felt I was getting from them. I found a medical practitioner who prescribed another anti-depressant, known to kick in faster than the one I had been taking, and began taking it with high hopes. I felt no improvement in the prescribed time, so on my own I decided to try the old one again. This might have made the difference for me, but unfortunately there are temporary side effects when adjusting to these medicines, also known as SSRI's (Selective Serotonin Reuptake Inhibitors) that were exactly what I didn't need right then. In five days I went from sleeping several hours a night to sleeping as little as ten minutes. I sat up, hour after hour, holding my knees to my chest and rocking back and forth. I became frantic to get the stuff out of my system, and after quitting it, walked incessantly to give myself the feeling I was hurrying the medicine out of my body.

I went to the library in search of self-help books. I found an excellent one, Worry, by Edward Hallowell, and took great comfort from its pages. I emailed the author and was touched to receive what appeared to be personal responses from both Dr. Hallowell and his secretary. Regrettably, they could not recommend a therapist any closer than Portland, and I was in no shape to drive alone across a wide swath of Oregon and navigate a sizeable town to find an office.

Thinking that my lingering grief for my mother could be a factor, I sought a grief group to join. My sister, in the small town of Blue River, had found a group that benefited her, so how could there not be one in a place as progressive as Brake? I did find one, but it was run by a pastor and based on religious tenets, and I didn't think I could relate.

I did, however, try Sunday services at a couple of local churches. It just offended me that A.J. would show up at 9 a.m. on a Sunday and ask if Leo could come out to play. I couldn't believe soccer teams had practice scheduled then! People were supposed to at least PRETEND they went to church, and expected others to. Sunday morning was, somehow, sacred! (Mainly I wanted a break from worrying about Leo with the other kids.)

At one service I attended, the sermon was called "Bloom Where You're Planted", and the minister began with "What are you doing in Brake, Oregon?" Oh my gosh, I thought. What *am* I?

Well, how about volunteering? In Athens, Leo and I had played with dogs at the animal shelter, so I called about doing that. In Georgia one simply showed up and was shown to the play yard with some dogs. But in Oregon, of course, there was an entire application and orientation procedure, which I found offensive and too overwhelming to go through.

Okay, it was time to get back to one of my lifelong loves—gardening. I began by weeding the beds in my yard, but dang, which ones were the weeds? I didn't recognize the desert plants, so I called the extension agency. They sent me printed information about the state Master Gardener program, another thing I looked into and never began. I continued to putter now and then in the yard, but weakly, and I felt like I was trying to grow things on the moon.

I was amazed whenever I saw myself in the mirror, because I looked normal. What would not have surprised me would have been a gaunt, haggard face with sunken, haunted eyes. That was the inside of me. The outside just didn't match.

John began to notice the shape I was in. For one thing, our sex life had completely ceased to exist. I was a frightened shadow of my usual energetic, wisecracking self. "I just feel so BAD here," I told him, as we sat on our back deck. It was a bit of a breakthrough for me to put it holistically, instead of saying that I was nervous and also that I had physical symptoms. I was beginning to play with the idea of just running away—to Blue River, where Leo and I could stay with my sister for a while, I could have some relief, and we could pass some of the time until school started. I felt like once Leo was in school and I got a job, things would stabilize for me—and they might have.

My husband didn't get it—how could he? I wouldn't have understood either, before it happened to me. And John is the son of a West Point graduate, from a family that doesn't approve of mental illness, so he had no frame of reference at all for what was happening to me. To him, I should have just had a stiff drink and snapped out of it. And how I would have loved to.

It is said that we can't ask more of people than they are capable of giving, and what true words those are. It simply wasn't in John to put his arms around me and say, "It'll be okay, honey. You're going through a tough adjustment, but I'm right here to help you. We'll get through this together, and we'll all love it here—you'll see, I promise!"

Much later I would express this to John, at a time when our marriage was falling apart. He would look at me coldly and say, "I don't think I deserve ANY blame for what happened in Oregon," and I would hastily apologize and agree. I bore enormous guilt for my anxiety for years, until I finally understood its genetic and biochemical basis. The beliefs we are raised with die hard.

And so we continued determinedly pursuing our life of leisure. We drove to a dog show in a nearby town. Spent a day in the resort town of Sisters. Went to a downtown bike race. Looked up friends of friends and attended their 4th of July fireworks party. John finally met some runners, and Leo and I joined all of them for brunch at an outdoor cafe after a Sunday morning run. Much as I wanted to curl up in a ball under the covers and whimper, I continued dragging myself around Brake, running errands, shopping, taking Leo to reading groups at the library and children's activities in the park.

On rare occasions, flashes of my former self emerged. The first was when Moose Slayer accused John of complaining to his employer about the cement mixer in the cul-de-sac. The next time I saw him, I accosted him and said, "Buddy, John and I did not call your company. You know that. You know we would have said something to you first". At this Buddy looked kind of sheepish and said, "Yeah, after I thought about it I figured that. Besides, I think I know who it is now!" and proceeded to finger another of our neighbors whom I was pretty sure was also innocent. In fact, all along I thought Lilly had made the call, but I wasn't about to get in the middle of THAT neighborhood's politics!

Another time, one of Lilly's charges told us, to our amazement, that he was no longer allowed to play with Leo or A.J. because his mother thought that they smoked.

Seven-year-olds!

This meant Leo was not allowed to go in Lilly's house or yard, and that the child in question couldn't play with Leo in the cul-de-sac or our yard, as he often had. When I asked Lilly about this, she was noncommittal as always. "I don't know why; I just know that's what the mom asked for, and I have to respect it," she said.

The Mama Bear in me woke up. That evening I sat in my front yard waiting for the mother in question to arrive to pick up her kids. When she did, I strode over there.

"Excuse me, are you Jason's mom?" I asked.

"Yes—" A guarded look.

"Hi, I'm Laura Anne, Leo's mom," I extended my hand. "Listen, I just wanted to ask you—Jason says he's not allowed to play with Leo any longer. Is that true?"

The mom shook her head. "I just said that Jason should maybe think more about who his friends are, after he told me that Eddie stole cigarettes from A.J.'s grandmother. I know Eddie and A.J. and Leo play together a lot, so I thought they might all have been in on that."

"No. No!" I said in amazement. "Leo is seven years old! Of course he doesn't smoke, for Pete's sake!"

"Well, I didn't think so…"

"And he certainly didn't steal any cigarettes! Eddie may have, I don't know. But Leo plays out here with these kids, and it was really causing a problem that he was banned from joining in, when they play baseball in the cul-de-sac or something."

"Oh well no, I never meant for that to happen."

"Okay, well, whew!" we were both smiling now.

Lilly, meanwhile, stood a few feet away, playing with some of the other children and effectively shrugging. I knew what had happened here.

Chapter 9
Chaos

The morning after the broken truck window incident, I had to get out. I had passed a terrible night, in spite of two anxiety pills, and I was in survival mode. It seemed crazy, and my heart was pounding, but something made me come out of the bedroom and approach John at the kitchen table, having his coffee.

I swallowed hard, and fought back tears. "Honey, I pray you love me enough to not divorce me for this, but even if you're going to divorce me, I have to go. I'm taking Leo and going to Blue River and I don't know if I'm coming back." Having gotten it out, I broke down.

"I'm afraid if I stay here, I'm going to go to pieces," I sobbed. "I've…I've even thought about jumping off a building but it wouldn't work because of that stupid ordinance that doesn't allow any buildings taller than two stories in town!" I ranted, and, in a way that only John and I could possibly understand, we both smiled.

He did not seem as surprised as I had expected. There was only one word for the expression on his face at the end of our conversation, and it was Grim. Since that day I have seen that expression many, many times, and it does not gladden the heart of anyone. John is such a naturally happy person that it takes something at least borderline catastrophic to bring that look to his face.

There ensued a very unhappy 24 hours. My husband's mouth was set in a tight line that did not relax. He seemed to know, however, what the decision had cost me, and he did not try to sway me. Although I maintained that I might very well come back, he never seemed to consider this a possibility, and was certain that his dream of living out there was coming to an end. Later he would tell me that on the final leg of our journey to Oregon, he had been looking around him and thinking, "This is just too good to be true. Something is going to mess this up." How prophetic his thoughts were, and how they broke my heart when I heard them. Surely the world had never known a bigger loser than I.

Leo took the news surprisingly well. After all, North Carolina had never been home to him, but a fun place where he visited his three cousins, played basketball, had snowball fights and wrestling free-for-alls. There was never any question of him staying behind with Daddy. Where I went, Leo went, and where Mom was, was home.

Packing was hard. What do you bring when you don't know if you are coming back? Don't know if you are staying in someone else's home or, possibly, your own rental place? Don't know if you'll stay until the weather gets cold? I packed the giant suitcase I had only used once, when we went to Russia. John booked the flight for me, and eventually his mouth relaxed.

We told the neighbors nothing; I was ashamed and furtive about my actions. My family back home was thrilled, being worried to death about me as well as having heartily disapproved of the move all along, but my in-laws were another matter. They are practical people, not given to a lot of "mush", and the idea that I was leaving our home without my husband, and might possibly do something as insane as not going back, met with their stern disapproval. It was simply not done by stable people in solid marriages—the only kind their family partook of—and worse, the financial bottom line of such a move was disastrous.

However, my sister-in-law, Karen, is an island of warmth in this mentally-disciplined clan. Luckily for me, she and her family lived in Raleigh, where Leo and I would fly in. We could spend the night there and be picked up next day by my more-than-willing dad and step-mom, who would drive us to Blue River.

I will never forget the feeling I had when I saw Karen and her husband Eddie at the bottom of the airport elevator. Relief washed over me like warm water, and I could not stop smiling. It was late, and they were concerned about the situation, of course, but I was happy enough for all of us.

My in-laws happened to be visiting at Karen and Eddie's home, and you could have cut the tension in their living room with a knife when we all walked in. I really thought, for a moment, that they weren't even going to get up, let alone embrace me as they always had. They finally relaxed somewhat when showing me pictures of their new granddaughter, John's brother's child, who had been born since we moved. I was practically bouncing on the sofa, my heart lifting and lifting with joy. There was no reason to be scared! I did not have to fear the knock on the door, the telephone bell. Someone else would take care of anything that happened, and what was more, nothing awful was going to happen here! I was back in the land of people I understood and related to. Not only that, there was green grass growing in red clay outside the windows, and it might even rain.

I called John to let him know of our safe arrival and tucked Leo into bed. Karen and I stayed up talking. She acknowledged her parents' bewilderment and disapproval, but when I talked of going back, she asked me, "Why would you do that to your health?" Late in the night, I took a sleeping pill and climbed in bed myself. After two months, at last, I could rest.

***

Karen and Eddie's daughter, Lynne, was two years old, and delighted to see us the next morning. After watching some of the 150 channels available on the household flat-screen TV, she and her big cousin Leo were allowed to play outside with Leo in charge. I had my breakfast while taking in all the indications of a successful, functioning family surrounding me. There was a note from Karen to her husband on the dry-erase board about some mundane household matter, signed with "I (heart) you!" The refrigerator was stocked with juice boxes, pudding cups, and other evidence of a young child in day care while her mommy and daddy worked at their fulfilling careers. Baby Lynne's room included her own pink Barbie TV set, as well as exotic gifts her mother had brought her from business trips to South Africa.

Eddie, the most dependable of his widowed mother's four children, needed to mow his mother's yard on this Saturday morning. Fortunately for the kids, her yard included a pool, so Agnes and I could take them swimming while waiting for my dad and Kaye to make the three-hour drive down from Blue River. It was a strange vacation-within-a-crisis, or, as Jerry Seinfeld once said to Kramer, "vacation from WHAT?" seeing as how I was unemployed.

I didn't swim, but watched the children from the side of the pool with my mother-in-law. Agnes looked me over in my sleeveless shirt and shorts and asked if I was losing weight. I seized on this as a chance to demonstrate to her that what I was suffering was real, that I hadn't just left my husband and flown across the country for nothing. I had lost about eight pounds at this point, and was not a person who could spare it. Agnes looked disapproving but did not comment.

When Eddie had finished his work, he sat under the deck to cool off, and I joined him. Karen's husband is what some would call the salt of the earth: a straightforward, hard-working family man, conservative in his outlook. I knew he thought leaving Oregon had been a drastic move on my part, but felt he would be less obvious than Agnes in his feelings. I don't recall how it came up, but he wound up telling me of his father's decision to move their family from the Northeast down to Raleigh, when he was growing up. It was a big change, of course, and separated his mom from her three sisters as well as her friends. She went into a depression after the move. But his father had moved for a job, and they remained in Raleigh. "It wouldn't have done any good for my dad to have moved us back," he said. He was reflective, looking out over the pool, leaning his elbows on his knees.

Somehow, it didn't come across as criticism. He spoke openly, letting me know that he knew I was suffering and why, but concluding that a family stays together and makes it work wherever they are. Of course the big difference was that John didn't have a job in Oregon, and neither did I, but his point was taken. It was the only time Eddie ever reached out to me personally, and I appreciated it. He knew John's and my final decision on the matter wasn't in yet, and he was sharing a personal experience he knew to be relevant. He wanted to help.

When we arrived back at Karen and Eddie's house, there was a bit of an uproar. "Now they're okay, and they don't want you to panic," Karen told me, "but your dad and Kaye have been in an accident. They can still drive the car, but they're going to be late." Everyone rushed to assure me there was no need to stress, and Eddie got a beer for each of us, which I pulled on gratefully. I can't imagine what would have happened to me at that point had one of them been hurt driving down the mountain to take their pathetic daughter home.

They arrived not long after that, full of stories of being sideswiped by an enormous truck on the interstate, and jazzed with the thrill of being alive and unhurt. My father was upbeat as always, so glad to see me and to take us back up the mountain. He also requested a beer, and we had a very relieved lunch together.

As we drove to Blue River that afternoon, with me feeling like a little girl in the back of my daddy's car with my son, Dad told us he had asked Agnes what she thought about the situation, and she had replied, "I don't know *what* they're doing."

I guess, in retrospect, it might have looked like I was leaving John, and after agreeing, nay SUGGESTING, that we should move across the country and buy a house. (John always said, in later years, that it was my idea.) I had assured Karen, who was my go-between with Rob and Agnes, that there was nothing wrong between the two of us, and that we had agreed on this turn of events. But I'm sure to Agnes, who had followed her husband (again, for a job), to Germany as well as all over the East Coast, I looked unstable and quite disloyal. Well, I couldn't argue with the unstable part. I'd argue even less with it now. The difference is, now I understand better what was happening to me, and why I made the "crazy" decision that I did. I was saving my own life—which would become obvious in years to come.

***

Although touching down in Raleigh had been an enormous relief, the time in Blue River was one of the strangest and most stressful of my life. Sara was working four days a week and her children were with their dad, so Leo and I were more than a little at loose ends at a time when I desperately needed support. The question arching over everything I did was, to quote The Clash, "Should I stay or should I go?" Not having the answer, it was hard to know how to proceed.

I didn't want to be a burden on Sara, and felt guilty even for the food we were eating, so I tried to help out a lot. I washed dishes and folded laundry, and some days I drove Sara to work so I could use the car to buy groceries or run other errands. I met with my dad and with Henry, who was remarried now, to talk about the situation and try to figure things out. I had long telephone conversations with a few select friends to whom I was willing to admit what I had done. I didn't know WHAT to tell my sister's neighbors. One Sunday when we accompanied her to church, one of the congregants said to me, "So you live in Brake, Oregon?" and I stammered for a long time before saying yes. Did I?

Leo got out his cousin Mason's bike and rode it all around the neighborhood, meeting any kid in his path. There weren't many, but a few were visiting grandparents, and with Leo's gregarious influence, they all wound up playing "Capture the Flag" one night well after dark. Sara looked out her window at the gang of kids in her driveway, and said, "That's amazing. It's NEVER like this."

I took Leo to the local park once or twice, and vaguely looked at the want ads, trying to figure out if they applied to me at all. I did need to see what the rental housing market was like, just to have that to factor into my decision. So I perused the local paper and made some calls, never quite sure how to answer the landlords' questions. Such as, where did my husband and I work? Oops. Can't say as I'd ever been in a position to look for a rental home without a job. John and I had owned three homes during the past ten years, and it was hard having people ask once again if I was a student, had pets, smoked, etc. I wanted to say, "It's not like that."

At night, sleep was so futile that I would go out to Sara's peaceful back porch, just a few feet away from a pasture. I would sit, ideally with a cat on my lap, and often drink a beer, staring wide-eyed into the night, trying to figure out how I'd gotten there and where the heck "there" was. Sometimes my stomach would growl until I got something I could handle to put in it. Sara began to joke about my 4 a.m. Cheerios habit.

I tried not to take medicines, but resorted to them at least every other night: a sleeping pill or anxiety med, so that I could rest a few hours. Although I was exhausted, I was so anxious that such a thing as an afternoon nap was inconceivable. One night when I was pacing back and forth, Sara said, "At least you're not in Oregon". And I realized and said out loud, "I never felt this bad in Oregon."

She and my dad and Kaye regularly campaigned against my returning—and to this day I am not sure if they merely didn't want me so far away, or actually knew how bad off I was. Nevertheless, one night, after Sara and I had gone to a play and were having dessert in a restaurant, I heard myself saying, "I think I better just go home".

I have always been considered sensible, and that was, after all, what a sensible person would do. My husband was there, my furniture, my dogs, my car, my life. I owned property there, for God's sake. A grown-up would definitely go home. And so I made the decision, although John didn't think it was a good idea. "Within a week back here, you'll be like you were," he said. But I had to. I just couldn't live with myself if I didn't.

Sara was almost in tears. "You'll go out there, and I'll never hear from you, and it'll be like you fell off the face of the earth," she said. "I'll never know if you're okay or not!"

Henry only said, sincerely, "I wonder what your mother would say". I had wondered the same thing, and I still do not know. I know that whatever she thought would have been an enormous influence on my decision, but her input was gone forever.

I could see that my father practically wanted to bar my way, but he very unhappily gave us a ride back to Raleigh and put us on a plane. I took two anxiety pills and prayed for sleep on the cross-country flight, but it eluded me. The medicine did, however, make me groggy, so that by the time I saw John, I was uncharacteristically inert. He was very glad to see us, and only later confided that he was disappointed by the greeting he received from me. Life was so strange to me by then that I think I was having an out-of-body experience at the time.

***

I was glad to get back to the house under cover of darkness. My heart always filled with dread when we turned onto the road to our neighborhood, but tonight I wouldn't have to face anyone in the cul-de-sac, and Leo wouldn't charge straight out to play. We went right to bed, and the next morning John joked, "See, you've been back in Oregon ten hours and nothing terrible has happened yet!" He was upbeat, having just seen his dream hanging in the balance, and then appear to solidify again—plus of course, he'd been lonely! I felt horrible to be back, but was trying to hide it and give Brake another chance. At the breakfast table, I waded through the pile of mail that had accumulated.

One letter was from Blue Cross Blue Shield of Oregon, to whom I had applied for health insurance for us all. John and Leo had been accepted, but I was turned down. Not offered a higher rate, but rejected, apparently because I had honestly answered their health history questions and I had, at one time, been on an anti-depressant for headaches. Headaches.

What would I do now? Going without health insurance was playing Russian roulette, especially at forty-plus. The letter referred me to a state agency, apparently a safety net for the uninsurable! which was very expensive and had a complicated application process. The feeling of being overwhelmed loomed large. "Well," I said to John after opening the letter. "Actually, something terrible HAS happened".

But I was back, and I meant it. I swung into action. I threw a small dinner party—three couples, including Sandy and Rita and a couple John had met while running. The woman was a writer of "Chick Lit", and brought a copy of her book, apparently only for us to admire, as she did not leave it. Sandy brought a large box of assorted bakery biscotti, tied up with a pink ribbon. We ate out on our deck and all was gracious and friendly—like normal people, in a normal situation. I was tired afterwards but had enjoyed it—shades of a potential social life in the Wild West!

I took Leo up to the local school to enroll him. I had all his records, and expected to breeze right through. But Oregon law required different immunizations and medical tests, which I would have to arrange first. Again, I felt as if I had started up a mountain in good faith, and someone had knocked me back down to the bottom.

Of course, it *wasn't* a mountain. It was a normal glitch in a procedure. All these minor setbacks were glitches. But to me, at the time, they were devastating.

Just before Leo and I left Oregon, a job had opened up with the county that was perfect for John. Although I'm not a fatalist, I thought of it as a sign. If he got the job, we should stay. If he didn't, it simply wasn't meant to be for us to live out West.

A couple of mornings after I got home, the phone rang right after breakfast. John answered and exchanged pleasantries with someone. With a feeling of unreality I heard his next remark. "Oh yes, of course, I understand."

He hadn't gotten the job. The burden of making the right decision settled its oppressive weight back on my shoulders.

Leo, who had jumped right back into the neighborhood gang, now came down with a fever and had to be kept inside. My panic button pushed again. He didn't have a pediatrician. What if it was serious? What would I do? I just didn't know what to do! It was a normal illness, really less than 48 hours of a moderate fever, and then he was right as rain. But in my mind, it was just more disaster piling on top of all the other disasters in a few short days back. When he did get back outside to his posse, he and A.J. got into a fight, and I ordered Leo back inside our fence since they couldn't seem to settle it. When I heard Leo yelling at A.J. to "Get your bike off my property!" I was certain that the Oregon sky was falling.

John's prediction had been accurate. On my sixth day back, I forced myself out on the patio to tell him, "I just can't do this." There were arrangements to be made.

My husband, of course, expected us to pack up together and trek back across the country. But I couldn't even handle that. I had to get out, now, with Leo. I think at this point I would have been too weak to even make that drive again. I got online and discovered that school in Blue River started August 8th, which was days away. I was in a panic.

John resigned himself to the perfectly shitty situation and got online to make my airline reservations. I was sure I would screw it up if I tried to make them myself. We arranged with a realtor to put the house on the market. We got quotes from moving companies. We broke the news, in North Carolina, where it was met with cheers from my family and consternation from John's, and in our own house, where Leo just figured his parents were crazy and whatever, dude.

And John drove us to the airport one more time. As we said good-bye, I could not stop crying. What I was doing was crazy—crazy! What if I didn't see John for months? What if the house didn't sell?

What if I was making the worst decision of our lives? What if Blue River was a disaster, we couldn't get jobs, we hated it? What if my marriage couldn't survive this? What *if?*

For the third time, Leo and I were pulled out to be searched, because for the third time, we were flying on one-way tickets. John could just see us from where he had to stop at airport security, and I was crying the whole time. The airline personnel simply went through the motions, averting their eyes from my grief-stricken face. I felt terrible for Leo seeing me this way, terrible for it being John's last glimpse of me. I just felt terrible.

***

It was pouring down the rain in Raleigh that night. Eddie picked us up alone, since Karen had just returned from South Africa and was in bed sleeping off jet lag. I kept thanking Eddie, and apologizing for being so much trouble, to which he would reply stoically, "That's what family's for". When we got to the house, he showed us to a room, where I assumed Leo and I were to share the only bed, and then went off to turn in himself. I had to find towels, and keep Leo quiet as we got ready for bed. It was a very different atmosphere from the night we had arrived so joyfully a few weeks before. I snuggled up to Leo and was amazed that instead of constantly wiggling and talking, he fell right asleep. It was so comforting to be resting with my arms around my child, safe at last in North Carolina. I remember very distinctly having the thought, "What if this is the last time in my life I'm ever happy?"

Chapter 10
Establishing a Beachhead

And now my work was cut out. First order of business: finding a home in Blue River. I had to know which school district we were going to be in, in order to get Leo enrolled, and school had already started. Sara's boys were back, and hustling off to school each morning in a flurry of backpacks, giant shoes and complaints. After they left, Leo and I would buckle down. I made call after call regarding rental properties, at last knowing that this was really going to happen. To the unavoidable questions about jobs, I answered that my husband was self-employed, and I would be securing employment in the immediate future. Fortunately for me, Blue River was a small town and plenty of people knew my family and wouldn't push the issue of secure income.

My decision made—and most irrevocably—you'd think at this point I would start to feel better. I didn't. I assumed it was the guilt; and the stress of missing John, finding a home and getting established—plus all the questions playing out on the other side of the country. But I was no better at sleeping, no better at eating, no better at smiling or laughing or feeling okay. It was a horrifically difficult part of my life I knew I had to get through—that I had created for myself, no less. I knew I had a lot to answer for to a lot of people. Leo was incredibly resilient, but he still gave me physical pangs of remorse one night as I was tucking him in to bed at Sara's house. "I just want to get someplace and *stay*, Mommy," he said plaintively.

Even with a clear path in front of me, I was still so incapacitated by anxiety that the thought of making a housing decision without John almost put me over the edge. I called him every night, when all the stresses of the day had taken their toll, and his voice and his words were like balm on my soul. I would describe each house I'd seen, how expensive they all were and how none was really practical for us, and he would reply, soothingly, "As long as we have a roof over our heads, baby".

"My people" were sure I had done the right thing, and were rejoicing in my decision. I couldn't rejoice in anything. At one point when Sara said, "You've done the right thing for yourself and Leo," I responded, "Maybe so, but what have I done to my marriage?" She didn't have an answer.

And so finally, with much hand-holding from my sister, to the cheers of my father, and with the help of a family friend in the rental business, I signed a lease on a house. It could not have been more different from our house in Brake. It was on a large, wooded lot in an established neighborhood, where the kids not only didn't play baseball with rocks, they didn't play it without batting helmets!

Sara and I together took Leo to his new school to enroll, two weeks into the semester. When we walked him down to his brand-new first grade classroom, he was holding my hand tightly and not saying a word. I knew he was scared—who wouldn't be? but he didn't cry or complain. He was "sprung" on his teacher, who had no idea she was getting another student and was not pleased; and I kissed him, reassured him, and said good-bye. I was so proud of Leo that day, but so nervous for him at the same time, that I had to go "home" to Sara's house and lie down on the sofa. My heart almost burst with relief when he came home saying Mrs. Wilkerson was "the most awesome teacher (he'd) ever had!"

The next few weeks were a labor of love. I drove around town in my mother's old car, lent to me by Henry, signing up for utilities, arranging for delivery of fuel oil, transporting borrowed household items from Dad's to our new home. I swept and cleaned and tidied the sprawling property, collecting bags of trash from the premises and dragging them to the street. I went several rounds with the ancient garage door and finally prevailed upon it to open. Finally one day, we were ready to "move" in.

I was thrilled to be getting out from underfoot at Sara's, but by any standards, our living situation starting out in the new place was difficult. We had almost no furniture and only a couple of lamps. There were few overhead lights except in the kitchen and baths, so I always felt most "normal" in those rooms. Once again I would sit on the toilet seat cover while Leo bathed, and read to him from borrowed story-books, pretending we were a normal family in a standard situation.

I borrowed a clock radio and telephone which I set up in the kitchen, and determinedly played music and listened to the news mornings and evenings. We had a card table and folding chairs, and Kaye had loaned us rudimentary kitchen gear, so I could fix tuna salad or scrambled eggs, and pack Leo's lunches in brown paper bags. I stocked our pantry with the most inexpensive of foodstuffs, feeling that one thing I could do to atone for—well, everything, was save money.

In the bedroom we shared, I had a twin bed my uncle had contributed, and Leo had a cozy palette on the floor. We took possession of a marble-topped dresser my grandmother had left me in her will, and set a castoff lamp from Kaye's attic on it. We even had a few throw rugs scattered about the place. At night we would curl up in my bed to read books, before I tucked Leo in on the floor. It was early September, and already cold.

I found out Leo's school bus, and each day walked him to and from the stop. After school I supervised his homework, and then we sometimes played "volleyball" with a lightweight play ball in our echoing living room, or threw a baseball out in the yard. I met a couple of neighbors and used my PR training to spin our story into something socially acceptable.

Unfortunately this was hurricane season, and torrential rains fell for much of the time. Several days school was canceled because of flooding in the area. One such morning I heard the announcement, informed Leo, and we fell back into bed and played "tickle monster", then celebrated with a cooked breakfast. That day, when the rain let up, we drove to the grocery store and I remember thinking I was going wild because I indulged in sugar, cinnamon, and a box of lime jello as treats! We had another outing that day, too, when my father invited us over for afternoon tea—and what a luxury it was.

While Leo was in school, I was now checking the want ads for jobs, and working on my resume on Sara's computer while our few clothes spun repeatedly in her washer and dryer. On the other side of the country, John had set a date for the movers, and was packing up all our belongings once more. We had our nightly conversation now with me sitting at my kitchen card table, lowering my voice so as not to wake Leo. I wrote in my journal for the first time since Athens: two entries, which were all I would write for the next 13 months. The first was a list of mantras to reassure myself that this too would pass, that John would come, the furniture would arrive, the other house would sell, I would get work, and we would be a functional family again.

The second entry, as I look back at it now, is very telling.

> *This summer, like Mom's death—and NOTHING had been like her death until now—has changed me forever, and increased my cynicism and bitterness. It has wrecked my self-image and our financial stability. I will never be the same. I have a level of fear in my gut that I had never experienced before. I carry the shame of being an adult—and a parent—who couldn't handle life, who was becoming mentally unstable, who felt she could only avoid drug addiction or suicide by running away…. I guess some people—even parents—have done worse. But I have lost all faith in my judgment. And I am not that far from paranoid.*
>
> *It would almost be easier to just have a breakdown and be hospitalized. I am just functional enough to have to retain all my responsibilities….*
>
> *At least I had some really good times up until now. Really. The sad thing is that you can go on being really unhappy for so incredibly long. It could last from now until I die, at 82. And you just endure on, because one thing I have learned is that I will never commit suicide. I will live on through anything.*

I wish I had written at all in the year that followed—my journals always provide me with insights into how I was feeling in the past. Sometimes I look back over my writing and remember so vividly; other times I completely surprise myself with how I was thinking and feeling at a certain time.

One evening I was surprised to receive a phone call from Agnes. There had been a very awkward moment at Karen's house when she suggested Leo and I should join her, her daughter Lynne, and some friends at her parents' beach house over Labor Day, and Agnes had responded stiffly that there "probably wouldn't be room" for me and Leo. It was almost as if Agnes sensed that it was the beginning of the end—that I was on my way out of the family. Had I been in a normal state of mind, I would have been shocked and devastated, but as it was I didn't trust my reaction to anything and just accepted the statement in a stunned kind of way. Karen, on the other hand, lit into her mom promptly.

Now, on the phone, Agnes sounded rehearsed. "Was wondering if you and Leo would like to come to the beach for Labor Day", she asked politely. I was immensely grateful for the gesture, but the thought of the trip overwhelmed me. "I don't know; I mean I'm driving Henry's car, and I feel like I shouldn't put extra miles on it," I stammered. Really I just wanted to curl up in bed for the three-day weekend, and not have to think about anything besides survival.

But Karen offered to drive from Raleigh if I could get us that far, and Henry had no problem with me taking his car, so in the end, I had no excuse to cocoon. I was packed and ready—not that I had a swimsuit!—when Leo got off the bus from school that Friday.

"What's this?" I asked, pulling an envelope addressed "To the parents of Leo Nicholson" out of his folder. Leo shrugged, and I opened it, my heart pounding.

It was a form letter, telling me that the school did not have Leo's immunization records and that he would be suspended if they were not provided within a week.

So much for having a good weekend.

Now Leo had had all his vaccinations, and I had already turned in the proof. Furthermore, had they *and* I lost them, it would have been a simple matter of a few phone calls to Georgia to get them again. But I was a parent alone (!) and in a general panic, and the word "suspended" triggered my intense fear response like something Lilly might have said. Although I headed on down the mountain, I ended up pulling to the side of the road and calling the school with my borrowed cell phone.

I had previously had a conversation with the school principal—who was married to one of my high school friends—in which I worried aloud about Leo's behavior issues. The principal chuckled at one point and said, "*Him* we can handle; you I'm not sure about!" I laughed shrilly, but was horrified to realize that others could perceive my anxiety. I was not normal, and they could tell.

Now the school secretary assured me that Leo would not be suspended over the vaccination issue, but my mind continued to race. I spent the rest of the day and part of that night imagining all kinds of nightmare scenarios regarding Leo's school career.

A few things stick out in my memory from that weekend at the beach, but most of it is a blur. I remember being so agitated when we arrived at Karen's house that I poured a beer into a water bottle to sip in the car as she drove us the rest of the way to the beach. I remember that I had used three blankets the night before in Blue River (and fretted about firing up the furnace without John there), but that when we arrived at my in-laws' house it was 88 degrees inside. And I remember how massively depressing it was to return to the cold, dark, empty house in Blue River when we got back, and how only Leo kept me going that night. Karen had given him a set of brightly colored plastic drawers for his room, and he was so excited about setting them up and arranging the few toys he had in Blue River in them, he didn't even notice that he should have been massively depressed, too.

Chapter 11
Regrouping

John hadn't had work all summer, and of course I hadn't worked in Brake. We had made our move west with a large nest egg that we knew we could live off until we both had incomes again. We also had plenty of equity in the house we bought there.

But turning around and coming back east, not knowing when the house would sell, and pretty much guaranteed a loss of *at least* the realtors' commissions, had not been in the plan. The backwards move ran us an additional eight grand, too, even though the move out there had cost less.

On her death, my mother had left me a small sum of money that ended up covering the majority of our losses, and I felt that she would have approved of me using it to save myself, as it were. But I still obsessed with our finances. I could have called all my North Carolina friends now for cheer and support, but I didn't. And even if the calls had been free, I wouldn't have.

I was humiliated by my actions; I hoped my friends had all heard I was back through the grapevine, and analyzed it among themselves before I had to face them. As I withdrew, other people's normal lives and issues seemed to have no relevance to me. My shrunken world included Leo, John, my dad and Sara, but except for a few other family members I couldn't see anyone else. *My* difficulties and fear were all-encompassing. Had a friend's husband been killed in a car wreck, I would have been terribly sorry, but I would have thought my problems were worse. I was a freak, someone nobody else could understand. Everyone sympathizes with a widow.

My problems weren't worse than being widowed, of course, but my condition was. I had lost my beloved mother to a car accident and since then have lost my husband to a heart-wrenching divorce, but through neither of these life events did I feel as bad as I did when caught in the steely grip of relentless anxiety, an insidious, life-draining disorder. That it is biochemical in nature would become clear to me in years to come. But while society supports those suffering from other illnesses, such as cancer, no one "gets it" about anxiety if they haven't been there themselves. Due to this lack of understanding, and the shame the sufferers feel, many of them go underground, pretending they are well while self-medicating with drugs or alcohol. They may not seek professional help, or may not find effective treatment; and as a result, many victims of anxiety disorders aren't around anymore to help explain.

And so, as the days stretched into weeks of Not Being in Brake anymore, I felt no better. John began his trip across the country, and we talked each night as he drew closer and closer. In typical fashion, he was getting the best out of the situation, taking a different route this time so he could see different states, and logging 600 miles per day instead of the 400 we had averaged. Each night he told me what he'd seen that day, anything that had happened, how the pets were doing. I asked what he'd eaten and if he was getting enough rest. I felt as if there were a cord stretched between our two phones and I was pulling him back to me, slowly, hand over hand.

The day of his expected arrival I met Sara for breakfast at a bagel shop. We talked, as always, about how badly I was doing. My sister assured me, "The hard part is over now." And I nodded—because any other reaction would have been disloyal—but in my heart I did not believe she was right.

That evening, on his last phone call to the house, John estimated he would arrive in 90 minutes. It turned out to take much longer, because of traffic, and Leo and I paced the house and yard like caged tigers, waiting for our husband/daddy and dogs. I came up with everything I could think of to amuse us, but naturally I had just gone in the bathroom when the Subaru turned onto our street. Leo yelled, and I came flying out in time to hear John say hello when he pulled into the garage. The greeting between my husband and son was incredibly anticlimactic. John sounded like he was coming home from any workday (back when he came home from work) and Leo seemed to be fixated on a bug he had located on the steps.

I, on the other hand, shrieked and shrieked, jumped up and down, enveloped John in a hug and then bounced all over the driveway with the dogs. My face about split with the grin I sustained for I don't know how long. My constant tension level translated into excited nervous energy for the entire evening of our reunion.

I gave John the grand tour of the house. I was so proud of it, clean at last, fully functional with utilities, and ready for his arrival. It was a great neighborhood and a huge, if wooded, yard. I scanned his reaction eagerly, and he was polite, but I could tell he was thinking that it sure was ordinary compared to our fancy place in the High Desert. And that it sure was cloudy and damp here, with moss and mildew proliferating around the house and garage. Plus now he would have to live in the same town with his in-laws! It had to be a comedown after the grand adventure of the Pacific Northwest. Now that he had finished his incredible journey back, the Dream was officially dead.

And poor Leo. He had been through so much, and now, after sharing a room with his mama for three and a half weeks, she had left him for another man (even if it was his dad). The first morning John was home, we found Leo curled up on the floor just outside the door to our bedroom, and he had a total breakdown about going to school. I was still in my bathrobe and told him Daddy would walk him to the bus stop, but he uncharacteristically had a fit about this. I sent him anyway, not being willing to walk a block in my pj's, but it was an awful good-bye for an already over-excited and guilt-ridden mom. But when John returned from the delivery, we fell back into bed and enjoyed our morning anyway. It was about dang time!

We continued the celebration with lunch at a pizza place with Henry and his wife, Loraine. We didn't have much to do, after all, since our furniture hadn't arrived yet. We had already hit the local Mexican place the night before with Sara and the boys; it was sort of an arrival tour for John. He wasn't at all crazy about hanging out in the house, since it was empty, dark (from both the weather and lack of lamps) and rather echoing. In fact, the first night as he held me in his arms, he looked up and down the long length of the house and remarked, "I'm glad I didn't have to camp out here for three weeks".

A few days later, the truck with our belongings arrived. First off the back of it was my car—what a glorious sight! I could finally return Henry's loaner. By the time we reached the last item on the truck, the rain had begun, and we covered my mother's piano with tarps while we manhandled it up the uneven brick walk to the covered porch by the back door.

The next morning, my family ate breakfast at a real table! with the steady downpour outside as an accompaniment. "It's really not always this depressing here", I prattled to John. "I think it is", he retorted without expression.

My husband wouldn't stand for the austerity measures I had been living by, and so there was rich coffee with cream and fruit pastries for breakfast now. Flooded with guilt as I was, I wasn't about to object to anything that made him happy, and I worried silently about our finances. We were now paying a hefty rent *and* a mortgage.

This time we unpacked quickly, finally hanging the pictures that had remained in their boxes the whole summer in Oregon. John made sure we got cable TV and Internet pronto, and started finding running routes in the new area. Both of us looked for work.

In October, in a run of good fortune I was sure I didn't deserve, the Oregon house sold for a decent price, I landed a secretary's job at the local university, and John started getting in work from his Georgia contacts. Somehow, somehow, we had landed on our feet, after our ridiculous bounce across the country and back.

And how did I feel?

No better.

A broken thermostat is broken—you can't fix it by moving it to a different house. I needed medical help now, not just a change of environment. My new employee health insurance didn't kick in for a month, and stubbornly, I refused to see a doctor until it did. This was one of my more foolish decisions, leading to another month of my life I can never get back, but I still didn't fully understand what I was dealing with.

At work, where I helped an old friend of my father's run the anthropology department, I kept up a professional and poised exterior. None of my new colleagues knew that each day when I signed the mail form I was thinking, "Another day down, thank God". No one knew that I scanned the newspaper obituaries every day, noting how old people were when they died and taking encouragement from ones that were closer to my age. Or that I walked across the campus on errands repeating to myself, "Just put one foot in front of the other. Put one foot in front of the other". Sometimes I hunkered down in a bathroom stall and folded my arms around my legs for a tiny bit of relief. Or I would purse my lips and blow when I breathed out, a trick the nurse practitioner in Oregon had taught me.

Lying awake in bed one night, I discovered that when I breathed out, if I focused and readied my entire mind and body, I could achieve one or two seconds of relaxation. On an individual exhale, for a fleeting moment, I could feel normal. I couldn't do it too many times, though, because it was so much effort and I was so completely spent.

That fall, I had my first-ever mammogram. When it came back abnormal, and the follow-up was also abnormal, I actually thought to myself, "At least I'll get out of here".

Of course I wasn't allowed to not be okay now. Look what my husband had done for me, just so I could be okay! John knew I was still not myself, and in despair several times he exclaimed, "But we're in BLUE RIVER!" I honestly don't remember what I thought about my lack of improvement in the first couple of months. I just promised John that I would settle down over time—I mean, I *had* to.

About this time Leo began to get in trouble in school. The honeymoon period was in fact very short. His teacher loved Leo, but was somewhat emotional herself, so they were an interesting combination. Mrs. Wilkerson often called me, and sometimes wrote me long letters about Leo's behavior and her concerns. One day in October she sent him to the principal's office.

When John told me this, I was so upset I couldn't think of anything to do but get into a hot bath. The enveloping warmth seemed to quell my rising panic. When the water turned cold, I drank a beer. I didn't know what to say to Leo, since I knew he would be upset and defensive, and I myself was not only an emotional wreck but had lost all faith in my parenting abilities and judgment. I could only tell myself it would have been that much worse if it had happened in Oregon.

November fourth I finally went to see a nurse practitioner. In a stroke of good fortune for me, Ginny had actually been through a similar trauma when she and her husband moved to his home state in another part of the country. She never told me how she overcame her difficulties, but she had no hesitation in recommending that I go back on my old medication. I gratefully agreed. This time I would stick it out.

Chapter 12
Reprieve

I remember it as clear as a bell. The first time I caught a glimpse of the old me, the person I had been until recent months, was one evening while John was brushing his teeth. I gave him a hug from behind and made a smart remark to our reflections in the mirror, and I felt it—a little flash of the real me. Wow. Could it be happening?

It was. I was on the road to recovery. Over the next few weeks, all my symptoms subsided, with the pounding in my chest the last to go. By Thanksgiving I had offered to host the family meal, and after that I have a parade of happy memories. Sitting in front of our first fire of the season, sipping a glass of wine as the first snow fell; coming into my own at work ("I'm not going to let my real personality show until my probationary period is over!" I cracked to my boss); and the joy of Christmas morning at Rob and Agnes's house, sitting on the sofa among the chaos of presents, wrapping paper, children and dogs, sipping delicious hot coffee—coffee! Several cups.

That Christmas for breakfast I made my traditional pot of grits for my Yankee in-laws, and along with them chowed down on eggs, pancakes, sausage, and bacon. I made a pecan pie with chunks of dark chocolate in it for Christmas dinner. I could, and did, eat anything and everything. The music was glorious, the wind on the beach bracing and invigorating. I loved it all! In spite of the abnormal mammogram yet to be resolved, I was happy and confident now. Chances were everything was fine, and if it wasn't, I would handle it. I would face it with my husband at my side and my wonderful family backing me up.

***

Medical technicians aren't supposed to tell patients what they are seeing during procedures for good reason: they can give false hope, or false terror. But I could have kissed the lady performing my breast sonogram when she told me, "It's a cyst, a simple cyst".

"Is that good?" I asked.

"It's perfectly normal", she answered.

I knew I had it made now: my anxiety gone, all of us established in Blue River, and I had my health! Still, the official word would come from my doctor after the radiologist reviewed the film.

It was definitely a sign of Murphy (of the Law of the same name) when Leo's principal called to tell me my son had gone to the office *twice* that day *before* I got the official all-clear. "Just can't let me be happy, can you?" I metaphorically asked God while digesting the irony. I hated it, of course, but the way I reacted compared to the way I had in October was like night and day. John and I spoke firmly to Leo and gave him consequences at home; John and I discussed it briefly, and that was that. My stomach didn't do flip-flops. Our evening wasn't ruined. We were a normal family (with a child who has gone to the principal's office twice in one day.)

I wrote in my journal later that everything had worked out "so much better than I deserved for it to". I blamed myself wholly for years, until it became a smart remark to John: "Did I mention that I'm sorry for that whole moving-across-the-country thing?" In fact, everything worked out so well that one evening, as we were driving through a gorgeous section of the county to eat dinner with some new running friends of John's, I looked around and then said to my husband, "You're welcome!" Which, too, became one of my regular quips.

Because not only was work coming in steadily for John now, he had also met a large group of people to run with, and he was faster than he'd been in years. In Oregon he had thought it would be a cinch to find running pals, but the only group he had discovered included septuagenarians (albeit extremely fast ones). Here he had discovered a training camp for competitive runners, where the athletes lived and trained full-time. They ran on the beautiful trails around Blue River and enjoyed pleasant accommodations, home-cooked meals, and many amenities at their bucolic location. They lived in an idyllic bubble devoted to running. It was something John would have given anything for, had it been an option, after college.

The night John and I got engaged, 15 years earlier, we went out with a group of friends in Atlanta, and John's future best man asked him, "Does this mean we're not going to get jobs as waiters, share an apartment and run all the time?" John had laughed and replied, "Nah, we can still do that!"

It had not occurred to me that my husband would ever blame me for not achieving the most he could as a runner. And it wouldn't occur to me for a few more months yet, but when it did, I would remember that remark.

***

When school let out for the summer, I felt like we, as a family, were cruising. Leo had done well (academically anyway) in first grade, and at year's end his teacher gave him a tiny carved Russian figure of a clown, which turned upside down to reveal the painted words, "Be happy". When I asked him why he was singled out to receive this gift, he answered guilelessly, "I was her most improved person."

Leo was on a baseball team at the time, and those cool June evenings sitting in our camp chairs watching 6-year-old boys play on fields surrounded by cool blue mountains were certainly the best of small-town life. We also signed him up for some day camps, where he got to swim and go on field trips, but he had plenty of time to just hang out and play with the dogs or the neighbor boy, or watch TV reruns. It was exactly the way I had spent my childhood summers.

Things slid to a virtual halt at my job, leaving me free to come in late, leave early, and run errands or go home at lunch. John continued to get work in spite of the season, but not so much that we couldn't take a vacation!

One of John's best friends was living in Costa Rica that summer, and John wanted us all to fly down for a visit. Tempting as it sounded, I didn't think Dan's bachelor pad was the best destination for the family, and I was still very much worried about money. Also, on some level, I didn't think I deserved an exotic vacation, and since John had gotten to spend three months in his favorite place on earth last year, I figured he'd survive without one, too. We perused a map for driveable possibilities and I suggested Hershey, Pennsylvania and Monticello, two places neither of us had been. John grudgingly agreed, as long as we added Harper's Ferry, West Virginia, which he had always wanted to visit.

Besides that vacation, the summer of '05 was marked by hikes with the dogs, visits with friends from down the mountain, dinners and hanging out at the running camp, and cookouts with my family. Dad was elated to have both his daughters and all four of his grandsons in town, and practically crowed whenever we were all together. My father has an almost unsinkable optimistic spirit, which floats determinedly back up after every event that has beaten it down, and he, too was cruising. What I had written in my journal as the medication was kicking in proved true: "It's getting to where I can just imagine, when I've had a beer and am around Dad, feeling okay again."

During one of our dinners out with the runners, an attractive blonde woman in her twenties announced to me jokingly that John needed to go with her to a high-altitude training camp in Ethiopia for a month that winter. I laughed along with everyone else. "As if!" I said. "That's what I need—to take care of a job, a child, two dogs and a house by myself in the middle of winter while my husband goes to Africa with another woman!" There was general merriment at the table, although I knew that the young people that comprised the group wouldn't actually have seen anything wrong with this scenario—having never been married!

At the end of July our lease was up, and this led to another marital spat. Steeped in remorse as I was for my husband, I felt worse for what I had done to our child, and I couldn't imagine moving him again after only one year. I definitely didn't want him to have to change schools. I think I was also subconsciously waiting for John to get a "real" job, either at the university or somewhere else in the Southern Appalachians, so that I would feel we were somewhere we were justified in being, not somewhere we had defaulted to. It would have been a nod to the equal importance of John's happiness in the marriage if we had moved away from my family and to a town where John had secured a job he wanted. It would have also made me feel better about "running back home with my tail between my legs", as I always described my defection from Oregon.

When I mentioned this, John countered, "What if you freak out if we move again?"

This got my back up. "Did I 'freak out' when we moved to Athens? or Atlanta? or Baltimore??" I demanded. "I've NEVER had a problem with moving until we went to the other side of the country! and I've never needed to live in the same town with my daddy, either—in my entire adult life!"

What it really boiled down to was this: John kind of liked Blue River. It was the mountains, it wasn't hot, he was loving his new running gang, and he didn't much feel like moving again. I had always kidded John about being "POLAR"—meaning he liked the Path Of Least Resistance, and the first time I said to him, in surprise, "You're lazy!" he responded dismissively, "You've known that for a long time".

Which brings me to something I have learned about distance runners. They may burn up 70 miles on the road per week, but when they're not training, all they want is a recliner and a cold one! I think the only reason any of them (men, anyway) ever do any home improvement projects is because their wives insist. And honestly, except for the vacation we took that summer, one trip to Mexico and our honeymoon, I think just about every trip John and I ever took revolved around a race or a track meet!

But for whatever reason, John wanted to buy a house in Blue River now. "We're throwing $14,000 a year away on rent," he complained. Somehow, though, I prevailed. When it came to Leo I was pretty insistent, obviously, on doing what I felt was in his best interests. After the year he'd had, I was more convinced than ever that our son had Attention Deficit Hyperactivity Disorder, and between that and my guilt over the instability I'd caused, I was determined to do right by him.

I think—I know, in fact, that I believed all along that John would love me no matter what. He always had, and we were so perfect together. I'd always credited him for that, saying that he was so easygoing he made it easy to be married, no matter how strung out I got. If asked to use one word to describe my husband, I would always say "honorable". Neither one of us had ever had a doubt that we would grow old and die together—and that we would love it.

We had been married three years when we had our first fight, and it was over money. I tended to be much more conservative than John regarding investments. But other than that, we were amazingly compatible: both smart, irreverent, honorable people who wanted adventures and happiness, and weren't particularly ambitious professionally. I grew up in a financially comfortable family, but John's was well off. I never cared about having more than we needed and could have a little fun with, and John only wanted more because he wanted to retire as young as possible and travel the world. Unlike most wives, I hadn't gotten especially upset over John's layoffs, because we didn't need alot and had always saved our money. Neither one of us cared about having a big house, pool, boat, or fancy cars.

And we laughed, so much! I think it was the strongest bond between us. Corny, dry, slapstick, politically incorrect or highbrow, humor was our thing. John was willing to be unbelievably silly for a laugh, and our marriage never lacked them. We called each other the same ridiculous nickname our entire life together, and we still "made people throw up" with our affection ten years into our marriage. In fact, I had printed on the invitation to our 10-year anniversary party, "Please join us in celebrating ten years of love and laughter".

And so I sailed obliviously right into our first—and last, as it turned out – serious marital trouble. And it started with the cessation of laughter.

Chapter 13
The Anvil

Years later, when I met someone who reminded me and everyone else of myself, I realized what an actress I am. Not to say I am insincere, even when I worked in PR, but I do like attention and I love to make people laugh. I can also pull some pretty good pranks on people without letting on.

But with John, what you see is what you get. As long as I had known him he had always been upbeat, unless he was injured and couldn't run. It was hard to say who suffered more when that happened! And you couldn't miss it—at least I couldn't—when he wasn't happy.

In August of 2005, not long after the family vacation, John became uncharacteristically quiet and distracted. I asked him a couple of times what was wrong. The first time he told me he was fine, and the second time he said, "I'm thinking about work."

Red flag. If anyone could put work out of his mind when he wasn't doing it, it was John. Even concerns about not getting enough work wouldn't have weighed him down, and I knew it. But he was not forthcoming with more information, and I let the subject drop. Besides not wanting to nag, I still had the 100% faith in my husband's devotion to me that allowed me to sleep like a baby when he was running with one of the young, lovely girls from the running camp. I might give him grief about it for laughs, but there was no concern in my heart.

Once I mentioned to Sara that John was running and then having lunch with a 23-year-old woman from the camp. "You must be pretty secure in your marriage that that doesn't bother you," she said. I shrugged. I didn't believe that, in John's eyes, I would suffer by comparison with anyone.

And so in spite of whatever was bothering John, I was perfectly content on that September night when John dropped the bomb on me. I was lying on the sofa, reading the local paper and chattering to John about a Hurricane Katrina benefit we should go to that weekend, when he announced, "We need to talk."

***

Too many folks out there have been through a divorce for me to put anyone else through mine. Although I am giving up my privacy to tell this story, I don't want to violate anyone else's any more than is necessary to achieve my goal of increasing understanding of mental illness.

But of course, divorce was not remotely in my head that September night. It didn't enter my head as an actual possibility until I couldn't deny it anymore, and when it did, I jumped up and walked for miles, all the way through downtown and out the other side before I turned back—at midnight. The thought of actually being divorced stunned and panicked me—but it was *normal* panic, and this is key. I was still taking my anti-depressant, and though the dissolution of my marriage put me through my worst nightmare, my reactions were all within the realm of normal feelings and behavior. There was one night after John had left, when I drank two Scotches and a beer, went to bed, and called John, sobbing, to come take care of Leo, "because I can't". There was a Christmas dinner where I threw a gift across the table at a restaurant in front of my son. In one argument I called John words I had never spoken in my life.

These admissions won't surprise many survivors of divorce. That particular trauma can make people almost unrecognizable.

I'm pretty certain that had I not been on an antidepressant, this would have been a much shorter story, had it been written at all. But I remained functional, working at my job, caring for my child, running our household without John, and reading about others who had been through what I was going through to not feel so alone. In a particularly cruel twist of fate, our dog Guinness was hit by a car and killed the morning John walked out of our 16-year marriage. I carried on that day, walking through the house to divide up our marital property with my husband, and then going on to work, where I attended a meeting, and covered two classes for professors who were out of town. Our remaining dog, Molson, stayed with Leo and me.

But that night, when Karen called and left a message for "Laura Anne and Leo" instead of the three of us as usual, I felt a physical pain in my chest.

We did the best we could, I guess. We protected Leo as much as possible, kept it civil most of the time, and worked out the separation agreement, once I could finally stomach it, between ourselves, bringing in lawyers only to make it official. I had held on to the idea that we would reconcile until John told me he had met someone else, at which point I was finally motivated to ask for his house key back, and tell him to get a lawyer to separate our accounts. My husband had not been unfaithful to me, he had simply been unhappy with me.

The inevitable feelings of anger and betrayal that the person being left goes through are necessary, in my opinion, to finally declare a post-mortem on a family. I fought and fought for the marriage, but it had already been too late by the time John spoke up. He just didn't love me anymore, and he'd been too polite to tell me in time to turn things around.

On our 17th anniversary, we met at his apartment to work out details about custody and child support, and I experienced a sea change in my feelings toward him. My husband said things that night that made me realize this was not my John anymore, and couldn't be again, even if *he* had wanted it. During that same week I signed a lease on a smaller house—my very own house for the first time, and that night I felt an unfamiliar feeling: optimism. It was a glimmer, like the time I made a joke when the anti-depressant was kicking in, and like then, it boded well for the future.

Chapter 14
Learning to Fly

I don't have recurring dreams, but I have recurring dream themes. One is that I am in college and don't know what my schedule is. The other has to do with homes, and specifically, with having to downgrade: from a house to an apartment, from an apartment to a dorm. It's natural enough to trace this insecurity to the 2.4 million times I have moved in my life, never staying anywhere more than six years during my childhood, and living in 15 places between the ages of 18 and 32. Kaye always quipped that she wrote my information in her address book in pencil.

But that 15th place was the first house John and I bought, in Atlanta. I will have a soft spot in my heart for it as long as I live. He and I (with loads of help from his parents) painted, papered, roofed, tiled, gardened and fenced that property until it was totally our own. We lived there seven years, only moving when John was laid off and got the job in Athens. While we lived there, I was surprised that I continued having the home-insecurity dreams, but I did. Moving to Athens, quickly followed by Oregon, and instantly followed by North Carolina, didn't help, of course.

The house I chose to rent three months after John left me was the perfect place to heal. It was at the end of a narrow gravel road that ran alongside the New River. There were four other houses in our "holler": one abandoned, one owned by a single man who was an incredible gardener, one rented to a young couple, and one occupied by "Miz Hallie", who was 102 but lived alone. The river bottom was hayfields, cut twice a year, and it teemed with deer, groundhogs, foxes, great blue herons and so many rabbits Molson didn't know what to do. There were beaver and trout in the river, and enough toads hopping around our porch at night that Leo set up a tank and caught them regularly. Fishermen (and women) came and went constantly, pleasant but saying little.

The property itself sat up high, with a stone retaining wall at the base of a hill allowing for a flat lawn directly in front of the house. The lush green view out of the kitchen window, with the stone wall on one side and a perennial border shaded by enormous hemlocks on the other, was one of the reasons I wanted the house. The sound of the river was another.

High up above the wall there were masses of blackberries, as well as apple and cherry trees. A very impressive treehouse was a huge plus for Leo.

Creeping up the steep driveway in my car for the first time, all I could think was, "I can't live here!" because of the access. Snow is a big factor in Blue River in the winter, and I had never lived on a gravel road, nor did I have the prerequisite four-wheel-drive car. But when I reached the top of the drive, my mom would have said the house "sang" to me. It was humble but solid, oh-so-homey, and I loved the covered wooden front porch and the cement patio, perfect for our outdoor dining set.

Inside, the house was charming as well. A small living room featured a gas fireplace and a huge picture window, and an arch separating the living and dining rooms gave a warm, retro feeling. The wood floors, scuffed and worn, gave way to brick-red tile in an enormous eat-in kitchen. (My dad eventually dubbed the house "L.A.'s Mediterranean villa" because of this room.)

As soon as I noticed the sturdy hooks on the ceiling of the front porch, I set my sights on a porch swing, which I bought as a kit from the local hardware store and assembled myself shortly after moving in. Between the gentle motion, the beautiful view, and the river sound, this became my favorite "healing place". It was also a source of pride for me that I had put it together without a man!

There was a lapse of a couple of months between signing the lease and moving in, and my outlook improved steadily as I got ready to relocate. Between John's departure in February and finding the new house in May, I had been through the hell of heartbreak, disbelief, panic and despair; I who never prayed, had actually knelt by the side of my bed and begged God to make him come back. When John had minor surgery I had insisted on driving him to and from the hospital myself, staying at his apartment to fix dinner afterwards, and bringing him homemade chicken soup and chocolate chip cookies the next day. Our emails during this time were sometimes angry and accusatory, but more often I was warm and affectionate, making my case that we could get through this and make it good again, and that all three of us would be better off in the long run if we did.

We had tried and rejected two unhelpful (and in one case, harmful) marriage counselors. One was a married woman with children, who made it clear she thought there was every hope for our family, and who stated that she didn't want to see divorce happen to "two such cute people". The other, a never-married man, started trying to steer us toward divorce in our very first session. ("We didn't come here for divorce counseling," I told him coolly. "We could break up by ourselves.")

But I had also heard my husband say, "I don't love you anymore"; I had argued with him about alimony and child support payments once we brought in lawyers. One day I was finally angry enough to order him to stop calling me our pet name of so many years. It was my first declaration of independence.

During this transformation, many people were helpful to me. My family was rock-solid behind me. They were too smart to turn on John, since they knew anything could happen, and weren't burning their bridges. But I was very lucky to have them in town for visits, home-cooked meals, shoulders to cry on, and encouraging notes. On the mantel that still bore the holiday cards from John's and my last Christmas together, I placed a card I particularly liked from Dad and Kaye. The verse said that when we are pushed off a cliff, we either find something to land on, or we learn how to fly. Although all I did was cry at the time, I was soon to be on my way.

I had two close women friends I had met since moving to Blue River: an older student in my department, and a professor in another. Although one has dropped out of my life since then, the other is my great friend Liz, whom I expect to be emailing when we are both 80, no matter what continent or tropical island she is on!

And at work one day, a scruffy 30-ish student walked into my office and introduced himself as Andy, a transfer and a new anthropology major, and although I found myself rather irritated by all his questions at the time, he ended up being a great friend and a crucial source of support for my sense of self-worth.

What people mean to us has so much to do with timing, with where we are and what we are up to when our lives intersect. The professor friend who was there for me only during the worst part of the crisis once wrote to me that "Even though I know you don't believe in all that mumbo-jumbo, I think our paths were meant to cross". Liz and I, on the other hand, will be compatible friends forever since we have so much in common: both (now) single moms, "of a certain age", animal-lovers, outdoorsy and outgoing. I foresee adventures with her whenever we find ourselves together in the future. And Andy, well, he was my anti-John. Whereas my husband had enumerated for me the ways in which I had failed him, Andy wrote me an email one day telling me how much my warm welcome and friendly smile had meant not only to him, but to everyone who walked into our department. This was apparently provoked by me referring to myself as "just a secretary" once, which bothered his sweet, sensitive soul so much that he said in his message, "There is no 'just' about what you do."

I also had a work-study student, Tony, who after watching his father walk out at a young age, had spent much of his life doing penance for other members of his sex by helping out women friends who had been left by their partners. Tony repeatedly offered to do odd jobs around my house, but I was reluctant to accept. Finally one day he just announced that unless I told him not to, he was coming over on Saturday with his wife and kids and seeing what he could do. And he was true to his word.

While I was packing up the house for our move, I noticed the mahogany chest containing John's family silverware was not in its usual place. Confused, I knelt down and rummaged through the cabinet. The chest was gone. I was stunned. John had only asked for what he needed for a bachelor household—nothing extra. I was pretty sure he wasn't eating his frozen pizza with sterling.

I'll never know whether he took it with him the day he moved, or retrieved it later on in our separation. We never discussed it. We divided up everything else together, because everything in our world had been ours, not his and mine. In all our years together, we had never even had separate checking accounts.

I wouldn't have argued had he asked for the silver set—would have told him to take it, in fact. But the planning ahead on his part made me cold inside. My husband knew he wasn't coming back—and he didn't trust me to hand over a family heirloom without a fight. I could just hear my mother-in-law saying, "Did you get my parents' silver? Be sure to get it. That stays in the family."

The forks and spoons would stay. I would not.

***

On moving day, I hired Tony as my truck driver and general project manager, and called in all my reinforcements. Sara's wonderful church sent their entire youth group to move me. Tony figured out how to get my mother's ancient piano across a very long lawn. And all I had to do was buy pizza, soda, and beer!

The first morning we woke up in our new home, Leo (age eight) shot video of the entire house, narrating the tour. When the camera finds me, very upbeat and ready to spend a day unpacking, I am putting on socks and expressing faux outrage that Leo has borrowed them and worn holes in the toes!

While Leo ran around the tiny new neighborhood, meeting people and videotaping wildlife and the mysteries of an abandoned barn across the road, I set up house. For the first time in my life, everything went where I, and ONLY I, wanted it! There were no "Johnpiles", as I had affectionately referred to my husband's things, strewn around the place. I and ONLY I decided where the computer would be set up, and whether we would get internet service or cable TV. As soon as I unpacked my teapot, I invited Dad, Kaye, and Sara over not just to help out, but for tea on the patio! The sun shone, Molson bounded around the yard, jumping off the retaining wall and totally belying his 12 years, and hope surged in my heart.

***

Where I live is a very, very big deal to me.

I never felt nervous alone in the house at night. Having lived in Baltimore and Atlanta for many years, where I was never the victim of a crime, I had no fear in this small mountain town I knew so well. There were no streetlights in my new neighborhood, but there was an enormous security light mounted on a pole at the top of my driveway, and its light flooded the uncovered windows that ran the length of the front of the house. When I saw that I was being charged for it on my electric bill, I asked the landlady if we could shut it off. She made noises about me being a woman alone, about people who parked at the end of the gravel road at night for subversive purposes…but I was really annoyed by that light. Honestly, if people wanted to do their marijuana deals at the end of the road, I didn't really care as long as they were quiet and left me alone. I wasn't particularly bothered by the guitar-toting homeless man who hung out by the river, either. Live and let live. Plus, I had Molson.

Molson and Guinness had been a pair for nine years, and of course we loved them both. But whereas Guinness was a sweet, pretty, nervous and not particularly bright Dobermann Pinscher mix, Molson was a smart, steady, loyal, and incredibly good-natured Brown Dog. The Humane Society described him as a "shepherd mix", Liz said he was "the L.L. Bean dog", and the vet said Molson was probably a "mix of mixes".

Molson never showed aggression to people or other dogs, but if someone approached the house his tail went up, his ears forward, and he barked just enough to alert me. He wasn't particularly into hugs, but he lived to play and chase. He had an enormous vocabulary, understanding not only commands, but many words we never taught him. When Molson was a puppy, John loved to buy him cheap stuffed animals and watch him rip them apart, shaking them and growling as the stuffing flew. Of course this became a problem when we were setting up a nursery. People laugh, but I swear I took that dog into the nursery, sat him down, and explained to him that these toys were not his and must be left alone. I didn't yell or say no over and over. And Molson listened intently, twisting his head from side to side in the mannerism that always made me say, "We know you're a human trapped in a dog's body, Molson. We know!" And Molson never once chewed one of Baby Leo's toys.

When Guinness died, Molson never saw the body. I always thought he should have, but John made the decision to ask the vet to dispose of her body before he came home from picking her up that awful morning. As a consequence, Molson often stood at the edge of the driveway of the old house, looking down toward the shopping center where Guinness had been hit. John had disappeared the same day, but he came back often to drop off or pick up Leo, so I don't believe Molson was looking for him.

We were all adjusting at that time, and one of Molson's coping mechanisms seemed to be asking for more affection. Whereas he had always tolerated a short amount of petting before looking for the Frisbee, Guinness had been a junkie, pushing her nose under our hands whenever possible, forcing an affectionate touch! Now Molson was doing that, "channeling Guinness", I told John in an email.

And the need was mutual. The first night Leo spent at John's new apartment, I literally got the gerbils out of their cage and sat on the sofa holding them, with Molson by my side, saying "We're not lonely, are we? No, we are just fine!"

John and Molson were extremely attached, but John knew better than to ask to take away my dog as well when he left. Once, when I was still at the stage of breaking down in tears over dinner from sheer heartbreak, Leo reassured me, "Daddy *has* to come back. He would never leave Molson!"

By the time we were in the River House, as I called my new place, I was not as needy, but I depended on Molson for the constant, steadfast companionship he provided. Although the landlady hadn't been crazy about the idea of a dog there, I won her over, and she wrote Molson specifically into the lease ("12-year-old family dog only"). Initially it was hard keeping Molson quiet at night, as the sound—and no doubt sight, through all that glass—of many wild animals kept him agitated and wanting to hunt. I finally let him sleep in my bedroom, which was more insular, and he got used to the country. Having him on the throw rug by the side of my bed was immensely comforting.

And how he loved living there! I had to tether him to the front porch during the day, but when Leo and I got home, we would count down "Three, two, one, blastoff!" as we let him go, and Molson would explode like a racehorse out of the gate, doing mad, joyous circles around the property, and leaping wildly onto and off of that retaining wall. He was so good to stay around that I let him wander when he chose, down to the river bottom or in the abandoned barn, where I'm sure a dizzying array of scents awaited him. Once he had eaten his supper, Molson was wherever we were, in the kitchen if I was cooking, or lying by the patio table if we were eating outside. On the many cool evenings that we tossed a football or Leo kicked the soccer ball while I gardened, Molson was chasing bees or rolling on his back, slipping and sliding down the steep bank above the stone wall. Aside from having lost his canine companion, I think Molson's life was idyllic at this point, as in many ways was mine.

Even Leo had it pretty good now. Although I will never argue, as John has, that he was better off with us apart, he adjusted as kids do, and he had a good life in both homes. At John's apartment, in a house in a lovely neighborhood, there were many children to play with, and eventually John, too, got a dog. There was even a Russian boy a few years older than Leo in the apartment upstairs.

At my home, by contrast, he lived like Tom Sawyer. He explored the ramshackle barn across the road and tracked wildlife. Once I heard him hollering from inside the house, and came out on the porch to see him, in the distance, terrifyingly high up in a tree in the river bottom. "Hi, Mom!" he called cheerfully.

"Get DOWN!" I ordered in alarm. "Only move one foot or one hand at a time!"

Then I paused, and added, "But hang on just a second." It was too stunning of a shot. I just had to have a picture, first!

Leo wasn't allowed to go to the river without me, but he could explore the neighborhood as long as he took Molson. The two of them brought home many treasures, ranging from broken tools to an old tire Leo rolled excitedly down the gravel road one day, yelling to me that he'd found us a swing. Whenever an adult (or older cousin) was available, he'd head straight to the river. Once he ran home and woke me from a nap.

"Mom! There's an otter in the river! There's an otter!"

I was sleepy, but I love otters, and furthermore, I was sure he was mistaken! So I let him drag me off the sofa and down to the bridge. It turned out the creature was a beaver, swimming placidly back and forth, taking sticks and branches to an underwater lair. I tried to startle it enough to make it slap its tail on the water, but that beaver couldn't have cared less that we were there!

***

When fall came, Leo got the teacher I had wanted for him in third grade: a dear friend of my mother's. I had put a bug in the ear of his second grade teacher that I hoped this would happen. The start of school was always a tense time for me, as I waited to see whether Leo would tolerate or hate his teacher, how he would handle the work, and how he would get along with the kids in his class. I relaxed somewhat now, and wrote in my journal that Leo and I had landed on our feet and were going to have a good year. John agreed to continue picking up Leo off the school bus (John lived in a different school district now) and delivering him back to me after I got home from work. One night per week and every other weekend, Leo stayed at John's.

One day at work, one of our best students walked into my office and asked, "Do you know of anyone who'd be willing to rent a room out to me three or four nights a week?"

I thought for a split second before saying, "Yeah, me!"

Teresa lived down the mountain, but was getting tired of the commute. She only had classes Tuesdays and Thursdays and would be graduating in December. It wasn't much of a commitment on my part, and I was sure she would be no problem at all in our household. She was an army veteran in her late twenties, intelligent and thoughtful, and I had always liked her.

Teresa ended up taking our tiny, closet-less bedroom sight unseen, and moved in shortly thereafter. I hung some wooden pegs on the wall for her clothes and made room for her in the pantry and bathroom. Leo, who loved having her around, decided I was running the "Laura Anne Inn" now and made signs for all our doors, bearing room numbers and names. He even drew up a registration sheet where he listed our roommate as "Terisasa", a name that stuck for years.

I asked my lawyer if the paltry amount of rent I was collecting would affect my separation agreement finances, and she laughed and said, "No, John'll just try to say you're a lesbian".

"Fine with me," I replied.

I had a nice variety to my evenings now: sometimes it was all of us, sometimes just Leo and me, sometimes me and Teresa, and occasionally just me (and Molson). Teresa's boyfriend visited from Germany for several weeks and was also a welcome addition, crammed in as we were. Sometimes he played his guitar on our porch in the evening, and I would sit in the porch swing listening and looking at the view of the mountains, thinking how lucky I was. I essentially lived in a vacation home.

One evening Sara and Mason came over for dinner, and afterwards we were playing cards. Somehow we got on the subject of answering machine greetings, and I was saying I just wasn't sure what to record any more. "I used to say, "You've reached the Nicholson family," I remarked, "but now that sounds wrong."

Mason studied on this, and then deadpanned, "'You have reached the sad remnants of the Nicholson family.'"

All four of us burst into peals of giggles, and Leo was on his feet in seconds, running over to the phone. He recorded the melodramatic greeting with the rest of us laughing in the background, and it remained our announcement for months. I always wondered what John thought when he heard it!

Leo's soccer season started, and John volunteered to help coach the team. I was pretty sure he did this to avoid having to sit with me in the bleachers, as he had at basketball games. We had felt uncomfortable initially at these games, then wound up having some laughs; but laughter is a bond, and I think my husband wanted to avoid it. He had broken free, even recording an answering machine greeting that welcomed callers to "John's Joint" at his new place, and he was not going to get sucked back into the wife-and-child thing. Though he detested dealing with lawyers, was hurting financially, and was doing without most of our furniture and household goods, apparently anything was better than living with me.

So he spent the soccer games on the sidelines with the team's head coach, while I sat on the bleachers alone or tried to strike up conversations with other mothers. I had never felt particularly a part of the "in" crowd of parents—the businessmen, professors, physicians, the stay-at-home moms; and now I felt even less accepted as a single mom. All of a sudden, through no fault of my own, I was a threat to married women—particularly those whose husbands had become quiet or distracted.

Another couple with a child in Leo's class were separated at the same time as John and I, and I marveled at their congenial relationship. They sat together at every game, smiling and chatting about their son. Neither one of them ever brought a date to a game; and when they each remarried, sometimes all four of them sat together. It was admirable, I thought—probably strained, but admirable nonetheless.

John and I couldn't quite pull it off, partly because I never dated, and John was in full find-a-replacement mode. I always found this ironic, since he had had a wife who was devoted to him, but unlike many men, he did not want to play the field. He wanted to be married.

Perhaps it's just me, perhaps it's the setting I was in, but I was not meeting anyone. John was using several online dating services, and to my dismay was detailing all his meetings and dates to Leo, who reported them back to me. His first girlfriend was a professor in a high-paying department at the university. Although I didn't know her, it was easy to look her up on the university website and see a photo and information. I never met Amber, but Leo told me when they broke up. Unfortunately he didn't tell me any details, but I would have cut out my tongue before I would have asked for them!

When Christmas rolled around, I faced my first major holiday without my beloved family of in-laws, not to mention my life partner. Of course it made things simpler, to halve a gift list and not have to travel, but how I had loved those huge celebrations! I guess I wasn't surprised when it turned out that my in-laws had expected to have Leo with them that Christmas—we'd been with my family the Christmas before—but at least John realized that when a husband leaves a wife and she faces her first Christmas without him, the least he can do is not take her child away, too.

Leo and I bought a Christmas tree without the first clue how we would get it home. The folks at the church parking lot tree sale seemed to have no rope or ability to tie a tree to the top of a car. Luckily for us, one of the third-grade dads was around, and while Leo and his son tore around the churchyard, playing, the dad offered to toss our tree in his truck and deliver it for me. I found that many kind souls want to help out a single mother, and most of them are slightly chauvinistic men, God bless them. One of my professors offered to help out around the house in addition to Tony, the work-study student; my dad became very protective, buying me four new tires for my car; and even John would email me when it was time to renew my vehicle registration or get the oil changed. This touched and irked me in equal measure. (Okay, mainly irked me with John, mainly touched me with everybody else.) I did not want to become a childlike person who needed a male authority figure. When John asked if I needed him to mow my new lawn or split kindling for me, I became huffy and said certainly not!

Although I welcomed my stepfather's help with buying a self-propelled mower, the whole point of that was being able to mow my lawn myself. And because it was extremely steep in parts, and nearly an acre, when I couldn't manage it because of a bad shoulder, I plied my now-teenage nephews with modest amounts of money and generous amounts of food. I *would* be the lord of my castle even if it required lots of Advil, or some extra cash!

Chapter 15
The Southwest

I was now in my third year of helping to run the Anthropology Department office, and every year I had looked yearningly at the itinerary for the American Southwest trip led by Dr. Jay. The Southwest had always appealed to me, and was really the only major section of the country I had yet to visit. As giddy with independence as I was that spring of 2007, it was my year to go.

So this time as I made the hotel arrangements, reserved the vehicles and arranged guides at national parks, it was all for me, too! The class associated with the trip met one evening a week for a potluck, so we had time to get to know each other and anticipate the trip together. Andy was in that class, and another student friend, Anita. It didn't take long for everyone to grow chummy in our mutual excitement. Sometimes after class Andy and I would head downtown for a drink at The Saloon, the spot where occasionally, during the worst of my divorce, I had escaped on my lunch hour for a beer by myself.

The Southwest trip involved camping, something I hadn't done in 30 years. If it hadn't been for Liz, I would have gone broke buying and renting all the gear I would need. But having hiked the entire Appalachian Trail (some 2000 miles), Liz had everything, and it was all light-weight and top-notch. She even went shoe-shopping with me and helped me select the hiking boots that would carry me all the way up the side of Arizona's Canyon of Death without a slip or a blister.

I was really worried about being twice the age of the rest of the group. I was in decent shape, but I still had trouble with the "frozen shoulder" I developed when Leo was a toddler, and it became very painful when aggravated. I couldn't picture carrying everything I needed to survive overnight in a canyon on my back without severe consequences. So I doubled-up on my physical therapy exercises and made room in my pack for half a dozen hot/cold pain relief muscle pads. I just couldn't let an injury keep me from having this experience.

And so I parked Leo and Molson at John's place, and set out with 24 others in the pre-dawn chill of a March morning.

***

It took two days for our little caravan (vehicles we dubbed "Peace Train", "VANarchy", and "Mothership") to reach Albuquerque, where our adventure began. It was an anthropology class field trip, so of course we visited ruins, petroglyphs, and Native American villages. While the other students vigorously took notes and made sketches of what we saw, I scampered around with the freedom of a course-auditor! My first view of a canyon (Canyon de Chelly, Arizona) was staggering. I took picture after picture, and practically ran up and down the trail. "It's like the Grand Canyon!" I squealed to Andy, as I photographed the view from every angle. "Are you kidding?" was all Andy replied.

We camped out that night, but it was "car-camping", and less strenuous than inconvenient. We lucked into an invitation to a tribal pow-wow in the evening, and ended up being, as we had been in the grocery store earlier in the day, the only white faces there. Everyone should have the experience of being in an ethnic minority at some point in their lives.

That evening in camp I told a sub-group of our party one of my favorite stories, which may or may not be true but frankly ought to be. There's nothing much more unpleasant than being flipped off by a stranger, whether in traffic or face to face, but the supposed origin of this gesture is actually rather noble. According to a website a friend of mine found, the infamous Bird dates back to the Hundred Years' War between the French and the English. The weapon of choice was the longbow, and the middle finger of the right hand was the bowfinger. The wily French, upon capturing enemy troops, would chop off the prisoner's longbow finger to incapacitate him for any future fighting. So the gesture of defiance was the middle finger raised high: "I'm still armed!" This plucky spirit appealed to me at this point in my life, so the lovely gesture became a standard between me and a few select friends who knew the story.

Most nights of our trip, we were at cheap motels, where I was lucky to share a room with a female professor, instead of three other students! (the "old-lady" room, as Andy charmingly put it—although he was in the "old-man room" with Dr. Jay.) During those evenings Andy and I both had the advantage of being able to hang out with the 20-year-olds as long as we liked, and then slip back to our own quiet rooms. I enjoyed spending free time with the students, who were wonderfully welcoming. I wasn't partying like they were—I'm long past that—but I was having a bit of a second youth feeding off their boundless energy, their music and dancing. One night one of the girls started straightening other girls' hair, and it wasn't long before the group started chanting for me, with my thick curls, to be next. I agreed and was surprised (and not displeased) with the result.

"WHAT room did you say you're in?" asked Andy drunkenly.

"Whooooaaa!" went the kids in response.

I glared at him, but I was loving it. I would have loved for John to have seen me now.

One night I was busted by Dr. Jay for breaking the rules. We had all signed agreements that we would behave respectfully and not be disruptive during the trip, which included not talking on the motel balconies after "bedtime". Anita and I were walking between rooms and paused for a photo with a friend who was outside for a smoke, when the camera flash went off unexpectedly, blinding us all. We were doubled over in giggles when Dr. Jay (aka Da Man) came out of his room below and spoke to us quite sharply. When Andy heard it, he loved this particular story. "I'm gonna tell your boss you were a troublemaker," he reminded me for the rest of the trip.

***

The first day of the big hike arrived. We would walk eight and a half miles down into the Canyon del Muerto with our Navajo guides, spend the night, and hike out equally far the next day. Dr. Jay was able to get us access to parts of the canyon off-limits to other tourists, and this would be the highlight of our trip.

We started out by ducking under barbed wire at an unmarked trailhead, which was a challenge with our bulky packs! I was lucky mine weighed only 25 pounds—other students were carrying 40.

We had only been walking a few minutes when we began to see small patches of snow among the sandstone and scrubby, fragrant evergreen trees. The student walking in front of me had tied his sneakers to the bottom of his pack, and they were swinging along with his stride. "I'm gettin' my ass kicked the whole way", he lamented.

The descent into the canyon was short and steep—steep enough that we sometimes walked sideways or even sat down and slid on our bottoms—but our native guides practically skipped. One, Daniel, was middle-aged; the other, Kee, was his father. Both wore cowboy boots rather than the high-tech walking shoes the rest of us had. But no one has invented the material that beats years of experience.

Most of our hike was across the canyon floor. Here there were new and exotic plants for me, pot shards and other artifacts for the anthropologists-in-training. We passed the hogans—mud huts—of the local people who still lived in them in summer to garden and tend their sheep. And we passed sheep, of course, and other farm animals, none of them enclosed, and many standing in the broad, shallow creek from which we would later draw our drinking water!

We stopped periodically at cliff dwelling ruins, to hear our guides tell us about the difficult lives of the Anasazi people who lived there for centuries, fending off both Navajo and white invaders. We saw their drawings, and joked that although they are now considered historic works of art, at the time parents might have been yelling at their teenagers for drawing graffiti on the building walls again! And who knows, maybe in some cases we were right.

We got to our campsite at dusk, and it was stunning. There were places to hide away, and enough room that everyone could have a prime tent-pitching site without getting in anyone else's face. We made camp and began gathering firewood. The mood was tired, peaceful, and excited all at the same time: we had completed our long journey, we were the only people for miles around with no sign that anyone had preceded us there, and we knew our evening would be a treat.

We spent the last half-hour of daylight tediously collecting and filtering water from the wide stream nearby. Had it not been for the threat of unknown parasites that could have made me miserable for weeks to come, I would have totally skipped the filtering. And it did occur to me that had we brought fresh fruit with us instead of the dried we chose for its weight advantage, we wouldn't have needed so dang much water!

As night fell, our guides, Daniel and Kee, started a campfire, which was so large and assertive it was nearly a bonfire. They got out their musical instruments—traditional pipes—and began to tell us Navajo legends and sing native songs. We had lucked into an absolutely cloudless night, and when we stepped away from the fire to learn an Indian dance, we were overwhelmed by the night sky. The moon was new, and there appeared to be layer upon layer of stars, nearly blurring together. "There are almost too many of them", one student marveled. Once we were back in Blue River, that sky would be one of the things we always remembered together. I doubt if I will ever see that many stars again.

After Kee and Daniel retired for the night, the rest of us started singing. We turned out to have some very gifted singers in our group. Our choice of material followed no pattern—from folk to rock to old Negro spirituals. Sometimes we all sang together, and sometimes one person would start a song nobody else knew and just solo all the way through it. I think most of us wanted to stay up all night, but our exhausted bodies won out in the end. After I crawled into my sleeping bag, I drifted off listening to Anita singing Joni Mitchell songs by the last embers of our fire.

***

The next day would test both my muscles and my nerve. We awoke to chilly temperatures in the shadow of the canyon wall. We filtered our day's supply of brown water, and to my horror there was not time to make coffee. The morning air was invigorating, though. We all looked forward to our traditional Indian lunch of "fry bread and mutton stew" which was to be prepared by some locals at an outpost across the canyon floor from our campsite.

We were cheerful that morning, all a bit proud of ourselves I think, and we enjoyed Kee's and Daniel's lectures on the ruins we passed, as well as the sight of some mustangs near the trail. At one point we were all following each other's footsteps across a damp patch of sand when the student in front of me, Kelsey, began to sink in with one foot. She quickly shifted her weight to the other foot and promptly went in up to her knee. We had all done the required reading about the canyon's history, and remembered the story of a horse lost to quicksand; as Kelsey reached out her hand to me, I admit I paused for a split second before grabbing it. My thoughts were not formed into words, but on some instinctive level I feared being pulled in with her. Hopefully none of my companions saw my moment of weakness!

I yelled, and Dr. Jay was with us in a flash; Kelsey was out of danger in moments. But while the professor and I were trying to get our heart rates back to normal, Kelsey only seemed bummed out by the dirt on her hiking boots and jeans. We were coming at it from two different perspectives, and age and experience were the difference. Once Kelsey realized how frightened we had been, I think she was a little unnerved. But we all shook it off and took pictures of her posing with her quicksand pants for our memory books.

What a crushing blow it was to arrive at the outpost and find no fry bread or mutton stew at all! Daniel had even taught us a song about the traditional food which we had been singing as our appetites built. There had been a miscommunication, and the only things available (for purchase, no less) were overpriced sodas and Girl Scout cookies. We were all in denial for some minutes, but finally accepted the loss and ransacked our packs for some form of lunch. One student changed the traditional song to include "crackers and crappy tuna". Personally, I ate gorp and a tortilla spread with mustard and mayonnaise for lunch!

Very shortly after that, we began the ascent out of the canyon. I'm sure Dr. Jay had warned us about it, but I must not have been listening, because I had no idea what was in store. The walk out, or climb up, as I should say, might have been a mile in length, but it took us an hour. Here it became obvious why ordinary tourists were not allowed on this "trail".

We were led by Daniel and Kee, or it would have been impossible to determine which way to go. They knew the ancient hand and foot-holds in the rock that had been used for centuries. These were only shallow impressions, and it was staggering to think of the people, young and old, strong or frail or even carrying babies, that had used these toeholds. After getting far ahead of us, our guides realized we couldn't see them anymore, and came back to help. My friend Casey was having leg cramps, and some other students were trying to massage them out. Kee took Casey's pack for her, but he ended up taking Casey herself on his back as he climbed up the rest of the way.

Toward the back, so I wouldn't slow anyone else down, I was taking it a few steps at a time, pausing periodically to get the shaking in my calves to stop. I was mentally thanking Liz for helping me choose those incredible shoes, which were giving me such secure footing. I was frightened in a primal way, like the time I witnessed a huge tree fall down in our backyard in Atlanta—but this time it wasn't a moment of terror, but a sustained period. And this time I couldn't scream! I could only tell myself that I had to do this, for so many reasons. I had to get out of the freaking canyon, obviously. I had to show the students I could do it, too. I had to have a reason to be proud of myself and frankly, to think, "In your *face*, estranged husband who thinks I'm dull!"

And so I labored on, ducking when the wind threatened to unbalance me and my pack. The poorer balance I have always suffered when taking an SSRI anti-depressant was a huge factor here, as was my bum shoulder—which so far had behaved very well! But I reached a point where I was going to have to pull myself over a ledge, and I simply could not do it. As Dr. Jay and my student friends Cutler, Taylor and Andy waited patiently behind me, I stood on a tiny ledge, my mind racing. I knew I couldn't, physically, go back. I couldn't go forward. I was picturing helicopter airlifts or simply spending the night there, when one of the kids, who was up ahead, asked if I wanted him to come back for me. I had to say yes. Derek pulled a good quarter of my combined body-and-pack weight up over that ledge without overbalancing himself, and I embarrassed him for the rest of the trip by repeating how I would STILL be on that ledge if it hadn't been for him. How the birds of prey would be picking my bones clean, the coyotes rummaging through what was left in my pack.

We all made smart remarks and conversation as we climbed, some of it not even related to what we were doing. It was pure distraction, at least for me, to mask the fear in my gut: fake it till you make it.

And finally we had joked our way over the lip of the canyon to where the rest of the group awaited us. They cheered each person as he or she clambered out. I don't remember ever feeling so exhilarated at any time in my life.

When Andy's head appeared on the horizon, I stood tall and flipped him a victorious bird! The folks in the know in our group laughed.

"Laura Anne, I am VERY proud of you," said Dr. Jay as he caught his breath on a rock.

"Dr. Jay, I am VERY proud of you!" I replied. "Something tells me when *I'm* 67, I won't be doing this!"

Later on in the Peace Train, I asked everyone if they had been scared. All the women eventually admitted that they had. Derek finally said, "Only when I went back to get you."

As we rode along to our next motel, I couldn't help telling the folks in the Peace Train how one complaint my husband had had about me was my lack of "adventurousness". My fellow Peaceniks were amazed. "You, not adventurous, L.A.? You, dull?"

"I wish there was a picture of me climbing out of that canyon," I mused. "Heck, we could set up a whole series of adventure shots to show him."

"Like L.A. taking out an elk," Cutler said.

"With a longbow!" cried Taylor.

"Oh yeah!" I remembered. "I've never told John that story! I should, so whenever he makes me mad I could just say, 'Oh honey!'" and I raised my middle finger high.

We all burst into giggles. I knew I was regressing in maturity, but man, it felt good!

***

And so our vans rolled on, through Colorado and into New Mexico. We had a full free day to spend in Santa Fe before our two-day drive back across the country. I had always wanted to visit Santa Fe, and was thrilled.

In fact, the whole trip had been a thrill, in one way or another. Every day I woke up excited about what the day would bring. I had never taken a trip like this in college, and now it was as if I were recapturing that age. I made such good friends among our group; we all did, and although Dr. Jay predicted the bond wouldn't last more than a few weeks past our return, it has been years as I write, and I still feel it with many of those people. Several have gone back and done the trip a second time.

On Santa Fe Day, I dressed to do the town, not to hike, and felt very young and hip in my orange tank top, black jeans and sunglasses. Some of our group had elected to spend the day at another archaeo-logical site, but I was ready for something completely different!

***

There is nothing I enjoy much more than being alone in a new and interesting place with time to explore. I don't have to accommo-date anyone else's wishes, and if I see something interesting on the horizon, I can strike out for it even if it wasn't in the plan. So although I started the day socially with breakfast with three friends, I set out on my own after that. I had my day pack with my money, camera, water bottle and chapstick (the essentials) and I was loaded up on caffeine!

The first thing I did was find the tourist center and get a map. After that I be-bopped all around the gorgeous terra-cotta city center, stopping at shops or by street vendors and taking a lot of pictures. I was so giddy with delight that I stopped at a table in a park and spent an hour writing in my journal about how happy I was!

I ended up spending some more time with fellow students: lunch in the square from a street vendor who inadvertently put me and another student on Salmonella Watch for the next 24 hours with the chicken fajita we split! and a side trip to the Georgia O'Keefe mu-seum. In the late afternoon, we headed back to our cheap motel on the strip, and I began my search for a place to salsa-dance that night.

Andy and I had been taking salsa lessons for a while at the uni-versity, and had told each other we would put them to use in Santa Fe. But being Prof. Jay's right-hand man on the trip, Andy had many obligations I didn't, and he wound up driving the professor to the Al-buquerque airport that evening. So I wandered around tourist traps near our motel, picking up fliers and picking the employees' brains about places to dance.

I finally scored with a Mexican restaurant and spread the word around among the group.

I had brought my "salsa outfit": a brown tank top and matching skirt cut shorter in front than in back, theater-curtain style. I paired it with strappy stacked-heel sandals that were the rare pair of high heels I could walk in without falling over. When one student, Nathan, saw me in this outfit on the motel balcony, he whistled and called me, "Miss Bring-a-Salsa-Dress-to-go-Hiking"! Of course, I loved that, too!

Dancing was the perfect end to our day, and Santa Fe was the perfect culmination of the entire 12-day trip. The women in our group vastly outnumbered the men, so we had to dance with each other quite a bit, which was fine. But after a while I got a hankering to dance with someone who knew what he was doing, and there were a dozen Hispanic men in cowboy hats just standing around the edge of the floor. I mustered my courage (and the $3 mojito I had drunk) to sashay right up to them and ask, "Quiere alguien bailar conmigo?" (Would anyone care to dance with me?) My new independence was driving me, but apparently the hombres didn't get the memo. To my horror, every single one of them declined!

One of the students, who had helped me out enormously on the hike, heard about my humiliation when I rejoined the group. In a vodka-fueled state of outrage, he declared, "That is SKETCH!"

I was vindicated later, when a couple of those gentlemen and several others as well asked me to dance, and I was able to swing through the rest of the evening. When Andy, finally back from the airport, joined me on the floor, he caught my eye and said, "We're salsa dancing in Santa Fe! You made it happen!"

***

The night before our final leg of the journey home, Taylor and I were leaning on the motel balcony talking it all over. "Are you nervous about going back?" she asked.

"No! not nervous", I answered, wondering why she would ask. But as I thought it over, I was. The trip had been pure getaway—no responsibilities, and so much new to see and do. But I would return home to lawyer-filtered negotiations of a separation agreement, and a husband with whom I still regularly had scenes. What's more, while I was gone Leo had been penalized a game on his soccer team for misbehavior he swore he had not committed, and John had yanked him off the team in protest and resigned as manager. Life at home was complicated.

Back in Blue River, which suddenly seemed claustrophobic and mildewy, the other Southwesters and I held each other up through a long period of readjustment blues. It began for me when Andy dropped me off at my house on the night of our return. There was not only no husband there, there was no child and no dog to greet me. After the social spin of the past two weeks, my beloved home seemed absolutely bereft.

As soon as Andy left, I called Leo to let him know I was back. "Mommy, can I come home now?" he asked.

"Yes!" I said, "You and Molson, too!" Even though it was after Leo's bedtime, I got John to agree and drove straight over to his place to pick up my boys.

Chapter 16
A Mistake

As I readjusted to normal life, I began to be really bothered by the frequency of my headaches. Obviously the SSRI was not doing the trick for them anymore. I had tried another medication prescribed by a neurologist, but when that didn't help either and the doctor ordered an MRI, I pulled the disappearing patient act. I was pretty sure, after suffering from headaches for 20 years, that I didn't have a brain tumor, and I was not interested in having an MRI. I am slightly claustrophobic, and I am severely averse to spending money on medical procedures I don't believe will help.

I had also been doing so well for so long with regard to being "single", I decided it was time to give no medication at all another whirl. So I tapered off the anti-depressant and suffered no ill effects. I was still frustrated by the headaches, but didn't have much faith in the medical system to resolve them.

As spring came to our "holler", Leo finished up third grade and I made my modest summer plans. We would visit friends down the mountain, host some friends at our house, and I would throw Leo a 10th birthday party in July. My "Thelma and Louise"-style getaway would be a road trip to Philadelphia with Liz.

Meanwhile, the one-year anniversary of John's and my separation came and went, and behind the scenes our lawyers continued to turn the wheels of the divorce process for us. Slowly. And expensively. I can't imagine what a contested divorce with real estate and considerable property costs! John's and mine was simple. His car was his, mine was mine; ditto with our IRA's; we didn't own a home, and we had no debt. Yet I still spent several thousand dollars on legal representation. The "left" spouse is really victimized twice.

In May, I let Liz and other friends convince me that I should break into the world of online dating. John had been doing it for a while with great success—in number of dates, anyway. He was now on his second relationship garnered through the web.

It was fun setting up my site, and I really tried to make it reflect me. I posted glamorous pictures, but also one in which I wore no make-up; pictures of me salsa-dancing and of me hiking in the Southwest. I was honest but brief about my personal life, and tried to be upbeat and funny about what I did and didn't enjoy. I pulled no punches—admitting that I am not religious and that I was looking for someone intellectual.

There was a flurry of activity when I "launched" my profile, but what it had in quantity it notably lacked in quality. I kept hearing from guys who couldn't spell, and ones I could imagine chewin' an' spittin' at a Nascar race. Don't get me wrong—I have friends and relatives in these categories, but I'm never going to have a husband there. Compatibility is key!

I had paid for six months on the dating site, and as these months wore on I began cracking wise about how it was the most money I'd ever spent to be humiliated. When a guy appeared that I could actually get excited about, he invariably ignored my message or "wink". I even contacted a couple of fellows I frankly thought I was being generous with, only to be snubbed. I wrote in my journal that "people out there are really kidding themselves, including, apparently, me." Thrashing about for the reason for my stunning lack of success, I could only conclude it was either because I was too honest, or because I didn't state my income, and maybe it's not just women who dig for gold in relationships. I can't believe this particular information is even requested on these sites—can you imagine being asked out on a first date and saying, "Wait a minute—how much do you make?"

Looking back in my journal during this spring and summer of 2007, it's surprising to me that I didn't notice the correlation between discontinuing my anti-depressant and beginning to complain quite a bit about my life. Of course my life was not a bed of roses, but I had been pretty darn happy with it for almost a year.

Attempting to cheer myself up, I planned a cookout at my home for my Southwest gang before everyone left school for the summer, and began planning a trip to England for Leo and me! We had friends living there, and having lived there myself in my late teens, I thought it would be great to show my son the land of Harry Potter. I went so far as to secure him a passport, which wasn't easy given his Russian birth and naturalized citizenship, and was expensive as well. But as I tried to set dates and reserve plane tickets, I became more and more discouraged. It appeared neither one of us could fly for less than four digits.

On April 10th I wrote in my journal, "I have decided to cancel my party, cancel my trip, and sink into a deep depression. I am pretty happy with my decision."

Which was me smarting off, of course, but why on earth didn't I see that I needed to get back on medication?

Three days later I wrote,

> I could only get dates with freaks, kids, and repulsive people. There is not one decent man out there who wants me. I am unattractive, old, and alone…. All I see in the future is menial work, penury, headaches, and single parenthood.
>
> I am terribly moody and irritable. I have no peers. I am out here all alone, on my own planet. My married girlfriends can't relate to me any more. My in-laws are phasing me out. I can't lift my lawn mower.

And even more alarming, on May 10th, the one-line entry:

> I *HATE* my life.

One of the last entries I made for the next 10 months is on May 27th, and it's one line as well:

> I think my whole life is payback for something I haven't figured out yet.

Chapter 17
It Never Rains…

Liz was leaving town. She had graduated with "Terisasa' in December, and now, like Teresa, was moving on to graduate school. Our last hurrah was the road trip to Philly, and it was a success. We traveled well together, explored the historic district of that rich city, and I got a kick out of meeting her parents, "the people who brought you Liz"! I convinced her folks to visit the Morris Arboretum with us, and she and I spent an evening at her brother's house, with his fun family.

But in late July, she packed up her house—in typical Liz style, making a bonfire out of everything she didn't want to move or give away! I showed up with milkshakes for her and her helpers, and tried not to cry when I left. Unsuccessfully. She had been the only in-town friend I'd had once my professor chum dropped out of the picture, and we had had loads of fun.

To top it all off, I was now the victim of a bank error. When a box of new checks went astray in the mail, the bank stopped payment on not only the lost checks, but the series of checks I was currently writing. My checks bounced all over the country. Credit card companies with whom I hadn't missed a payment in 10 years raised my interest rate and threatened to report me to credit bureaus. Utilities hit me with late fees, and department stores sent my checks back. Through a long and harrowing process, I straightened out each situation individually, asking the bank for letters to the national companies, and sweet-talking the local ones. Eventually my credit score was returned to its rightful solidity.

In August I made a vet appointment for Molson for something other than shots for the first time in his life. Now 13, he was getting bony and seemed tired, and I wanted to make sure he was okay. I scheduled it for a Saturday when Leo would be with his dad, as Leo didn't take seeing our animals frightened or in pain very well.

As the days passed, I began to wish I had made the appointment sooner. It alarmed me when I noticed that his belly seemed swollen, while his hipbones stood out in relief. One evening I took him for a walk and he had to stop to get his breath repeatedly. By the time we got back to the car, I knew it was the last walk I would ever take with Molson.

At the veterinary office, the doctor took all Molson's vital signs and listened to his heart and lungs. She then took him to the back of the clinic for an x-ray of his chest. When she came out with the films, she didn't mince words. "I think he's dying," she said.

I wrapped my arms around my dog's mighty chest and said, "I think so, too," as the tears began.

***

I was glad Molson was only my dog now. John and I had discussed Molson's "end of life issues" long ago and found we disagreed on the subject. John would have spared no expense and traveled to Raleigh to seek any treatment that might have prolonged our dog's life. I didn't want to put Molson through it. He was the most devoted companion I had ever had, and I would not let him suffer. I have always thought people should be so lucky as to have the one who loves them most decide when their life is not worth living any more, and be able to peacefully go to sleep in their arms, unaware and unafraid. You couldn't ask for more.

But only animals get this mercy. I called around until I had found a veterinarian who would come to my home to put Molson to sleep, and I put her on notice that the time was near. I did not want my dog to be afraid during his last moments, as he always was at the vet's. Then I declared the "Week of Molson"!

Everyone, human and dog, was invited to visit Molson at our home whether we were there or not, and I know at least a couple of people came and sat with him. I'm guessing one of them was John. My soon-to-be ex-husband cried when I told him the news, and I'm sure he cried more when the two of them were alone.

I took Molson on car rides until he couldn't get into the car anymore, and kept him close by whether we were inside or outside the house. Every day I hand-fed him meat—he had lost interest in dog food. I walked him out on a leash when he had to do his business, because otherwise he got confused and began wandering down the driveway, then couldn't get his breath coming back up. There was an almost unbearable tenderness in our interactions. Molson didn't know what was happening, but he knew something was. He trusted me to take care of it, and him, and I watched closely for the signs that it was time.

John came over and dug Molson's grave in advance. I couldn't physically do that, and I had to be ready. Molson was a large dog, and it was summer, and wild animals everywhere—I had to be practical. But it was unspeakable seeing Molson sniff around that grave when I walked him. Thank God he couldn't know.

Finally I made the appointment for after work one day. I didn't tell Leo, because I couldn't imagine making the decision understandable to him. As I lay in bed the night before, I listened to Molson's labored breathing from the floor beside me and tried to imagine not having his presence in our house.

The next morning I looked at him as he stood at the kitchen door, with the look of patience and acceptance he had developed in his illness. "I'm going to make it stop, Molson," I told him. "I promise you. It will stop today."

Molson was laid to rest that evening in his favorite blanket, all dirty and smelly like he liked it. Leo, who accepted my decision better than I expected, helped his father fill in the grave. He then heaped rocks over the site and placed wildflowers on it. From a piece of wood he found in the yard, he made a marker and wrote on it in black: "Here lies Molson Nicholson, November 1994—September 2007. He was the Best dog in the World. His reward will be awsome".

Afterward I asked John if he wanted to split a beer and sit on the porch as a family remembering Molson, but he declined and asked if he could use my bathroom to "freshen up". He came out of it dressed for a date, and headed out.

The next day I wrote emails to people who had loved Molson telling them the news. John sent me a florist's gardenia. I felt the need to make a tribute, and ended up posting my first-ever "status" on my

Facebook page: *"L.A. Nicholson* is thankful that she had the greatest dog in the world for 13 years".

***

Molson died on the Tuesday after Labor Day, the same day I went to my doctor for my yearly checkup. Ginny learned that I had never had the MRI the neurologist ordered and promptly scheduled one for that Friday. On Wednesday, my lawyer called to tell me I needed to come in and sign my final divorce papers. On Thursday, my marriage officially ended.

Chapter 18
Not Again

I knew the feeling when it came. It started Thursday night, before the MRI. I found myself sitting on my bed, without Molson beside me, ruminating about the MRI process. The doctor had given me three sedative pills, and I knew I could zone out during the whole thing. So why was I worrying?

Well, what if the test DID show something abnormal? But I knew I didn't have a brain tumor—if I did, it would have to be the slowest-growing tumor of all time! But what if the procedure detected those plaques that are associated with Alzheimer's, which my grandmother died of? I wouldn't want to know I was going to get it—that would ruin my life! My *divorced* life. My life alone, without a dog, with headaches.

This is how my thought process was going that evening. I had trouble falling asleep, although I did eventually. The next morning I took only one of the sedative pills, since I planned to go to work from the hospital. The MRI turned out to be no big deal, and only took 20 minutes. The whole time I could see the technicians in a mirror visible through an opening in the machine, and I had a "panic button" in my hand, just in case. So that hurdle was over.

But I still felt nervous. Fortunately, Ginny had started me back on my anti-depressant at my recent appointment. It would kick in within a few weeks.

I didn't have a good weekend. Leo wasn't with me, which gave me too much time to think, and on Sunday I found myself in Dad and Kaye's back garden, saying frantically, "I'm starting to feel like I did in Oregon".

These were alarming words to all of us, but the obvious reason for my distress was waiting on the results of the MRI. Kaye, who had had several, tried to reassure me, but it didn't work, and I didn't know why. Intellectually I didn't believe anything was really wrong with my brain.

On Monday, I got the all-clear from the doctor's office. My MRI was fine. Flooded with relief, I hung up the phone and hugged the first person I saw, which fortunately was Andy.

"I don't have a brain tumor!" I cried, to his dismay.

Even as I stood there, explaining my outburst, I realized I was still nervous.

The thermostat. It wasn't resetting.

***

There is a documented "feeling worse before you feel better" syndrome when starting an SSRI. It had never happened to me, but I had read the news stories about people having suicidal thoughts and behaviors during the first few weeks of treatment. I had only ever had a little dizziness, a wave or two of nausea, before beginning to feel much better.

The insomnia began. I split sleeping pills and told myself I could only take half of one every other night. I have always feared becoming dependent on medication. For some reason, maintaining on an anti-depressant had not seemed like a dependence. For one thing, I never felt it wear off, like I did with anxiety or pain medication. Being on an SSRI seemed kind of like being on birth control pills.

Ginny prescribed a little more anxiety medicine for me to take during the adjustment. I used it, sparingly, but I was starting to feel really freaked. The feelings coincided exactly with the resumption of my medication—almost as if the medicine had caused it. Had operated in reverse. But how could that be?

I called the doctor again. "I really think you'll be happier if you stay on it," she advised me in a late-night conversation, as I lowered my voice so as not to wake Leo. Or let him hear.

Intellectually, I understood her thinking, but I still balked at the advice. I felt like I was poisoning myself—what sense did it make to take something that made me feel awful? I had been fine—okay, not happy, but not anxious—before I started taking this medicine. Now I was in a tailspin. Why would a logical person continue?

After several conversations with my wonderfully sympathetic pharmacist, I decided to taper off the drug. I would be very careful, do it gradually, so as not to upset my system. If I didn't feel better once

I was free of the stuff, I could always go back on it. But I would never know if it was causing the problem, if I didn't conduct this experiment.

My calendar from this time has recorded the amount of SSRI I took each day. I didn't just split pills, I shaved varying amounts off them. This irrational behavior was very unlike me, but I didn't recognize it at the time. When I was finally off the medicine, I gave myself 10 days to make sure it was completely out of my system. Now I would be okay.

But I wasn't. I went back to the doctor.

"Let's try a different drug in the same category," she said. "Your relative does well on it, and I have a friend who loves it so much she says she going to make up T-shirts!" That sounded like a plan. Even better, she gave me enough anxiety medication to get me through the entire adjustment.

"I want you to give this a good three weeks to take effect," she admonished me. I promised I would.

In my neurotic state, I began with half a dose of what the doctor recommended. I felt no ill effects, so after a week I went up to the full dose. With that, my digestive system rebelled. Except for the time in Oregon, during which I could still eat but just didn't want to, I have always had a stomach of iron. I have literally eaten a corn dog and an ice cream cone and then gotten on the "Devil's Drop" at the State Fair. I have never experienced car sickness or sea sickness. I have always reacted to stress with my head, not my stomach.

But this was bad news. Within days of going up on the dosage, I simply could not eat most foods. Soon I could tolerate only about 10 things: poached eggs, bagels and cream cheese, potatoes, noodles, and rice; very plain chicken and lean pork chops, and occasionally peanut butter sandwiches. I could eat chicken soup and small amounts of bland boiled vegetables like carrots and corn. I began to lose weight.

I still had to feed my child balanced meals, of course. I was getting weaker with lack of sleep and nutrition, but I had to take proper care of my son. At ten, he knew vaguely what was going on, that Mom was adjusting to her "headache medicine" and it was causing some stomach upset which should pass. One night I fixed spaghetti and actually put a little of the tomato sauce on my own noodles. "What are you doing?" Leo asked in surprise. "I know, I'm living dangerously, aren't I?" I laughed, feebly. Another night I went out on a limb and ate a strawberry.

Shaky and semi-panicked, I went back to Ginny for my three-week follow-up. She was alarmed. After my previous stunning success with the first SSRI, I think this reaction was the last thing she expected from me.

"I'm not trained to help you at this point," she told me. "You need to see a psychiatrist."

I thought so, too, as serious as it sounded.

Blue River had, at the time, a whopping four psychiatrists in practice. None were taking new patients. Ginny called a local mental health clinic to see if she could get me in, but was told there would be a very long wait, as there were "homicidal, schizophrenic people" ahead of me on the waiting list.

Obviously flustered, my doctor asked me, "Do you want to be admitted somewhere?"

"No!" I cried. *Admitted* somewhere? What did that mean—a psyche ward? Our county didn't even have one! Besides, what would I be admitted for? I hadn't done anything crazy; I was just miserable. Who would pay for it? What would my family and friends think? People like us didn't *get* committed.

Ginny called me at home that night, to recommend a psychiatrist in Warrington, about a 45-minute drive down the mountain. She had heard good things about him and he had agreed to take me on. I was relieved, although the thought of having to drive that far and find a new office overwhelmed me, like going to the grocery store had in Brake.

"When I suggested admitting you somewhere today, I think you got mad," she said.

"No, no!" I interrupted. "Not mad. It just scared me—that is a really scary thought."

"It's not as bad as it sounds," she answered. "Those places are there to help people, to keep them safe while they get stabilized on medication, and they have a lot more resources and experience than I do."

"I know," I said. "But let me just get started with Dr. Bernard and we'll see how it goes."

***

Even with my doctor's help, it was a couple of weeks before I could get an appointment with the shrink. My entire family was very worried by now, and Kaye offered to drive me down.

One beautiful Saturday morning as I was sitting up in bed watching the sun stream through my window, I began talking out loud to my mom. I had had a bad night, as always, but at least on weekends (especially when Leo was at his dad's), I could continue as long as possible with the sleep that usually came just before the alarm clock went off. I didn't even have a dog I had to let out, or a cat that would jump on my face and demand breakfast.

So I prattled on. And I had an epiphany.

Obviously, I needed to go back on my original anti-depressant and stick it out. It hadn't ever upset my stomach, and it had *worked*. All this going on and off and trying new things was silly and traumatic; I needed my old standby back.

I know a lot of people would probably say this was my mom "talking" to me. Skeptic that I am, I just said that I had had a realization and that I knew my mom would agree.

I was a bundle of nerves the day Kaye drove me to my appointment with the psychiatrist. Once we had filled out the paperwork and I had been shown into the large, dimly lit office, Dr. Bernard, a young, well-dressed man, offered me a seat. It was a couch. I looked at it for a moment before sitting and said wryly, "Well, here I am, on the psychiatrist's couch." Part of me still couldn't believe it. But I knew I needed to be there.

It was a long story to go through for the doctor, going all the way back to when I had started the medication for headaches, 10 years before. When I was finished, Dr. Bernard looked at me, nodded, and said, "I know what *I* think."

"Yes?"

"I think you should go back on your original medication," he said. It was exactly what I wanted to hear.

Chapter 19
Make It Stop

Now I would be okay. With that horrible second medicine out of my system, I would be able to eat again, and gain some weight back. My old standby, after whatever initial quirks or upsets it caused, would, within three weeks, be balm on my troubled soul. I knew now it hadn't caused my anxiety. I was just falling off the cliff anyway, and it was coincidence that I started it at the same time. That medicine was my friend—my salvation before, and it would be again.

This was the beginning of November 2007. I wish I remembered more about this time, or had written in my journal. My calendar shows the painstaking "stepping up" I did to get back on 20 mg of my old standby, with daily notes about whether I took any anxiety medicine, how much, and any stomach trouble I had. The only thing I remember specifically is calling the nurse at my psychiatrist's office and asking her why my stomach was still upset 10 days after quitting the second SSRI.

"I wouldn't worry about that," she replied. "It takes a good two weeks to get out of your system."

I tried to keep the faith. But my mind was racing. Could that stuff have permanently messed me up? Could the trauma have somehow sensitized my stomach to all SSRI's? What was going on?

***

When I went back to Dr. Bernard, he suggested that my persistent stomach trouble was due to anxiety, and wanted to up my medication dose. I didn't like that idea at all, and refused. He then prescribed a second medication to "augment" the SSRI. He began asking a lot of questions about my mood, until I finally asked him if he was trying to suggest I was bipolar (because my grandfather was? because it was the Disease of the Week?)

"Perhaps," he replied. "You seem very down this time, and last time you almost seemed manic."

"I was 'manic' last time because I was so glad I had finally gotten in to see a psychiatrist!" I cried. "And I'm down now because nothing's working!"

Dr. Bernard gazed at me thoughtfully. "I'd like to try something else," he said at last.

"You mean instead of the SSRI, and the augmenter?" I asked.

"No," he replied. "In addition."

"What kind of medicine is it, what class?"

"It's a non-traditional anti-psychotic."

"Anti-psychotic? I'm psychotic now?"

"Look, I can show you the Harvard case book if you want."

"Never mind, fine; I'll try it," I said. After all, what are we paying them for, in the end, except their prescriptions? Medications were the only thing he ever wanted to talk about, anyway.

I did look up the prescription before filling it, and I had to admit it made sense for me, on paper. I could see where he was coming from. I was starting to feel like a pill bottle, though.

My family was keeping close tabs on me, and I talked to them and a few friends. I kept going over and over the facts, how it just didn't make sense, searching for someone who could explain what was happening to me. There HAD to be a logical explanation. I have always been a firm believer in logic. But this defied it and I couldn't accept that. If logic didn't work, the foundations were slipping out from under me. If my old standby couldn't fix me, what could I do? I could be like this for years, if I could survive that long on so little food and sleep. Life as it was right now was insupportable, unsustainable, utter misery! When was the last time I had felt joy? Why could I see the gorgeous autumn colors of the mountains and not feel anything? How could I be a mom like this? What would it do to my son?

I began to wish that I could fall asleep and not wake up. Of course, to do that, one would have to fall asleep in the first place. I couldn't cry over Molson anymore—I couldn't cry at all. Dinner each night was more and more of an ordeal, because it was so exhausting to cook for Leo, and then fix something different that I could eat.

I began to pace the floor of my living room at night. It was a squeaky hardwood floor, and I had to find a path I could take without waking Leo. By using my tiny dining room and living room together, I could trace a figure eight. Once I was sure Leo was asleep I would walk it, over and over, my mind racing or even talking to myself out loud. I would tire quickly, and sit on the sofa, the slightest bit relaxed from the physical effort. Within minutes, I would start pacing again.

I kept going over the chronology of this illness in my head, trying to figure it out. There had to be a solution right there—why couldn't I grasp it? Why couldn't I solve this? It was maddening, terrifying, soul-defeating.

The most effective way I can describe how anxiety disorder made me feel is to go back to an incident from childhood. When I was 12, a friend and I were cutting through someone's property, walking down their long gravel drive. We were barefoot. A dog we didn't know—a bulldog—was on the screened-in porch, hurling himself at the screen and snarling at us. I don't know how it happened, but I will never forget seeing him push the porch door open and start down that driveway like he'd been shot from a cannon. As he bore down on us, my friend and I ran for our lives. The fear was absolutely primal.

Those sensations, in my arms and my legs and my gut, were there all the time now.

By mid-November I was fantasizing about death, the only peace I could comprehend for myself. I thought of ways I could end it all, rejecting many as impractical (buying a gun) or too scary (jumping out of the fourth-story window at my work). Just thinking about suicide, the fact that in theory I could do it, brought a small measure of comfort—that there was a way out. That I was choosing not to take it, but it was always there.

The thing that stopped me, of course, was Leo. I couldn't do that to him. It would be the ultimate betrayal, worse than his father walking out the door. How could a 10-year-old boy ever be expected to recover from something like that? Especially one who had already coped with so much?

I remembered a friend whose sister-in-law had attempted suicide three times after leaving her husband. They had two children adopted from Ukraine. My response to this was, "I just wonder how much some kids are supposed to take."

I remembered what I had always said about suicide. "It's cowardly, selfish, and—for people who have children—inexcusable," I had pronounced. Kind of like I had always blamed the parents for the kids' poor behavior, until I had a child of my own.

I confided in John. He was one of the only people who knew the full extent of what I went through in Oregon, and he was my child's father, after all. I invited him in one day when he brought Leo home at dinnertime, and I took him to the back bedroom while Leo watched TV.

I was curled up on the bed holding a pillow against my stomach while we talked—the position I felt most secure in. John sat on the edge of the bed looking extremely uncomfortable. I gave him the rundown, told him I was back on my anti-depressant. I told him I needed my entire support system around me now, and might sometimes need help caring for Leo. He looked grim but agreed, and got my promise I would stay on the drug that had turned me around before.

Ever since the anxiety began, two months before, I'd been trying to find a counselor. No way would I go back to the folks John and I had seen for marriage counseling (we saw how well THAT turned out!) The only other financially feasible option in our town was the local behavioral health clinic. During my "intake" there, I had curled up in a stuffed chair this same way, and recited my long, sad tale to a largish young man who assured me in a bored way that he suffered from panic attacks when not on medication and in counseling. It was always a relief to pour out the story to someone who either cared or was being paid to. By the end of our session, I felt I had given him a clear picture of the mental disaster that was me now. But I didn't "click" with him, as the literature says one should with a counselor. He listened but took notes only when I mentioned medication, which I thought portrayed a vastly incomplete picture of the situation.

Eventually someone from the clinic called back with a therapist for me, a lady whom I would meet with only twice. She had suffered major depression and took issue with my statement, "With this kind of anxiety, I'd give anything for a good depression about now". She turned my statement around backwards, convincing me that we might as well be from different planets, for all the understanding I'd get from her.

One chilly Sunday afternoon, when I was determined to feel better, I told Leo we should play outside in spite of the gloom. There had been so many happy times when we had tossed the football or a baseball in the front yard, and I had been healthy, the sun was shining, life was good. Surely if I recreated the action, I would feel that way again. But on that day, even the heavens conspired against me. We set up the soccer goal on its end and used it as a volleyball net, but it was a sad little game, with me trying to lunge for the ball and getting out of breath and lightheaded. The winter light was pale and our hands were freezing. Defeated, I called it off.

***

Over in the non-bizarro world, John was now dating the woman he had "freshened up" in my bathroom to see after burying Molson. Leo liked Carrie, unlike the previous girlfriend, who had offended him mightily by not loving dogs. This one was a reasonable age, lived in Blue River, and taught at the university. She loved animals and seemed outdoorsy. I was relieved for Leo.

In fact, I could picture the three of them fixing dinner together, John's dog at their feet, in his cozy apartment. It would be like a family—like we had been, only without me. Maybe Leo would find everything he needed there, and decide he was tired of going back and forth all the time. Maybe it would be better for him not to have to divide his time between two homes. He would only have one mother figure and one father figure, and he wouldn't have to try to keep up with all his school things and clothes between two households. I was sure the in-laws would like her, and my replacement in the family would be complete.

I knew this was bogus even as I said it to myself, but still I allowed myself to think it. This was the last link in the chain that I needed to break to get out.

***

The following weekend, Leo was to be at John's place. At lunch on Friday, instead of curling up in my car for a nap, as I often did, because of my weakness, I decided to go home and curl up in bed.

As usual, I took a long time falling asleep, and then jerked awake after only a few minutes, with my heart pounding. I lay still, staring out the window.

I could not get up.

I just couldn't do it, couldn't go back to work. I couldn't keep pretending I was anything but a miserable shell of what used to be a human being.

An idea began to hatch in my mind.

I got up and called my boss, thankful when I got his voice mail. "Greg, it's Laura Anne. I'm not feeling well, so I'm going to take the rest of the day as sick time. Sorry. If you need anything, I'm at home—you know the number. Sorry. Bye."

I crawled back in bed, but I was sitting up now. I thought of how good a milligram of anxiety medicine could make me feel for 24 hours. I extrapolated to imagine how good 10 milligrams could make me feel, or 100! I thought of blissing out, in total relaxation, and drifting on a cloud of pharmaceuticals into oblivion.

How long it had been since I had been happy! How very happy I would be during those minutes before sleep took hold. Especially knowing I would never have to get up.

I would never have to awake and feel the miserable tingle of anxiety revving up, my heart starting to pound as fear flooded my entire system. I had the power to do this, to *make the misery stop*, forever.

I got up and walked into my bathroom, got out the bottle of anxiety medicine. There were 31 pills left. But what if I threw them up before they could take effect? I could take them slowly. I got my anti-nausea pills, too.

What if it didn't work? I remembered a movie I had seen years ago, in which a man tried to kill himself with an overdose, and ended up living out his years in an institution, a horribly damaged version of his former self. One friend stuck with him, visited regularly, and took walks with him by a lake on the grounds of the hospital. I remembered making a completely irrelevant "note to self—never try to commit suicide with pills".

I couldn't botch this. How would I ever face people again if I did? I looked back in my bathroom cabinet. I found several pills of another anxiety med, which I took out as well. For good measure, I also collected some over-the-counter sleeping pills. I filled a tumbler with water and went back to my room. I placed everything on my bedside table.

It was 2:30. I was due at my dad's house for dinner at 7:00 that night. Four and a half hours ought to be plenty of time.

Had I had a dog at this point, or even a cat with me to pet, I might have had misgivings. But the house was inanimate, lifeless, except for me. The stillness beckoned me—inanimate objects felt no pain. Mine was the only suffering within those walls, and I had the means, here in my hands, to make it stop.

I poured some of the pills into the palm of my hand. Slowly I swallowed two. Then two more, and then a fifth. "I'm really doing this," I thought. I looked at my watch. A few minutes later I swallowed several more. Then a nausea pill. I waited. I was not going to blow this. Soon, I would feel the wonderful calm settling over me.

I didn't feel anything, but I kept swallowing the pills. After 20 minutes or so, my hand was empty, and I poured the rest of the bottle into it. For probably an hour, I steadily consumed pills.

Finally finished, I lay down on my side, pulling the quilt over me, and waited to feel marvelously peaceful, or at least very sleepy. It didn't happen. The moments I had been willing to sacrifice everything for never occurred. There was nothing.

***

Someone was shaking me awake. My father and Kaye were in my room, really bothering me. The light was dim. They were talking. Kaye's voice asked, "How many pills did you take?"

"All of them", I answered. Their voices continued. I heard Kaye making a phone call. She hung up and said something to my father. They were getting me out of bed. I didn't want to get up, but I couldn't fight it. I was amazed that, propped up on either side by the two of them, I could walk. We were outside. We were walking toward their car.

***

A voice, asking me what I took.

"Thirty-one Medicine A, half-milligram," I answered obediently. "Four Medicine B. Two Medicine C, and some D so I wouldn't throw it up."

Then, nothing.

I woke up.

"I need to use the bathroom," I said. There were motions, and someone put something under me.

"Just go ahead and go," a voice said. I did, and somehow I didn't wet myself.

Nothing.

I woke up. The light in the room was very dim. I saw Kaye at the foot of my bed.

"What time is it?" I asked.

"Time?" she repeated, in a conversational tone. "It's twelve-thirty".

I wondered what that meant. Night, or day? What day? Were we inside or outside? Why was it so dark?

Nothing.

I opened my eyes. I can still see my sister's face, clearly, on the left side of me in the dim light. Her expression was confused. Disturbed. It was the face of someone who knows something terrible has happened, but can't process it. A vague feeling of misgiving stirred within me.

Nothing.

A black woman with very short hair was making a telephone call. My father's voice. "She's finding somewhere for you to go, honey".

What did that mean?

Nothing.

My father's voice. "The police will drive you there, and we'll be there in the morning".

A policeman and a policewoman, their faces carefully blank of expression.

"Sorry we have to do this, but it's procedure. Anyone who has hurt themselves or someone else has to be restrained in the squad car."

Shackles being put on my ankles. Handcuffs. A parking lot with fluorescent overhead lights. My father crying, standing beside Kaye.

The officers pushed me gently into the back seat. I curled into the door. I was starting to wake up. I didn't want to.

Their quiet voices in sporadic conversation on a drive that seemed very long.

When we stopped, the male officer took my shackles and hand-cuffs off to walk into a building. Flourescent lights. A nurses' station. People talking.

A kind woman took me to another hall. She helped me undress and asked what I liked to eat for breakfast.

"I've been eating a poached egg on toast and a bagel with cream cheese," I answered. I was surprised that they cared.

A few minutes later, I was in a bed.

Nothing.

**

Given that a modest dose of anxiety medicine could make me "cruise", as I told my sister, for 36 hours, you would think I would have simply taken it regularly, and lived my life. I was afraid to. I was sure I would need more and more, become addicted, and anytime it wore off I would be a basket case. I was more afraid of becoming addicted to a drug than I was of committing suicide with it.

**

I had a roommate. I don't remember who she was. Our room was very much like a dorm room, except it had an attached full bath. I was not remotely interested in taking a shower.

We were called to breakfast. A large room with tables, a group of a dozen or more people. Some were employees, but it wasn't obvious who. I was the only one wearing a nightgown, hospital-issued.

Some of the people were friendly, mainly the men. They were talking like ordinary people, and drinking coffee. A television was on, with sports news.

A woman came in with a cart full of trays. One by one she called everyone's names, and each person, including me, went up to retrieve a box containing breakfast. Mine had a hard-boiled egg and a bagel with cream cheese. I tried to eat some of it.

There were meetings, a schedule. Meetings with names like, "Coping with Stress" and "Anger Management". I didn't want to go to them. I wanted to sleep.

Sara, Dad, and Kaye were there. We were in my room. Sara was curled up with me on the bed.

"You have to promise us you will never, EVER do anything like this again. Promise me", she said.

"Okay," I said dutifully.

"I've talked to John," Kaye said, "and told him you're sick, and he needs to keep Leo tomorrow, too. And your dad has told Greg that you won't be in to work on Monday. So you don't have to worry about any of that."

"Okay," I said. None of it had occurred to me.

I was sad when they left. I closed the bedroom door to take a nap.

"No ma'am!" said a large nurse, forcefully. "As long as you're here, that bedroom door will be open! There are consequences for what you do!" She was practically yelling. I went back in the room and lay down.

I didn't have shoelaces. My family had brought me clothes, but I wasn't allowed shoelaces. I didn't have a watch. I didn't know where my purse was, and that bugged me. I had my glasses, though. Someone had thought of that.

We had to fill out menu cards for our daily meals. It was amazing; you could order whatever you wanted, but there was almost nothing I could eat. I tried to find the blandest things: chicken, bread, potatoes.

I went to the meetings. It was starting to occur to me that you didn't get out of this place with the bully nurses unless you cooperated. When the well-meaning social workers and counselors gave us "homework", I tried to do it, even though none of it had anything to do with me.

I wished they would turn the TV off. It was always football. Some of the men tried to get me to talk, and began telling me their stories. Several were alcoholics. They couldn't figure out what my problem was, so I admitted I had taken an overdose.

Then they began telling me stories of their own suicide attempts. One man, fairly young and attractive, with a ponytail, said he had tried multiple times and that as soon as they let him out, he would try again. I wondered if they would let him out. He asked me where I was from, and told me of football games he had been to in Blue River, that he liked it up there.

Some of the guys began cheering me on when I tried to eat. At snack time, they saved their packets of saltine crackers for me, knowing it was one of the only things I could eat. I could only eat a small amount at a time, so I saved them, hiding them in my room because we weren't allowed to have food there. And sometime during the day, one of the employees would find them and take them out. I wondered what kind of harm they thought I could do myself with an extra packet of saltines.

I watched the other people tuck into cinnamon-swirled French toast at breakfast. How could they need to be here if they could eat? How could they be suicidal if they could enjoy food—which they certainly seemed to.

In the mornings, people got up dreadfully early. I would hear them in the hall, talking to employees. I wished they would be quiet so I could sleep. But insomnia was a problem many of them shared.

A woman checked in one evening. I heard them come into the ward, and saw her because of course my door was open. She was young, and pretty, and someone who appeared to be her husband was there with her and hugged her before he left. I thought, how can she need to be here if she has a husband who loves her? I walked past her in the hall on my way to the medication window to pick up whatever it was they were giving me, and I looked in at her and said, "It'll be all right". She didn't respond.

At the medication window, we were given our pills in tiny cups, and we had to take them in front of the nurse. I don't remember what they were giving me or why I didn't want to take it, but I remember knocking back the pill cup while holding the pill in it back with my finger. Me, the good girl, the rule follower. It was so easy to fool them! I couldn't think what to do with the pill—flushing it never occurred to me. I ended up putting it in my jeans pocket. If someone found it in my room, I would be in trouble.

On the third day, I was led into a room with a large group of people around a table, and introduced to each one. I was Exhibit A. They asked me questions. I was articulate now, and tried to say the right things to get out. I just wanted to be home. I wanted my purse, and my shoelaces. I wanted my car keys. I wanted to stop being treated like one of these crazy people.

On the fourth day, a nice Indian doctor ruled that I could go home. The guy with the ponytail said that sometime when he came to Blue River and I was eating well again, he'd take me out for a cheeseburger. Another man came to the door of my room while I was gathering my things and asked if he could see me sometime. I paused, and asked if he was married.

"Separated—the divorce will be final in June," he replied. That was an easy out. "I don't date separated people", I said. He nodded in resignation.

"Maybe I'll look you up after June," he said.

"Sure", I responded.

Fortunately, neither of these suitors had my last name, and neither seemed to think of asking for it. Almost as if they knew it was hopeless.

I wasn't attracted to either man, but I also wondered just where they got off, being crazy people, asking ME out?

And then I thought how laughable it was that in six months on a major internet dating site I had struck out completely, and in three days in a loonybin, I had two offers.

***

Before I ever landed in the hospital, Leo and I had tried living with Dad and Kaye for a while. I couldn't handle the cooking and child care, and just needed looking after. I even said to my dad at one point (curled up on the guest room bed), "I just wish I could go somewhere where people would take care of me". I imagined a genteel convalescent home, with well-dressed patients in lounge chairs dotted about the manicured lawn. The psych ward of a small-town hospital was not what I had in mind.

But although staying with my relatives lifted some burdens off me, it multiplied others. For one thing, it was just bloody inconvenient. I was in a brain fog from the anxiety and found it hard to dress and prepare for work from somewhere other than home. I kept having to make exhausting trips back to my house to pack up clothes and toiletries. Meanwhile, Leo slept on a pallet on the floor of the guest room. It was comfortable and cozy, with Mom right there—but it wasn't home, and he had trouble settling down. It wasn't right, and he knew it.

So after I was released from the hospital, I did not wish to try that again. I went back to my house, Leo came back from John's with neither of them knowing what had happened, and I tried, feebly, to soldier on. I went obediently back to the local Clinic to see another counselor.

I didn't really think that much about what would happen if John found out. It was simply a given that he couldn't know. Somewhere, intellectually, I knew he could use it to take Leo away, but my tunnel vision wasn't letting that in, and on some level I believed he couldn't manage his running/dating life as the full-time dad of a 10-year-old, and therefore wouldn't fight me. He knew how bad off I had been in Oregon, and he knew it was happening again. In fact, he had yelled at me once during our break-up, "You were semi-suicidal there, what was I supposed to do?" I assumed there would be some shred of understanding from him about my condition, or at least the acknowledgement that I had never endangered Leo, no matter how bad I felt.

So I picked up where I had left off with my life. I went right back to work, told my colleagues I was "Feeling better, thanks", and no one at the department was the wiser. I kept taking my SSRI and waiting for the magic to happen. I rationed myself small amounts of anxiety med, and ate as much as I could manage. I kept small bottles of gingerale and club soda on my desk, along with baggies of oyster crackers that I nibbled on as much as possible.

And very little changed. I was exhausted, overwhelmed, anxious, sleepless, sick to my stomach and watching the time run out on the last vestiges of hope for my miracle cure. I continued to lose weight that I couldn't afford to lose. And now, I was under the microscope with my terrified and betrayed family.

I remembered a dream I had had years before, a powerful one, in which I was walking down the stairs in my family home, with my parents and sister watching, and policemen waiting to take me away. I had done something terrible, disgraced myself and my family, and was being led away in handcuffs. Now it had happened. I was that person now, a shame to the family name. No one knew but the four of us, but we could never change that reality. Or as I said to Sara, "I can never again be a person that didn't do this."

I went back to Dr. Bernard, assuming he knew what had happened. He did not. "I guess you're horrified," I said wearily, as I sank down on the sofa.

"I'm surprised," he replied. "You've really just started treatment. I would have thought you'd give the medications more time to work."

What went through his head at that point, I wonder? More importantly, why the hell didn't he know that one of his patients had tried to commit suicide? Shouldn't the hospital have immediately ascertained whether I was under psychiatric care, and contacted that care provider? Didn't they want his opinion on the dramatic development in my case, his input on my ongoing treatment; didn't they for Christ's sake want my prescription records? It amazed me that the various physicians taking care of me didn't communicate with each other. Should the psychiatrist who released me have given me a prescription for 90 pills, with a refill, of the medicine I'd tried to kill myself with? Was there no coordination at all?

And so a week passed, then two. There was no explanation for me not starting to feel better at this point. Whether it had actually harmed me or not, the medicine definitely wasn't helping. My despair deepened. If the old standby couldn't help me, then nothing could. As I would try to explain later, to myself as well as others, I panicked.

On a Saturday night when Leo was at John's, I called Sara and asked if I could come over. I just wanted to be away from my lifeless house, that I had once loved so well. I hadn't been able to read or watch television for months. I couldn't even remember what I used to do in the evenings—I was completely at a loss when I got home. I knew that her warmly lit living room, with her and her son, and one of their cats on my lap, would bring me a measure of comfort.

Sara welcomed me, tucked a blanket around me on the sofa, and put on the movie "Little Women". I didn't want to watch a movie, since I couldn't concentrate on anything, but Sara (being normal) had no desire to just wrap her arms around me on the sofa and listen to my fears for the 47th time. So the movie played, and at the part where Beth died, Sara pointed to the distraught Jo on the screen, and said pointedly, "See that? Do you see that? That's how I would be if anything ever happened to you!"

The next day, Dec. 2, was Sara's birthday. I had bought her a piece of pottery, and had ice cream in my freezer that was to be my contribution to the family party that night. Normally I would have baked her cake, but everyone knew I was too weak, so Kaye was taking that on, and hosting, too.

I didn't go to church that morning, but I told my sister I would come to a special event, the "Hanging of the Greens", at the church that afternoon. It sounded like such a wonderful activity, launching the holiday season with beauty and Christmasy smells.

My father called that morning—someone called just about every day now—and invited me to come help him and Kaye plant bulbs that afternoon. I was not at all interested, and made the excuse that I planned to do some Christmas shopping before heading out to the church. That was the kind of thing my relatives liked to hear. I guess I may have actually thought I would do it, too.

I don't remember much else about that day. I was thinking, like I always was, how amazing it was that the overdose had not worked, and how limited my other options were. I thought a gun would be the surest method, but the only place I knew that sold them was Walmart—and what if I ran into someone I knew? I was more worried about being embarrassed than dying.

Many, many times that day—and many times before—I had gotten a kitchen knife and held it against my wrist. I couldn't imagine quite how it would work. What if the blade wasn't sharp enough? What if I didn't bleed enough? Where would I do it, so as not to make a mess? So funny the things I worried about when I wanted, above all, to be dead.

But every time, I put the knife back. I turned my thoughts back to whatever task was at hand. I'm told I was paying bills that day—was in fact in the middle of writing a check, when some thought process made me stop, get up, and walk down to the basement. I look back at that entry in my check register and try to remember, but there's nothing.

I try to remember what I was wearing. Apparently I was dressed for church already, wearing a skirt and boots. To this day I don't know what outfit it was, because nothing is missing from my wardrobe. I wonder if I was wearing my glasses or my contacts. Did I have on makeup? Had I washed my hair?

When I got to the basement, I found the loose razor blades I was after—too quickly. We always used them—John and I—when we scraped paint off windows. I thought to myself, now *this* will work.

I walked back up the basement stairs, which came out into the yard, and back into the house. It was early afternoon. John was supposed to bring Leo home at 3:45—earlier than usual, so John could go to a recital of his new girlfriend's. I wondered if I had enough time. Somehow, in my illness, I thought it would be okay if I was good and dead by the time my son got there—I just didn't want him to see me dying.

Whenever I hesitated, I thought about how it would be two more weeks before Leo would spend another weekend at John's. Fourteen days I would have to get through—when ten minutes was unbearable.

There were many feints and starts, but at some point I knew it was now or never. I do remember making the first cut. It was on my throat. I was in my bathroom, with all the doors locked, looking in the mirror. The immediate swell of dark blood was shocking. I could have stopped at that point. I could have bandaged it up—it never did require stitching. I don't know how I would have explained it to anyone, but I could have still stopped.

I didn't. When I was done with the razor blade, I couldn't believe how normal I still felt. In spite of the blood loss, I didn't feel myself dying, didn't even feel lightheaded. I wasn't dying fast enough. They were going to be here. The horror of it panicked me. I unlocked the bathroom door, walked to the kitchen, and chose a knife. I was terrified I would be seen through the windows by Leo and John. I got back to the bathroom and locked the door again.

The knife didn't hurt. I was amazed. It was as if I was not in my body. I kept on. I did everything I could do to ensure my swift and certain death. And then I heard them arrive.

My memories after this become dreamlike. Certainty followed by hallucination; unconsciousness, then awareness again.

There were repeated knocks on the door, and then the windows, becoming louder, more urgent. People were calling my name. I heard them walking around the house, talking, bewildered. Then John's voice outside my bathroom window. "She's here! I found her!"

Oh, *please go away.*

There were other voices with John's; his father and mother were there. I hadn't even known they were in town. I curled up on the floor, trying to make myself smaller, wanting to crawl into the shower stall, but I was finally too weak.

Suddenly there was a thud, and the sound of glass shattering. John and Rob had rammed through the outside door with a telephone pole. The inside door, to the bathroom, gave way easily to someone's shoulder.

The two things I said to John, over and over, were, "Don't let Leo in" and "This is not because of you."

Thank God, no one let Leo in. At one point, I saw my mother-in-law step over me, but most of the time she must have been outside with Leo. I heard John on the phone. No one talked to me. There was all kinds of activity around and above me, but I was not a part of it.

The scene came into focus again when the medics knelt down beside me. I struggled to fight them off. *Let me go, just let me go! I've gone to all this trouble.* "I want to die!" I said frantically.

"Not today," replied one of the men.

They were stunningly calm. They see terrible things, but I'm willing to bet this was one of the worst any of them had ever seen on a call. Still, they maintained the same unflappable, reassuring manner with me that they would have with a child who had broken a bone.

I was fading in and out. I don't remember being put on the stretcher, but I remember the sunlight when they carried me out of the house, the normal afternoon sounds around me, feeling faintly embarrassed by the melodrama I had caused.

The last thing I remember is the sound of the siren and the bumps of my rutted gravel driveway as the ambulance pulled out. It was the last thing I would know for days.

Chapter 20
Dreams

A hospital corrider. I was parked in it, on a bed. I heard voices—black voices, calling me "Ms. Nicholson" very cheerfully. They were competent, matter-of-fact, as they went about their tasks. "Now we're going to roll you over, Ms. Nicholson," "We're going to check your blood pressure, give you an injection". I couldn't see, but I sensed that I was in limbo, waiting to be established somewhere.

It went on forever. It seemed like hours, maybe days, and I was frustrated and bored. If my mother were alive to hear me tell this, she would say, "Only YOU, Laura Anne, could be bored in Intensive Care!"

I wanted to see what was going on, to be able to talk with people, to know where I was. I wanted something to change, something to happen, things to become clear. But there was no relief from this muddled quasi-reality.

***

For days or perhaps weeks, I slid in and out of consciousness. I later learned that after the Herculean efforts of the local trauma team finally stabilized me from the blood loss, I had abdominal surgery and was then transferred by ambulance to a larger medical center down the mountain. At that hospital, an eight-hour surgery was performed on my trachea. At some point after that, I developed a lung infection, then another, then a third. I was transferred out of ICU and back into it twice. Under the miracle of morphine, I felt no pain, but my fever exceeded 105, and in my feverish delirium there were elaborate, convoluted dreams. Some of what I remember actually happened, some obviously didn't; and some of it I don't know about to this day.

I was looking at my fingers. They were swathed in bandages. I thought, "I didn't hurt my fingers," then, "but I must have, because they've bandaged them up."

There was a pretty nurse, cheerful, with short blonde hair, named Susan. My dad was visiting me, with a friend from the university, and the atmosphere was decidedly upbeat, holiday-ish. For weeks after that I waited for that nurse to come back, but she never did. I wondered if she had left the hospital. I decided I wanted to be a nurse when I got better.

I was in a large, empty room, the only patient. There were two nurses talking. One said she had to drive her son to work on her lunch hour. When she came back later, she told the other nurse, "One hour exactly—I did it!" They began talking about their work. "This is not like a job, it's like a marriage," one lamented.

I was in a cafeteria. A large cafeteria, with many food options. I finally decided what I wanted to eat, but then I didn't know where to sit. I didn't know who I was supposed to sit with.

A coworker and I were talking about Christmas. "Oh, I already got all my gifts for Greg's children," she said. "I got them a lot of clothes from this website they like, and a guitar." I felt bad. I had never bought gifts for Greg's children, and he was my boss. "I know!" I thought. "I'll get them a bunch of clothes from that website they like, and a guitar."

I was at the Hanging of the Greens. Other people there were working hard, accomplishing so much, enjoying themselves. Now they were talking about bedding plants. One was going to go home and plant out pansies. I couldn't do anything but watch. But at least I had gotten to the Hanging of the Greens.

I wanted to know where my car was. It really bothered me. After all, I had driven to the hospital, right? Was I getting ticket after ticket? Had I been towed? My family were all around, but had anyone thought of this? I couldn't talk, but the bandages were off my fingers now. I tried to ask my sister in sign language. She got a few letters, then became frustrated. She called over a nurse, who tried to follow my labored spelling-out of the words. No one ever understood what I was asking.

Why were my fingernails so disgusting? There was black dirt under them! Had I been gardening? Well I couldn't have, because I was in the hospital. I puzzled and puzzled over this phenomenon.

I watched the action in the ICU. There weren't rooms after all, just bays we were parked in. I could see a long line of desks, and watch the employees at computers, talking, buying drinks from a vending machine that dispensed them with a startling clunk. I watched them sanitize their hands, put on gloves, and, when they had to do something particularly awful, don yellow bibs I thought of as "splatter aprons". One day a man and a woman put on splatter aprons and came over to me.

"We're going to take out your breathing tube," they told me. "You're breathing on your own now." That must be good, I thought. But I was afraid.

"The worst part of this is getting the tape off," joked the man as they scraped at the tape on my nose and face. That wasn't bothering me, so maybe it wouldn't be bad. The man counted to three and they heaved a massive, dripping, mucous-covered object shaped like my collarbone out of my chest. It didn't hurt so much as shock me. But immediately I was in breathing distress. Later on I would try to reconcile the shape of that object with the pathway of its removal. I never did figure that one out.

I was in a disco, a brightly-colored club, with people dancing to loud music. I was trying so hard to breathe. A nurse I recognized walked by, stopped, and said, "Hi Laura Anne," at the foot of my bed. I recognized her. I was dying, strangling, but no one would help. It was the worst sensation of my entire life. I told myself that in a little while, I would take something to fix my breathing. I just had to hold out until one hour had gone by. I became very sleepy. I had made it.

My sister was there. "You're getting all the oxygen your body needs," a nurse said. A man came up and introduced himself as a Respiratory Therapist—who knew there even was such a thing? He put a mask over my nose and mouth and said, "This cool mist will help you breathe." It didn't make any difference, but I held it in place.

"You're getting all the oxygen your body needs," my sister said.

"You're going to have a tracheotomy," my dad told me. "It's to help you breathe".

"Is that permanent?" I whispered.

"No," Kaye answered. "They'll make a small hole in your throat and insert a tube. As you start breathing better, they'll put in smaller tubes until you don't need one anymore."

My surgery was scheduled for 6 a.m. I woke up and asked the nurse what time it was. "Five-thirty," she answered. I didn't know if she meant a.m. or p.m.

Hours passed. A doctor was examining me. "You're scheduled for a tracheotomy this morning," he said, "But that doesn't necessarily have to happen." He was down at my face, listening very closely. "You're breathing normally," he said.

Oh my gosh. I was. I was just—breathing.

A nurse was talking to my family. "People think of a hospital as a place to get better, but actually a lot of people come here and get pneumonia," she said. We were in a large room with equipment like they have at children's playgrounds at fast food chains. The nurse and I were on a red slide. She had given me a can of Pepsi.

"The doctor said only clear liquids," she said. "But this is—almost clear!" That Pepsi was really good!

Music played. Someone sang, "To the left, to the left," and started dancing. "You so crazy!" laughed someone else. I had never heard that song before.

"What's your name?" the nurse asked me.

"Laura Anne."

"What holiday is coming up?"

"Christmas."

"What's the next holiday after that?"

I thought hard. "Valentine's Day," I finally answered.

A man was admitted in the bay next to mine. He was groaning and groaning. "When I was young, the worst thing that could happen to us was getting pregnant," said his wife. She was well-dressed and had glossy blonde hair in a page-boy. She was chatting with the employees as she waited for her husband to pass his kidney stones. She didn't seem concerned. Eventually she and her husband checked into the luxury room to spend the night, because they were rich.

"You need to sign this paper to give me power of attorney," my dad said. "That way I can pay all your bills and keep your business in order while you're here." A clipboard appeared on my lap. I tried to sign it, but my fingers didn't work. I made a mark like an upside-down letter V.

"That's fine," said the security guard, who was evidently also a notary public.

"We're taking care of everything at your house," my dad told me. "We've stopped your papers and had your mail forwarded to us. I'm dripping the pipes on cold nights, and we're checking the mousetraps. Everything's fine."

"Thanks," I whispered. I didn't care.

"I make mincemeat pies every year, a dozen of them," the woman said. "I make fudge, too, and my daughter-in-law makes all the cakes."

"Did she try to kill herself?" asked her husband.

"We don't know, and we're not going to ask!" his wife answered severely. "And if she did, we're not going to judge!"

We were on a screened-in porch; I was in a chaise lounge. The former Volunteer Coordinator of the Atlanta Botanical Garden was trying to get me to eat.

"You like jello?" she asked, peeling the foil top off a plastic cup of bright orange gelatin.

"Yes," I said, and she began spooning it in my mouth.

"You like juice?"

"Yes."

"How 'bout chicken broth?"

"Yes," I answered dutifully. She spooned some in my mouth, and immediately I wanted to stop eating. Within minutes, my stomach was doing somersaults.

"When we were young, no one talked about depression, or taking medicine for it," she told my father. "If I was depressed, someone would just give me a hug!"

They were moving me to a room. "That's a good thing!" my dad exulted. "You're gonna be out of intensive care!"

I wasn't sure about this. I always had a nurse, and people around me, in the ICU. Would I be left all alone in a room?

I was having dinner with my psychiatrist from Wilkesboro, who had come to see me in the hospital. We were at his house, and two of the ICU nurses, who were married and had two small boys, were there, too. The mom nurse, who had been at the disco, was discussing what videos the children could watch, and which games they could play. The dad nurse was exulting over the parking space he had gotten. I wanted, more than anything, to go to the bathroom.

"We're going to the football celebration," one of them said to me. "It's out on the street. We'll be back soon."

When they got back, they had sets of little footballs with the team's name on them. I wanted a set for Leo for Christmas. But more than that, I wanted a bathroom.

I motioned the ICU nurse over. "I can't go to sleep, because I need to go to the bathroom. Can I just get up and walk to the bathroom?"

"You're on a catheter, Sweet Potato," she answered cheerfully. "You don't need to get up to go the bathroom!" She was pretty, she looked like a country singer. "You just rest, Sweet Potato, okay?"

It was cold, we were outside. I was being trundled to a regular room again. The nurses were upbeat. "Now we love you, but we don't want to see you back here again, you hear?" they told me. We finally entered what looked like a room in a motel. They dumped me gently on the bed. I was no longer on an IV, but I still had a feeding tube. I was afraid no one would remember to put liquid in the feeding tube here.

There was a television on, and a matronly black lady, my Acute Care "sitter", was watching a lurid story about a young man viciously killed. I turned to her, trying to ignore the horrific images flashing on the screen.

"Do you have a family?" I asked in my whisper. "Yes!" she answered, and began to tell me about her children. "Do you have pictures?" I asked, and she gladly got them out.

"I have a son," I said.

Kaye was sitting by my bed, yelling at me. She was right in my face.

"Laura Anne! Laura Anne! Answer me!"

I stared at her. Why was she so upset? Her face floated close to mine, and she slapped my cheek. Why was she yelling?

"You need to cough," the man said. "Cough!"

I tried to cough.

"More than that!" he said. I tried again.

"If you can't do any better than that, I'm going to have to suction you like I did yesterday, and I don't think you liked that very much," he warned. I looked at him, and wondered what he was talking about.

"What's your name?"

"Laura Anne"

"Who's the president?"

I thought about which name to use. "Dubya,' I answered, and the nurse laughed.

"What hospital are you in?"

"X." Dammit! It was Y. I *knew* that one, but I didn't have enough breath to speak again.

I was back in ICU. One of the nice nurses was there. "I think you could sit up for awhile," she said. "Do you want to sit up?"

I didn't want to, but it seemed rude to say no. "Okay," I said.

It took several of them to lift me out of the bed, and into a chair, transferring tubes and wires. "Do you want something to read?" the nurse asked.

"Okay," I said. She placed a women's magazine on my lap. Giada di Laurentis and her teeth and cleavage beamed from its cover. I looked at it. What did it have to do with me?

Could I get back in bed now?

"I'm gonna do your hair, girl," cackled the young nursing assistant. When I assented, they propped me up and began to try to work a comb through the tumbled mass on my head.

"There's blood in here, girl! What happened? Did you fall and hit your head?"

"Yes," I said.

The nice nurse and the nursing assistant gave me a dry shampoo, talking all along about how pretty I was, what a pretty smile. They arranged my hair and showed me a mirror. I liked being propped up in bed because I could see all the action in the ICU. Lots of employees said hi to me, and seemed to know me. The nursing assistant put my hair in a French braid, and rearranged my hospital gown on my shoulders. "Can't let the fruits show!" she chortled.

"Now you just need some lipstick, and a little red dress," said the nurse. "You'd be a knockout!"

I was tired now. They laid me back down.

It was Christmas. The whole day had passed, I thought, from the dim light outside. Was anyone coming?

My sister and father appeared, holding gift bags.

"Merry Christmas!" cried Sara, and burst into song. She had rewritten the words to a Christmas carol for me. She opened each of my presents and showed them to me. There was a black cord bracelet with a silver heart charm from Leo. I loved it. She hung a Christmas ornament with Leo's school picture in it on my IV pole. I looked at it all the time, sadly but with pride. "That's my son," I would say to each new nurse when she came on duty.

Somebody had found my glasses, and brought them. The nurse put them on my face. Now I could see everything in the ICU. Everyone was talking about Christmas presents, and trips, and holiday recipes. I couldn't believe I had missed Christmas.

I was in a regular room again, with a different "sitter", and Kaye. It was hot, and stuffy. I was very high up. I didn't like the room. It was lonely. I couldn't see into the hall, and nothing was happening there, anyway. I missed the bustle and the nurses from the ICU.

The pastor from Sara's church, Shelly, was there. "Do you want me to recite the 23rd psalm for you?" she asked. I was back in ICU; perhaps they thought I was dying.

"Yes," I said. She held my hand and got right down at my face to recite it. Since then I have memorized the passage.

Henry was there. I couldn't talk, but I could turn my head and see him. He smiled, and said several pleasant, conversational things. In what seemed like less than a minute, he was gone. I was sad that he had left so soon.

My high school friend Sheila stood over me, with tears in her eyes. "It's just so good to see you," she kept saying, over and over again. I listened while she and Kaye talked. "This is the first time I've been able to talk all I want, without Laura Anne interrupting me," she laughed through her tears.

Chapter 21
Reality

"Now, this better be the last time we see you here," the nursing assistant said with mock sternness. "We love you, but we don't want you comin' back here no more, no ma'am!"

I was being trundled across the huge hospital to another regular room. This one was big, and looked more like a motel than ever. I liked it better, though. It was near the nurses' station on the floor and didn't seem so isolated. And it wasn't high up and hot.

"You sure are looking better, Laura Anne," said a nurse I didn't recognize. "It's really good to see."

"You know me?" I asked.

"Sure, I saw you in your old room, before you went back to ICU. Do you want some ice chips?"

"I can have ice chips?"

"Yes, as long as you eat them slowly".

"Yes!" I answered.

How nice it was to have something on my tongue other than the solution they always cleaned my mouth with. I savored the chips while I took in my new surroundings.

There was a computer monitor next to my bed for the nurses to check orders on. While no one was using it, a variety of images rotated onto the screen. "Beware of S.A.L.A.D.—Sound Alike Look Alike Drugs!" read one. Another was a checklist to complete while preparing a patient for surgery. One screen reminded caregivers to wash their hands. It didn't inspire great confidence in me, especially after the Swiss-clock-efficiency of the ICU, to be in a ward where employees had to be reminded of this.

"It's time for your bath," the nurse said. I assumed this meant the sponging down I always had, an exhausting process that nevertheless always left me feeling better. But the nurse called a coworker, and they lifted me into a chair. I was amazed when they placed a bowl of warm water, a bar of soap, and a towel next to me and told me to go ahead.

"I don't think the service here is as good as in ICU," I said. They laughed. "Time to start doing things for yourself again," one told me. They didn't realize I wasn't ready.

***

The next day, I was ordered to sit up in a chair for an hour. The nurse asked if I would like to watch TV. I was always asking the sitters to turn the TV off, but now I said okay, and searched around til I found an episode of "Frasier". It didn't interest me, but it passed the tedious time sitting up.

Before they helped me back to bed, the nurse told me she had a doctor's orders to remove my feeding tube. I didn't want it out. Then I'd have to deal with the whole eating thing again.

"How do you do take it out?" I asked.

"Just pull!" she answered.

I actually giggled as she hand-over-handed that tube up all the way from my small intestine through my nose. It was a strange and ticklish feeling, and very freeing to finally have nothing taped to my face, no poles to be strapped to. But I dreaded being expected to eat.

Shortly after darkness fell, an orderly brought my dinner. There was no broth, jello, or juice. It was some kind of a fried chicken cutlet with a semi-congealed lemon sauce. The smell hit me like a volleyball to the face. I tried to psyche myself up to eat it, but the aroma really put me off. Finally I flipped the styrofoam cover closed on the dish and announced, somewhat petulantly, "I'm not eating it."

The nurse lifted the cover and looked at it. "This is probably the worst thing they could have brought you," she said. "Is there anything you *would* like to eat?"

"No," I said. I supposed I would die now. I was back to where I had been, unable to eat, and now there was no lifeline to a pouch of liquid food.

***

Later that evening, I became extremely dizzy. I had never felt like this. It was horrible. I ran my hands through my dirty, sweaty hair over and over, rolled to my side and clawed the mattress. The misery went on and on.

When the nurse finally appeared, I told her what was happening. She asked me a few questions, then said she would call the doctor. The doctor never came.

"And did you eat tonight?" asked a mean nurse.

"No," I said.

"Then you need to eat," she announced, and placed a cup of pink liquid in front of me with a straw. "You like strawberry?" she asked.

"Yes." I sipped it. It wasn't too bad. The nurse was busy at the computer. "The doctor has ordered you some anxiety medicine," she said.

"No!" I cried. "That will make me worse! I'm already horribly light-headed!"

"Are you refusing your medication?" she asked furiously.

"Yes," I replied. (Who knew it was that easy?)

She hmmphed. "Drink more."

I sipped.

"The doctor is coming to check you out soon. Drink."

I drank.

***

"What happened last night?" I asked Kaye. "Did the doctor ever come?"

"No," said Kaye. "You fell asleep."

***

My Acute Care "sitters" ranged from 18-year-old boys who watched rap videos on computers to motherly women with bags of knitting. Mostly, they were a fairly depressing lot. I found myself having to ask one girl with a nose ring to turn off a horror movie she was watching at 11 p.m. while I was trying to sleep. She was quite indignant, and complained about me on her cell phone to a friend.

The nights were the worst. The various employees on the floor would practically hold a party in the doorway of my room, with food and drink, lights on, and loud conversation. No one seemed to care that I needed rest. Sometimes in the wee hours of the morning, I lay and waited for it to turn light outside, watching the wall clock and dreading the arrival of my breakfast tray.

The food was god-awful. It's hard to mess up breakfast, but they did. I was only allowed to drink thickened beverages, and there is probably nothing worse than "nectar-consistency" instant decaf coffee when your stomach hasn't had solid food in weeks. I would sit up and nibble on the biscuits and bits of scrambled eggs. They always brought me a boatload, including all kinds of things the nutritionist wanted me to eat to gain weight—protein shakes and some bright, artificially-colored cream in a cup. I did what I could, but another couple of human beings could have gotten by on what I sent away.

The only reason I could eat at all was because the Swallowing Disorders Specialist (who knew?) came to my room one day and put a tiny camera up my nose—- and that is just as toe-curling as it sounds. She showed my fascinated father and uncle, who were visiting, live footage of me swallowing spoonfuls of green-dyed applesauce, from inside my throat. Because my lungs weren't completely sealed off yet as I swallowed, I couldn't drink regular liquids yet. As nasty as the thickened milk, water, and "lemon-flavored beverages" were, I was sure I would become dehydrated without the insurance policy of the IV. And I did, repeatedly.

Eventually a physical therapist came to work my legs some, and to walk me, strapped securely to her with a belt and leaning on a walker, a few steps down the hall. It was a seasickness-inspiring challenge, but it also felt like an accomplishment, and everyone smiled at me and was encouraging. I finally got to see what the world outside my room looked like.

My sister regularly brought me cards, and told me of large amounts of chocolate that waited for me at her house, sent by friends. Sometimes I didn't know who the card-senders were, which invariably meant someone from Sara's church. One day I got a large box, which held a beautiful bunch of alstroemeria, my favorite flower. It was from Lisa, along with a soft stuffed rabbit. It seemed that John, as well as two high school friends, had tried to send me flowers in Intensive Care as well, but flowers weren't allowed there. Finally I had some.

Lots of people visited. Joni surprised me one day along with our Third Musketeer, Chris. The three of us had been inseparable in college, and Chris's and my friendship went back to our freshman year (or "fresh manure" as we always called it) in high school. Chris had brought her two youngest daughters, no doubt explaining to them beforehand not to ask any awkward questions. Before the four of them had left, Sara arrived with Drew and Mason, and my room was quite crowded for awhile. I had never understood people saying someone was "too tired for visitors," but I got it now. As glad as I was to see folks arrive, and sad to see them leave, I still felt like a hostess, having to smile and talk. If I could have just dozed off whenever I wanted to, with their conversation floating around me, it would have been very nice indeed. Who knows? Maybe I did.

So, was I anxious? The thought occurred to me one day. Actually, I wasn't. I was weak beyond words, overwhelmed, guilty, depressed, confused, sick to my stomach and fairly hopeless about my future, but I was not jittery or unable to sleep. The doctors had been giving me my anti-depressant intravenously for weeks, and at long last it had kicked in. My muddle-headedness was a mercy, because had I been thinking clearly, I would have concluded that the obstacles facing me were insurmountable. I was now a disgrace as a mother and as a human being. I couldn't picture ever being able to do my job again, or run my household. I had put everyone through a nightmare, I was covered with scars, I couldn't eat. Hell, I couldn't *walk*. I was a sad, pathetic freak of nature. As for what would happen with my son, I couldn't even go there.

One day, Kaye asked if I would like to see Leo. "Yes!" I cried, although I was taken by surprise and more than a little nervous. John was passing through town with him, and could bring him to the hospital. Leo was too young to visit by a couple of years, but I was pretty sure we could sneak him in if everyone just acted like they knew what they were doing. I told Kaye to make sure he knew I looked different, and had stitches and scars all over me. She had thought to warn him, of course, and so I sat, like a girl awaiting her first date, looking at the door.

My son looked great, and was wearing the football jersey I had picked out for him for Christmas. He did not come over to hug me, and I was too shy to ask him to. John had taken him to Disney World, so I asked all about that, while Leo nervously wandered around the room, touching everything and asking what it was.

I ran out of conversation too soon, and lay there feeling like the failure I was. When it was time for him to leave, I asked for a hug, and he manned up and gave me one.

I had not seen John.

Various professionals began to visit me now—psychiatrists and social workers. They talked to my family outside my room, and I figured they were cooking something up, but I didn't know what, nor did I care much. Dad finally talked to me one day about going, voluntarily, to the mental health ward of the hospital.

What could I say? I was obviously *nuts*, and moreover I was nowhere near being able to take care of myself. The doctors said I was well enough to be released, but they just didn't know. I could still barely eat, still wasn't allowed regular liquids. It wasn't as if I had a husband waiting at home to take care of me.

So I agreed, and signed lots of papers on the line that said "Voluntary", and when they loaded me into a wheelchair that night, I kept cracking, "I'm going to the PSYCHE ward!"

It was the first time I'd been in a wheelchair, since all my previous moves had been on a rolling bed. I didn't know the nurse who took me, and she rolled me a long, long way, with a paper grocery bag filled with my cards, gifts, and stuffed animals, sitting on my lap. I was quite un-nerved about the change.

I didn't feel better when we got to The Center, and there were heavy locked doors, like at the other hospital I'd been in for those three dreadful days. They wouldn't let me bring along my beautiful glass vase of flowers, or even the stuffed bunny with the tiny pink ribbon around its neck. "What, I'm gonna hang myself with a six-inch ribbon now?" I asked. It was an awful feeling, going back to security guards and laceless shoes. For three and a half weeks, I had been treated like a human being; now, I was a specimen again.

When we finally arrived at the psyche ward (for that's what it was), the nurse parked me in front of a check-in desk and left. Feeling deserted, I faced the tall, beautiful woman across the counter. Her expression was cold. It seemed I was expected to go through a large stack of paperwork with her, in spite of the fact that I was alone, exhausted, and it was late at night.

The nurse never cracked a smile as she instructed me on the ways of the ward. I was to spend my time in the day room, and not in my room. I was to attend classes. If anyone wished to see me, they would have to have my number code. If anyone called who did not have the code, the staff would tell him or her that they knew nothing about me. Meals were brought in at eight, twelve, and five, and I was to eat with the others. Lights out was at eleven. I could use the communal phone during limited hours, for toll-free calls only.

She told me some patients had to be restrained and/or isolated when they showed behaviors threatening to themselves or others. "I'm going to put you down as high probability of needing to be restrained, because of what you did," she told me, never meeting my gaze.

"This is an ambulatory unit," she continued. "You are expected to get up and walk to the bathroom. Because you are a Fall Risk, your bed will be alarmed so that, should you get up during the night without help, a nurse will be summoned."

It must have been a great deal like being checked in to prison, and had I had the energy, I would have panicked. Instead, I listened and nodded dumbly, my mind reeling, as she told me I should get a living will and a medical power of attorney. By the time she and another nurse finally wheeled me to a room and helped me to bed, I was completely overwhelmed and thankful just to curl up in a ball in the semi-darkness (I wasn't allowed to shut the door). I slept.

Someone snapped the lights on and walked into the room. Blinking in bewilderment, I beheld a young doctor with a clipboard. I was weakly enraged that I had been disturbed.

"Sorry to wake you," the doctor said briskly. "Things got behind in the ER and I couldn't get over here till late."

He then proceeded to ask me almost all the questions the check-in nurse had asked me on my arrival. She stood by, towering over him.

Had I ever been sexually molested? Had my husband ever hit me? Did I still wish to die?

I protested the treatment several times, but was dismissed.

Finally, I was left alone, except for my roommate on the other side of the curtain, who was talking to herself incoherently. I lay in a daze, wondering what the next morning would bring. Finally, I slept again.

Chapter 22
The Center

"Attention, your attention please. Breakfast is now being served in the dayroom."

It seemed there was a loudspeaker in my room. The clock on the wall read eight, and the calendar beside it said January 2nd. They always had those clock/calendar combos in nursing homes when I visited elderly relatives. I guessed crazy people needed them, too.

Was I really supposed to just get up and walk, and eat? Wasn't someone going to bring me a tray? My question was answered a few moments later when a nurse entered with a medical cart.

"Good morning," she said mildly. "I'm going to check your vitals."

I sat up in bed while my temperature, pulse and blood pressure were taken.

"Okay, I'll get a chair to take you in to breakfast," she said. "You can wash up and get ready while I'm gone. There's towels in the bathroom."

Ummm…whatever. I made no move to get up, but looked out the window while the nurse retrieved a wheelchair. My view was of a section of the hospital roof, and there was an impressive blue-and-gold helicopter parked there.

When I was wheeled into the large dayroom, I saw a bustle of activity. A hot meal cart radiated cooking smells, and people going through a line were helping themselves to eggs, bacon, cereal, juice. Some stared as I entered, but most ignored me. They looked normal enough, I thought. Some patients were eating at tables, but most were in overstuffed chairs lined up in front of a TV. Nurses moved among them, distributing medication. The television was tuned to an episode of the type of sitcom that generally goes straight into syndication.

I was vaguely pleased that I could get grits and bacon for breakfast, although the grits were lumpy of course, and I still had to sip that damned thickened liquid. Seeing as how I'd been asleep moments before, I wasn't hungry; but I knew I needed desperately to eat and that I wouldn't have another chance for hours.

I noticed that the teenage boy in the chair beside me had slashes on his wrist, stapled closed. I had only recently noticed my own cuts, which were stitched with blue thread that had been snipped anywhere from a centimeter to a good four inches away from the wound ("It's like they were practicing," Sara said.) Why did I have five cuts on one wrist? And why did the first one go around the sides of my arm?

The young man saw me looking at his wounds and introduced himself. He was pale with dark hair, and I could picture him as a Goth. He wore a heavy-metal band T-shirt. "I can throw away your trash for you," he offered.

"Thanks."

When he returned, the boy told me the story of his "incarceration." I don't remember the particulars, but he had been handled roughly by police, and lost some of the staples in one wrist. This apparently made him so angry that he pulled out the rest of the staples in the ambulance on the ride in. I didn't ask why. He was nice. I expressed sympathy.

"I really need to get to the bathroom," I murmured a few minutes later, looking for the nurse who had helped me in.

"Do you need help?" he asked, and offered his arm. I assented, and he was walking me toward my room when a nurse materialized in front of us.

"I'LL help you," she insisted, ordering my friend to sit down. Oh, well.

There was a nice nurse, Caroline, to whom I felt I could express concern. "I've been lying in bed for a month," I explained, "barely sitting up at all, and not walking. And now this lady last night tells me I'm supposed to be up all day, going to classes and sitting in that room."

"We'll do two up, one down," Caroline said. "Up for two hours, in bed for one. See how that works." I felt slightly better.

I was given a walker, like my grandmother used after her stroke. One of the women patients said, "It's good to see you getting around better." I was confused. Hadn't I just gotten to this place? Did this woman know me? I smiled and thanked her.

I was the only person in a hospital gown, so when Kaye called later and said she was coming to visit, I said, "Bring clothes. They wear clothes here".

There was a routine to The Center, more structured than that of the other hospital. Lots of classes, that met in stuffy, windowless rooms where I squirmed miserably on the hard chairs and sometimes felt faint. Whenever we weren't in a session, relentless inane TV in the dayroom that made it impossible to read. Daily tribunals with half a dozen doctors, and people drawing my blood every ten minutes. The meal cart brought heavy, cooked food three times a day, and a "snack window" opened in between meals and at night. In the afternoons there was some free time, and I always snuck off to my room to collapse on the bed, but that was when visitors were allowed, so I was usually called back out. We weren't allowed to have visitors in our rooms.

My dad was determined I would have company every day, but my most frequent visitor by far was his wife. He came sometimes, too, but Kaye was Old Faithful. Sara made it as often as she could, and other people surprised me. Henry and his wife, Loraine. My boss, Greg. Sheila came again, and so did Chris. My high school friend Flynn visited several times. He had come to see me in the ICU as well, bringing a great stuffed dog that reminded me of the time in high school when a bunch of us had gone to Carowinds, and the boys knocked themselves out to load all us girls down with prizes they'd won. How very anthropological. Flynn had been the only one, ever, to ask me what I'd been thinking when I cut myself up. I had looked at him, considered, and then answered, "I don't really want to talk about that."

When Greg visited, I looked dreadful, as I always did in The Center. Personal grooming goes completely by the wayside in a mental health ward, even if you have the strength and give a rip, which I didn't. No nail clippers were allowed, no razors or tweezers. We couldn't use hairdryers, but had to let the staff use them on us. I hadn't even had a shower. Though I tried to always dress now, it was hard to tell the difference between my day and night clothes. Since none of my pants would stay up, I tended to stay in three-quarter length pajama pants, with T-shirts and some heavy brown shoes my sister had brought me. My skin was cracked and flaky either from dehydration, or the dry air in The Center. Certainly not from soap!

After Greg and I had greeted one another, he sat down in the chair beside me. I was so ashamed of how I had let him and the rest of the department down. I looked at him and swallowed hard.

"I am so, so sorry," I began.

"Don't," he interrupted, his eyes wet. "Just don't. How do you feel?"

"I feel about how I look," I answered wryly, "in other words, like hell!"

The anthropology department was getting by without me, it seemed. Greg was reticent about how well it was going, but he told me to take the time I needed and assured me my job would be waiting. I thanked him, although I couldn't imagine ever working again.

After a couple of days in The Center, Nurse Caroline asked if I'd like to take a shower. It sounded like way too much effort, but I figured I'd better say yes. She and another kind nurse both helped, bringing a shower chair for me to sit on and shampooing my hair for me. It felt great. For the first time, I saw the strange bandage strips, black sutures and what looked like the reinforcers used to keep notebook paper in a binder, all over my bony torso. It was the first time I'd seen my body.

"This is so nice of you all, thank you," I said, as they helped me dry off. "When I first got here I wasn't so sure about this place."

Nurse Caroline frowned. "We heard about that. That never should have happened."

"Oh, really?" I asked, "You heard about my check-in?" How nice that Nurse Ratched was not approved of by the other staff! I felt reassured.

But after this, I was unavoidably aware of just how desecrated my body was. In addition to the slashes on my wrists, I had cuts on the inside of my elbows, the top of one leg, and multiple places on my neck. I had stabbed myself twice in the throat, and three times in the torso.

The surgeon's incision that began at my throat ran nine inches down my body. A second incision ran six inches down my belly. There were 4 small cuts for "viewing holes" on my stomach and under my arms. Although it seems patently ungrateful to question the professionals that saved my life, I would like, someday, to understand why so many cuts were made—some not anywhere near my wounds. I would like to understand why my chest was broken open as if for heart surgery, when the only injury anywhere near there was at the base of my throat.

Moreover, I had the physique of a refugee. I stand just over five foot seven, and the first time I stepped on a scale, I weighed 93 pounds.

I began to tell myself, each time I endured the jolt of seeing my naked body in the mirror, "This is the worst you will ever look. It will only get better from here."

My Goth friend's staples notwithstanding, very few people in The Center were noticeably scarred or injured. I am amazed in retrospect that the other patients didn't avoid me or avert their eyes from my multiple scabs and sutures. But they did not, and in spite of The Center's policy discouraging patients from getting to know each other, I talked with anyone who was willing to pull their eyes away from the TV.

I tried "What are you in for?" only once, then learned to use more subtle icebreakers when someone new arrived or I was bored to distraction in the dayroom. I thought the staff's idea that we should avoid interrelating and "focus on ourselves" was counter-productive. On the contrary, I believed that distracting myself from my own problems by showing concern for others—and maybe receiving friendly overtures in return—was the best possible therapy. At one of our group meetings I raised my hand and made this point, reciting my favorite quote, "We cannot always feel happiness, but we can always give it."

But I was just a patient in the nuthouse; what did I know about mental illness? The trained professionals dismissed my suggestion indifferently and moved down to the next item on their agenda.

There were several middle-aged, normal-seeming women patients who were pleasant to me, and I wondered what was wrong with them. The friendliest told me quite clearly why she was in the clink. "I

tried to commit suicide seven times in six months," she told me cheerfully, and went on to describe some of her attempts. She had three
children, but had lost custody of them; and an accounting job that she
said might or might not be waiting for her. While I was there, she had
electro-shock therapy, which I thought was only from old movies, but
is apparently still used in a more sophisticated form. She seemed to
feel it helped.

The most cheerful person among us was a 40-something man
in a wheelchair. He was a hearty-looking individual, with bushy hair
and a beard, and he joked so often and ate so enthusiastically that I
was completely flummoxed as to why he had slammed his car into
a tree at 70 miles per hour intentionally. He had children whom he
home-schooled, and a girlfriend whom he seemed to be hiding out
from (an easy thing to do, in The Center). Todd was a football fan and
also got excited about certain TV shows. Unlike me, he always stayed
up until lights-out, at 11 p.m. I sometimes snuck off to bed before the
8:30 "wrap-up meeting," which was as lame as all the other meetings
in the place.

Some patients in The Center were sprung occasionally, for a
trip to the mall or some such activity. I never was, but then I was way
too weak to manage, anyway. I did look out the dayroom windows at
the grass and trees below and wonder, now and then, when I would
breathe outside air again. But I didn't care much, yet.

I made efforts to avail myself of all the resources, including the
"leisure counselors". They asked if I wanted music in my room (I said
yes, but never got it), and helped people exercise. One counselor had
me walking on a treadmill, which encouraged me, since until recently I
hadn't been able to take a step. (The treadmill, of course, had handles I
could keep a death-grip on!) One day I struggled to sit up long enough
to play Scrabble with three other women. One had spoken to me nas-
tily the night she was admitted, then snuck contraband chocolate to
me in my room, perhaps out of guilt. One was a lady who seemed as
nice and normal as anyone I'd ever met, but told me she heard voices
saying terrible things. The last was a young wife and mother who was
a cutter ("I don't want to die," she explained. "I just like the sight of
blood.") My bottom was so bony that the chair hurt it like crazy, but I

got through the game, even making the word "loony" on the board. "Like all of us," I quipped, but I was the only one who laughed.

I was walking with a cane now, and occasionally being visited by a physical therapist who assessed my progress. I tried to walk circles around The Center, but whenever I had a visitor I wasn't allowed to do this. We couldn't go out of sight of the nurses' station with people from the "outside". I even felt like I needed to justify myself to the nurses at the station when I walked alone, as if I were doing something weird.

One morning walking to the dayroom for breakfast, I became dizzy. It turned out my blood pressure was dropping radically whenever I stood. The doctors put me on an IV, which was a relief, but they told me I had to stay in the dayroom at *all times* now. Including night. Apparently I was going to strangle myself with the cords.

I needed my rest so badly, that this almost panicked me. The thought of being forced to sit in a recliner by the nurses' station with lights on and people talking all night frustrated me beyond belief.

I ranted—in a very sane way—about this. One couldn't carry on too much. First I used logic, then I asked to speak with whomever had issued this cruel order. I was told she would be by later in the evening, but I never saw her. I asked for a bed to be wheeled out for me, but was told this wasn't possible. I had a distinct feeling, always, when I spoke with the staff, that I wasn't really someone whose opinions they had to worry much about. What was I going to do, after all? If I made a fuss, it was the "Quiet Room" for me.

I requested bedding and situated myself on a two-seated sofa as far from the lights as possible. I was furious at the treatment, an automatic order from someone who had never met me, rather than a thoughtful decision that actually considered my well-being.

This was one of the amazing things about The Center. In all my time there, no one ever counseled me one-on-one. You would think that would be the main thing happening at such a place, but instead each patient had a few minutes with a group of psychiatrists once or twice a day, discussing our symptoms and medications—where I always felt very much on the hot seat as the entire group stared at me and wrote on their notepads, God knows what. I was always aware that I might be saying the wrong thing, digging myself in deeper. During these sessions, I never sensed caring people reaching out to help, only detached scientists studying me. Although the internists who began coming to see me after the hypotension occurred were funny and friendly, the psychiatrists I met never smiled. Once one of them bullied me into crying, asking how I could have done this to my son. "Do you know what it's like for a motherless child?" he demanded.

"Look, I'm very ashamed of what I did, okay?" I pleaded. At this the doctor shrugged and remarked, "It's nothing to be ashamed of; you're depressed; you have a mood disorder."

I stared at him in disbelief, but said nothing.

The nurses were much warmer people. LaSalle was a big, big-hearted woman whom I always enjoyed being assigned to. "Are you named after a car" I asked her disingenuously.

"Honey, that car is named after ME!" she replied.

After one awful night in the dayroom, I was permitted to go back to my room, IV cord and all. I had developed a fever and thrown up, and they had to acknowledge my physical needs at this point. LaSalle was my nurse the first morning back in my room. I had just woken up when I heard her cry, "What is this? Hmm? I go away for two days and come back and you're on an IV! What is this?"

I wished I could kid along, but it seemed like I was dying. I had been getting stronger and now I was flat on my back again with God knew what. Later that day, another sympathetic internist examined me and said, "You know, a recovery is not always a linear process. Sometimes it's two steps forward and one step back".

Is it ever one step forward and eight steps back? I wondered.

The staff were making so many allowances for me now that my visitors were allowed in my room! This was a treat, for we had privacy, and it was also very necessary, since I was weak as a kitten. Once again I was getting trays for my meals. Once again, rather than bringing me broth or jello, a nurse would deliver something like turkey, gravy, dressing and boiled vegetables, with Boston cream pie for dessert. I asked for dry Cheerios.

After a few days of bedrest, I was raised from the semi-dead again to toddle with my IV pole into the dayroom. Sometimes someone helped me, sometimes not, as I found an outlet near one of the recliners and plugged myself in. One day after I had settled down to attempt to read like this, I witnessed actual crazy behavior in the psyche ward.

The woman had been checked in for a couple of days. When the self-labeled "vampires" approached her to draw blood yet again, she put her foot down. (I myself had protested once, only to be firmly rebuked by a young doctor nearby who heard my unmitigated gall.) The woman began to yell and gesture. Everyone's attention was caught. Several people at the nurses' station dialed the phone simultaneously. I watched with interest from directly behind the woman, as a male employee attempted to calm her down.

Some kind soul had brought us fresh fruit, and there was a bowl of oranges and apples near at hand. Seizing the only weapon she had, the woman began to hurl the apples and oranges at the male employee. What amused me was that the man not only didn't duck for cover, he didn't even attempt to protect his privates from the close-range, flying fruit! It seemed like he felt he would lose face, or authority, if he backed down. That must be something they teach you in Dealing-with-Crazy-People School, I thought. The woman emptied the bowl with fairly random shots, screamed her last expletive, and sat back down, apparently satisfied.

I have to admit, I was pretty entertained by this encounter. Nothing interesting had happened in The Center up to this point. People slowly resumed their stations, and a minute or two later, the security detail—seven men, no less—came through the heavy, locked doors with their hands on their weapons. They consulted with the Center personnel while shooting uncomfortable looks at the patient, who was sitting calmly in her chair now, beside the empty bowl.

To his credit, the head Security Dude approached the woman courteously and asked if she would come with him. I was amazed when she nodded, murmured assent, and took his arm. They led her to the Quiet Room, and I have no idea what happened after that. I never saw her again.

***

Although no one had mentioned cost yet, it eventually occurred to me that my medical bills had to be astronomical. I had insurance, but my God. How far could it go? There were limits; there were co-pays and co-insurance. Was I destitute?

My dad, always the businessman, brought me the happy news one day. "I went to your insurance office to find out what your part of all this was costing," he told me delightedly. "The woman there looked it up and wrote down a number and handed it to me. Four hundred and thirty-five dollars! That's all! I thought she'd made a mistake!"

Well, that was cause for huge relief! I supposed. Although really, as knocked off its tracks as my life currently was, what difference would another crisis have made?

About two weeks into my stay, I began to notice that almost everyone who had been in the unit when I arrived was gone. Many people came and went in two or three days. I had also caught on, finally, that the classes were on a one-week cycle, and they were all reruns for me now. I still doggedly went to the vast majority, but I was getting restless.

I was talking to Leo on the phone now, as well as Liz, who was like a breath of fresh air among the staff and my other contacts. "It had to've been that cocktail of meds you were taking," she declared. "Because you never would've done that—not when Leo was coming. That just isn't you!"

Her solid belief in me, as well as her lack of expressed shock or horror, was reassuring. Everyone else had changed how they acted toward me—I saw the careful expressions, the well-chosen words. Liz was still good ol' Liz, pulling no punches. Her own family has a history of mental illness which fascinates her, and she is completely non-judgmental about it. As long as I've known her, Liz has understood what I only came to understand through my own awful experiences, that mental illness is just failure of the neurological system, like heart disease is a failure of the cardiovascular system, or renal disease a failure of the kidneys.

Talking to Leo stirred the dormant mother-instinct in me that had fallen by the wayside in the months-long focus on myself. The first thing I did was apologize to him, and tell him I hoped someday he could bring himself to forgive me. The second thing I did was give him my solemn vow that nothing like this would ever happen again. My son impressed me with his candor. He came straight out and asked me, "Why'd you do it?"

I reminded him of how I had been struggling throughout the fall, and explained the despair I had reached as best I could. I brought in Liz's prescription theory, something concrete he could understand, but still took ultimate responsibility for my actions. He didn't say much in response, but he was listening.

I asked him all about Christmas, made sure he had gotten the football I had hidden for him in the attic before my attempt, and the Tom Brady jersey I had asked Kaye to buy. I asked about school, avoiding the subject of whether any of his classmates knew what had happened. I promised that over time we would rebuild the good life we had had, thinking all along that it would never be good for me again, but I could make it good for him.

Muddle-headed as I was, I was never sure whether I had told people things or not. When I began to repeat myself, I would see the careful expressions come over their faces. The only thing I knew for sure was that I had made an enormous, horrifying mistake, put everyone I loved through hell, and that I would never, EVER, attempt to harm myself again. No one else believed this, of course—not my family, who had thought I had learned the first time; or by any means the hateful psychiatrists, but I knew it for myself as soon as I was fully conscious again.

I said to my sister sadly one day, "I've made my life a lot more complicated, haven't I?"

"Yes," she admitted. She had brought fingernail clippers, and I was so weak that I couldn't squeeze them hard enough to cut my nails. She was doing it for me.

"The rest of my life is going to be penance," I said hopelessly.

My dad spoke up. "I don't know about that," he said. "Everyone makes mistakes."

I scoffed. "Not like this," I said. "This is the Mother of All Mistakes—well, except maybe for murder."

"Maybe someday you can help someone who is feeling like you did. Maybe you can stop someone from committing suicide—and maybe they'll listen to you because you've been there."

Well. There was that. We had had a volunteer from a mental health advocacy group visit us one day, and I had paid him no attention until he said, "A year and a half ago, I tried to commit suicide."

At that point, I had jerked up my head and paid attention for the rest of his visit. The professionals could yammer on and on, but this guy knew what he was talking about.

An idea began to grow in my mind. That was the first thing anyone had said to me that offered me absolution for my crime. I am analytically inclined, so it occurred to me that if I could stop someone, I'd break even. But if I stopped two people, I'd be ahead! I would have actually done some good in this world! In spite of everything! The first glimmer of hope started somewhere in me, somewhere down so deep that I would not tap it for a long time yet.

But I did make progress. One amazing day the lunch service lady told me I could drink regular liquids now. She was not the person I was expecting to hear this from. I had been told I would have to have the damned camera up my nose again before I'd get the green light.

"Are you sure? What happened?" I asked.

"I don't know, but it says here you can have regular liquids."

"You mean…" (I could hardly believe it) "I can drink iced tea, like everybody else?"

"Uh-huh."

I was thrilled, but scared too. In an interesting reaction to not successfully ending my life, I was now completely obsessed with my health—mostly, I think, because of fear of the ventilator. So I carefully took my first sip of tea, with a nurse watching. It went down fine.

"Just be careful," she told me, and bustled off. That day I would drink water after brushing my teeth, instead of having to spit it all out. Small victories!

Eventually people began talking about what would happen when I got out. Where I would stay, what kind of follow-up care I would receive. My father kept discussing counselors, clinics and doctors, and I kept nodding and letting him answer his own questions. One night Kaye made me fill out forms to receive medical leave from work. The thought of working overwhelmed and depressed me, although I supposed I would have to. What I really wanted was for Kaye to leave me alone and let me watch "Jeopardy", the only decent show I had ever seen come on the dayroom TV.

People pressed me for answers now: what were my plans? Did I know I needed follow-up care? Did I realize that if the doctors gave the word, I would be legally required to receive it, and if I missed an appointment, a sheriff's deputy would come to my door and escort me to the clinic? I just stared when my father said this. I figured I wouldn't miss any appointments, and if I did, I didn't mind if a deputy gave me a ride.

My father was my biggest cheerleader through it all. He would literally cheer if I ate a good dinner, and he regaled me with assurances that he and I would hike Mount Rogers again soon, as we had a year before. He never blamed me or pointed out what I had put everybody through, never uttered a word about his own fear, shock, grief and horror, not to mention the betrayal he must have felt. But he didn't visit as often as Kaye, and he almost never came alone. In retrospect, I imagine he psyched himself up for each of those visits for hours in advance, and I imagine it was an enormous effort.

One day I was resting in my room when one of the young psychiatry interns came in and began to talk about my legal status in The Center. I had signed myself in voluntarily, which meant that in theory I could have checked myself out at any point. I had not felt the need to as of yet, being too sick and weak to care for myself, and I also knew it was in my best interests to wait until everyone approved.

But now, it seemed, my status had changed. Somehow, I was becoming an involuntary patient—one who would stay in indefinitely. A little bit of my old fire stirred, and I began to sputter—carefully, of course.

"What? Why? What have I done wrong? I've gone to classes, cooperated with everything, kept a good attitude. I don't understand. Why would you do this?"

The young man, as humorless as all of them, didn't feel the need to justify the committee's decision. I reiterated my good behavior and outlook.

"Nevertheless, that's what's going to happen," was all he would say. Just when I had started to think that my release would come any day, I had been magically transformed into an inmate—someone who would have to appear before a magistrate to overturn the doctors' decision and walk out into the world. I would have to have a lawyer, which the hospital was inexplicably providing for me—oh good, I thought, one of their own retainers; *he'll* be fair.

"You want to talk about depression and anxiety—this is a good way to bring it on," I said angrily. The boy didn't even bother to shrug. He stood to leave, then glanced at my wrists.

"I'll see about getting those sutures out tomorrow," he remarked, and left the room.

Ironically, of the handful of days that I did not have a visitor, this was one of them. I sat in my recliner in the dayroom while all the other visitors came and went, and tried not to despair. It was fortunate that I was still out-of-it enough to not react to this incarceration as I would when I was healthy. I knew it was serious, and wrong, and I was a little scared, but my emotions were still muted, as was my intellectual understanding of things. My sister said later that everyone noticed how "detached" I was this entire time.

Most remarkably, I was not asking anyone about Leo. It took a year for me to realize that I hadn't, and even longer to understand why. I think I probably felt too guilty to have the right to ask about him—to have the right to even be his mother.

Whereas I hadn't been terribly concerned about getting out initially, now as the figurative bars slammed shut behind me, I became obsessed with it. I complained bitterly about the awful food, the uncomfortable bed, the nurses coming in at night and shining a flashlight in my face to see if I was sleeping! I argued that I wasn't getting anything out of being there—I'd heard all the lectures, done all the activities, and no one was counseling me anyway. I pointed out indignantly that I was a mother, and my son needed me (the one I wasn't asking about). Furthermore, I was disgusted that the head doctor had sent the flunky to do his dirty work.

My nurse that afternoon was a sympathetic one, and I told her what had happened.

"You know, there's a patient advocate you could contact," she told me. "I mean, I don't know the doctors' grounds for the change, but if you're concerned, I would urge you to contact her. I'll get you her number."

Bless her heart. It was not the first nor would it be the last time that a nurse stuck her neck out for me, offering to help me fight the system. I thought they were remarkably brave. I, on the other hand, wasn't, and feared that bringing in the patient advocate would be used against me, to show that I was difficult. There is nothing like being involuntarily held in a psychiatric ward to bring on paranoia.

I got through that evening somehow, and the next morning I was called before the psychiatry team for my daily grilling. Fortunately I remembered that I had been changed to involuntary and confronted them about the decision.

Dr. Helly raised his chin in my direction. "We've talked to your local clinic," he said. "It seems you weren't very good at keeping appointments."

I gasped in amazement.

"I missed two appointments, and they were both *after I was admitted to this hospital!*" I cried.

Dr. Helly dismissed that and continued. "You never talk about what happened."

"No one ever asks me to!" I cried in outrage. "No one, once, has ever asked me to talk about what I did."

"We'll send someone around to talk with you this afternoon," he replied. "The violence of what you did to yourself, coupled with the fact that it was the second attempt, makes you very high risk for another suicide attempt. The statistics say that you will try to kill yourself again; why should we let you out to do that?"

I didn't have an answer, of course. Defeated, I said, "I know you don't believe me—I wouldn't believe me either, but I KNOW I will never try this again."

"We *don't* believe you," Dr. Helly said, and the session was over.

No one came to my room to talk that afternoon, or ever.

***

One of the nurses who had helped me shower the first time tried to explain the doctors' justification to me.

"They want you to be on involuntary follow-up care, and only patients who are committed involuntarily can be legally required to do that."

"But I would GO to follow-up care," I wailed. "I DIDN't miss appointments at the Clinic until I was in Intensive Care. It's not fair!"

"Also you act too normal, for someone who's just done this to yourself," she said. "They think you're not dealing with it, so it could happen again.

"And believe it or not, some of us would worry about you after you were released," she continued. "They can't keep you here forever, so they're just making sure someone will be monitoring you after you leave."

"It's not fair," I repeated. "I came here in good faith because I knew I needed help; I signed a million forms that said "Voluntary", and now they're just slamming the door behind me. It's a bait and switch!"

I said this out loud to other patients, too, within earshot of the nurses, who gave me warning looks. I didn't care what they thought now. This was just wrong.

***

When the lawyer came to my room, I made sure I was dressed and had made my bed. It was my belief, naturally, that the more sane I appeared, the harder he would work to get me out. I wasn't sure how he would judge my sanity, since he was a lawyer and not a psychiatrist, but he had to somehow, I figured.

I was wrong. The attorney was pleasant, but not interested in my mental state, or really anything I had to say. He simply explained the logistics to me, of appearing before a magistrate on Wednesday, the only day these hearings were held, and getting a ruling based on I-wasn't-sure-what. He left after a few minutes.

When Wednesday arrived, we woke up to snow. The few inches wouldn't have made a difference in the operation of most cities, but here in the Piedmont of North Carolina, it was enough to shut things down. I watched the window fretfully, waiting to hear some sort of news. The staff knew nothing about what would happen. It was just another day to them.

My dad and Kaye appeared mid-morning. The courthouse was closed, they told me; they had spoken to the lawyer. It meant another week in the slammer for me. We all sat in the dayroom, stunned, with even my father in a bit of a funk.

When his cell phone vibrated, my dad jumped up so quickly I didn't even know what he was responding to. He yanked the phone out of his pocket and made a beeline for the ward door. (Cell phones weren't allowed inside.)

"What's going on?" I asked Kaye, but she was right behind him. I paced in frustration until they returned.

"That was the lawyer," Dad said excitedly. "He found a judge willing to hear your case. We've got to go right now!"

"Wait, what about me?" I called after their rapidly disappearing backs. If they answered I didn't hear them; they left as if shot out of a cannon.

This was just stranger and stranger. How on earth could someone judge if I should be released or not, when they had never clapped eyes on me? I didn't understand the system and still don't; it works—when it does—in mysterious ways.

While they were gone, I had my daily grilling with the psychiatrists. When I brought up Leo, I broke down in frustration. At this, Dr. Helly raised his chin at me in a characteristic gesture and remarked to his colleagues, "We may have to reconsider this. We'll follow up with Risk Assessment and discuss this case again."

What? Why the sudden change of heart? Was it because my representatives were standing in front of a magistrate even as we spoke? Was the committee saving face? We had been told the courts ruled with the hospital 90 percent of the time; it didn't seem like the doctors had anything to worry about. And who the heck was "Risk Assessment"? Was I a human being or just a liability now?

But soon after this meeting, I was speaking with one of the social workers when she said, "After you pack, you'll meet with Dr. Egan about your prescriptions and follow-up care."

"What?" I asked in amazement.

"Oh, you didn't know? The judge overturned your involuntary status and your involuntary followup; you can leave any time." She betrayed no emotion.

"Really? I can, really, I'm leaving today?" It was too good to be true.

"Yes," she answered. "I think it was because you cried in your session today. Before, you had never shown any emotion."

It was a miracle to me. I hurried to my room to pack with trembling hands and was waiting in the dayroom when my dad got back. Without a cane or any assistance I walked up and threw my arms around him, ecstatic. He was laughing and elated.

"You know what that lawyer said?" he chortled. "He said the hospital was keeping you here because you have insurance, and so many of the patients don't. That judge just slammed the folder shut and said, 'I'm overturning both rulings!'"

My dad would tell that story with great glee many times in the future. I was sprung!

Chapter 23
The Long Road Back

The reality of my freedom kicked in very quickly. Kaye was going to stay with her mom, who was ill, for several days. She wasn't coming home with us.

My heart sank like a stone at this news. My dad was my hero, but he wasn't a caregiver, and he certainly wasn't a cook. I listened in disbelief as he said that we could go to the grocery store together, and I could decide what I wanted to fix.

For a while, I sat in silence, then finally said, "I don't think you have any concept of how weak I am." He didn't, and it was terrifying. Had I been released from my captivity only to die of starvation?

But the first evening actually turned out to be grand. There was much more snow in Blue River than down the mountain, of course, and my father's legendary steep driveway was impassable. He stopped at his neighbor's drive, where the homeowner and another neighbor were talking, snow shovels in hand. It was dark by now, and in the cold wind I felt more frail than ever beneath my winter clothes.

When the men decided Dad's car should stay where it was, I blanched at the thought of walking up the steep street to his driveway, let alone up the driveway itself. But my dad and his hearty neighbor, who happened to be a doctor, each took one of my arms and outright powered me up that hill. All I had to do was move my feet!

Even better, the neighbor said his wife had made some lovely lentil stew, and would a bowl of that sit okay on my stomach? Nothing could have suited me better.

Within 20 minutes, I was curled up with a blanket over my knees on the sofa in Dad's study, which is the coziest room on the planet; and my father was proudly presenting me with a tray of hot lentils, crackers, and cheese. He bowed with a flourish.

"Would Madam care for anything else?" he asked me. I giggled and assured him all was perfect.

When I snuggled down into the blankets of the four-poster bed in Kaye's luxurious Victorian guest room a bit later, I was happy in the moment. I was still scared to death about the yawning maw of the task before me, but for tonight, I was "home" and I was free.

Reality kicked me in the teeth again the next morning when Dad hollered up to me from the kitchen, "I'm going for a run—you know where the food is!" and the garage door slammed shut.

***

We muddled through the couple of days until Kaye returned. Though Dad had promised me I could sleep as late as I wanted to, my first morning there he awoke me at ten asking, "Are you going to sleep all day?" There he stood, still flushed from his run, the very picture of 71-year-old health. I opened my eyes a slit and murmured "Yes" before closing them again.

When Kaye returned two days later, the three of us fell into a routine. I unwillingly hauled myself out of bed each morning between eight and nine, and came downstairs in my robe to sit on the small sofa in front of the woodstove and stare straight ahead. Once I could finally face it, I fixed myself something bland and stodgy for breakfast. Afterward, I dressed and performed a minimal amount of grooming before returning, exhausted, to the sofa to sit and stare some more. The rest of the day was punctuated only by meals and trips to the bathroom, naps, and halfhearted efforts on my part to appear to be doing something: picking up the newspaper, straightening up my room, or hobbling around the house using my dad's handsome carved walking stick for support.

Other people had agendas for me now, but I was simply getting though each day, each hour. My dad was in touch with my boss, and forced me to call him, but I couldn't even think about going back to work. Hell, I couldn't even *think!* Dad wanted me to go for walks outside on nice days—crazy talk! He was constantly on about my upcoming appointment at the behavioral health clinic, which I knew would be a total waste of my time and minute supply of energy. I was so thin that I didn't want to expend any extra calories at all, hoping every one I consumed could go toward rebuilding my body, rather than powering actual motion.

Left to my own devices, I would have stayed in bed till noon daily, had a bite, and gone straight back down for a nap. But Dad wouldn't have it. If I wasn't up at a reasonable hour, he came in to wake me. If I wasn't in bed or having my afternoon nap, I was strongly discouraged from lying down. This was tough, as most of the chairs at The Center had been cushy recliners, and I had spent very little time vertical.

But did anyone applaud me for sitting up? Oh, no! They wondered why I didn't DO something, at least read or maybe watch TV. I didn't want to read. I couldn't concentrate, and further I didn't care about anything anyone had written. As far as television was concerned, I had had enough of that in The Center to last me a lifetime! Of course, Dad and Kaye only watched recorded PBS shows, so it was a far cry from what I'd been subjected to. Still, each evening when the three of us gathered in the den to watch an episode of "Masterpiece Theater" or "Mystery", all I really wanted to do was go up to bed.

Eventually I started talking on the phone. Dad approved of this activity, because it *was* an activity, so I could get away with doing it lying down on the sofa. My voice was still very weak, as were my lungs, so conversations were difficult, but at least I could thank all the well-wishers who had sent cards and gifts, and update those who had driven all that way to visit me in the hospital.

People came to see me now, and I tried to get away with lying down while we talked. The first time Leo came, however, I sprang to life. I got my child an after-school snack of cookies and milk, and sat up with him at the dining room table. I had pictured us spending some cozy time over homework, and then snuggling up in the den to watch "Arthur" on TV. But Leo didn't like the cookies, and he didn't want to snuggle. Furthermore, he wanted to watch bad sitcom reruns, which made me want to run screaming from the room.

I felt like a total failure after his first visit, and stared at the fire while my dad assured me that it would take time to rebuild my relationship with Leo, but that it would certainly happen. His words slid off my consciousness like his ideas about me cooking or starting to clean my own bathroom—completely irrelevant. No one could understand me now, or ever again. I was one of very few people on earth who had raised their hands so savagely against themselves, and I had managed to botch it anyway. Many, many times I lay in that beautiful bed and thought how much easier it would have been if I had just "succeeded".

One of the first things I had done after being released was call John to tell him I was back in Blue River and ready to be with Leo. I didn't expect to break down, but I did, thanking him for being our son's only parent all this time, telling him how much it meant to know Leo was well-cared for and loved. I secretly felt John had been a solo parent long enough, and had expected that Leo would stay with me at Dad's instead of at our own house, five nights out of each week, as he always had. But this had never occurred to Dad and Kaye. They felt their hands were completely full taking care of me, and that I, too, needed to concentrate on myself right now.

Well, I was doing that. Heaven knows I wasn't putting much thought toward anyone else, except my child. I ruminated about how I couldn't breathe well, how my stomach wasn't right, how I'd never gain weight at this rate, how my dad was crazy! and had no idea how sick I was. I thought how I would never again do a single thing that wasn't necessary for survival—like read, travel, give a rip about anything. My sister had given me a brass cookie cutter in the shape of a teapot among my Christmas gifts, and I had looked at it and thought, that's nice, but I'll never bake cookies again. Why would I?

I was very disheartened about being able to be seen in public again, once warm weather came. Even my winter clothes weren't all turtlenecks, for Pete's sake! Would I always have to wear long sleeves, like my coworker at a previous job, who had tattoos? Was there make-up that would cover the scars? (but what a pain!) Jewelry, maybe? But then I'd have to shop for it, and I would never care enough to shop again.

I worried incessantly about a relapse into pneumonia. It was February now, and flu season, and my thoughts ran from flu to pneumonia to hospital ventilator in seconds flat. And the horror of having the breathing tube removed—still the worst thing I have ever experienced.

So when my dad announced that I needed to get ready for my first appointment at the local behavioral health clinic, I rebelled all-out.

"That clinic is gross!" I stated as forcefully as my lungs and vocal cords would allow. "The waiting room will be full of people with colds and flu, and my resistance is nil right now! Plus the weather is awful! I'll reschedule and go next week." But my father put his foot down. He had promised the judge who released me that he would personally see to it that I got follow-up care, and he felt that his word was on the line. I argued and argued, but I do believe he would have picked me up and put me in the car, so I got up and went, with tears of anger and frustration streaming down my face.

The folks at the Clinic couldn't have been more solicitous. They seated me in a cushy chair in a dimly-lit room, brought me a glass of water, and carefully asked me questions. They described two different patient groups at the clinic that I could join. I didn't really get it, but they seemed to want me to join one, so I picked the Team Group, which did activities like walking together. Not that I was interested in meeting any more messed-up people. In spite of the fact that I'd done the worst thing possible to myself, I still somehow thought I was saner than any of their other patients were likely to be.

Joining that Team turned out to be the best decision I've ever randomly made. It hooked me up with a great counselor, Audrey, who came to my home, instead of me having to go to the germy Clinic. I was also assigned to a psychiatrist for medication management, which meant I wouldn't have to drive down the mountain for treatment now. My Warrington shrink, Dr. Bernard, had made the interesting decision to refuse to take me back as a patient. What lay at the heart of this, I wonder? Was he worried about a lawsuit stemming from the three medications he'd had me taking when I tried to kill myself? I'm not the sort to blame others, but I guess some patients would.

I kept my winter gloves on through the whole Clinic appointment, and worried as soon as I sipped from my water glass, whether it had been well-washed or not. I was glad as hell to leave the place, and went defiantly up to my room to lie down as soon as I got back to Dad's!

***

I had only been home a few days when I came downstairs from a nap to learn that Kaye had had a revealing conversation with my ex. There was a court hearing scheduled for the *next day*, in which John was planning to ask for full legal custody of Leo.

I really don't know how these things work, having had mercifully few dealings with courts, but apparently this hearing could go forward whether I was there to defend myself or not. After all, John hadn't had to call—I would have thought his attorney would have had to contact mine, or me, but I had heard nothing. My lawyer didn't even know I'd been hospitalized.

I could not possibly have gotten my attorney, a desperately busy woman, there with me and prepared for any sort of legal defense on 24 hours' notice. I was not in good shape to represent myself, obviously, but that would have simply justified John's claim that I was unfit. There was nothing to do but talk directly with John.

He agreed to come over to meet, by which time my dad had met with his own counselor, who was not reassuring.

I was on the phone with my attorney when John arrived, and my father, who was furious, left John out in the cold until I hung up. Dad could barely speak to his former son-in-law as he walked in the house. I led John into the study and closed the door.

We hadn't communicated, except for my call when I got back to Blue River, so the meeting would have been monumental anyway. But with the hearing pending, it was the stuff of which nightmares are made. Nevertheless, we were able to get through to each other—John explained that he hadn't meant to keep me from seeing Leo, only to ensure that he made the decisions for our son. I'm not sure what decisions needed to be made at the moment, other than when he would be where, which apparently wasn't the issue; but I believe pressure was being brought to bear on John from outside sources. At any rate, not only did I get through to him to the point that he agreed to cancel the hearing, but we actually were sharing a laugh as we walked out of the study, and my ex-husband spontaneously hugged me before he left—something he hadn't done since our separation.

Dad and Kaye were stunned by John's turnaround, and couldn't seem to accept it at face value. Dad's discussion with his counselor that morning had made him even angrier.

"Do you know what Kierstin said?" he asked furiously. "She said, 'If someone tried to take away my children, I'd be suicidal!' She said we'd better lock up all our sharp knives!"

I didn't really care if my former husband had an agenda, as long as he wasn't taking away my parental rights. "Well, he's dropped it," I said tiredly.

Later on that day, my lawyer expressed a similar opinion. She had seen the papers from John's attorney. She lowered her voice to that of a girlfriend sharing a confidence. "I saw what they said about you—terrible things," she told me. (Probably all true, I thought.) "I think they were trying to push you over the edge", she went on.

As if the situation weren't dramatic enough already! I didn't think for a minute that John wanted me dead—how could he wish that on our son? How could he ever live with the guilt? As for his lawyer—I didn't see why he would care. If anything, I was a source of income to him.

My ex and his family were flailing, trying to do damage control for Leo in a situation they couldn't possibly understand. Hateful as the whole thing sounded, I knew that on some level, we were all just doing the best we could—even the lawyers, I supposed.

***

It was just a little too good to be true, as it turned out. The subject came up again within days, when John said he was "taking a lot of heat" for canceling the hearing, and asked for some sort of guarantee, in writing, from my psychiatrist that I was not still suicidal. Of course psychiatrists don't give such warranties on their work, so I told him that wasn't possible. Which didn't leave me much room for arguing when he told me okay, but he needed a bit of a grace period on his back-alimony from the time I had been hospitalized (I wasn't asking for child support for this time, of course).

I believe the expense that had come up necessitating the delay of payment was probably an engagement ring. Leo had spilled that news the last time he'd been with me. John knows our son cannot keep a secret, so maybe he preferred that Leo drop that bomb; at any rate, it neither distressed nor particularly shocked me. Leo liked Carrie, and didn't seem to object, and I certainly was not carrying a torch for my ex. Also, my emotions were still somewhat muted, thank goodness, or I would not have come through the custody scare as well as I did.

So I congratulated John, and he told me the wedding would be in June. Then he asked if Leo could stay with us the next night, as he and his fiancee had plans.

***

My first outing was to a church-league basketball game of Leo's. My dad has a policy against going to grandkids' games ("When I was a boy, we played in the sandlot! We didn't have uniforms or refs—we worked it out among ourselves. My parents would have LAUGHED if I'd suggested they watch me play. They had work to do!" etc. etc.) but I still needed to get there and back, and I wasn't driving yet. Eventually Sara agreed to go to the game with me.

I covered up my wrists and neck well, as you can imagine. I didn't know how many of the parents in the community knew what had happened. I couldn't disguise my emaciation, but I tried to put color in my cheeks with makeup. I dreaded the public appearance, and knew it would exhaust me, but I also wanted to see Leo play.

I'll never forget how hard those bleachers were. Even though I sat on my coat, I squirmed through the whole game. No one said a word to me about being gone, or being sick, or being back; but then no one said much to me at all. I was now even more of an outsider than I'd been when I appeared in town two years earlier under dubious circumstances, two weeks after school started and noticeably minus my husband—or when it first got around that John and I were separated, the year before.

Even though John had left me in February 2006, I hadn't told any of the other parents all that spring. I couldn't face it, and until May I was holding out for reconciliation. That first summer I was picking Leo up at camp one day when a third-grade dad walking through the parking lot with me asked how I was doing. "Fine," I answered. He was peering at me pointedly, as if he expected something else. Finally he asked, "How's single parenthood workin' out for you?"

"Oh. Heard about that, did you?" It was all I would say. I didn't know I was enough in the local crowd's radar to be a topic of conversation!

Anyway, now, at the basketball game, I felt like a spotlight was shining on me, but it was probably my imagination. I was very grateful that Sara was there. As luck would have it, my in-laws and Carrie were also in attendance, all sitting cozily together with John, and there was no avoiding conversation with them after the game. How do you face someone who last saw you lying in a pool of blood on a bathroom floor, of your own doing? They don't write etiquette books for this stuff. Even my mother, Emily Post of the Blue Ridge, could have only winged it (she would have winged it well, though!)

I hope I emulated what she would have done. I first hugged and congratulated Leo, who played well (I'm not one of those moms who praises a child after he coasts through a game or goofs around), then smiled and greeted my in-laws. Rob's hug was glancing, but Agnes held onto me long enough to tell me she loved me, twice, to exclaim over how thin I was, and then to hold me at arms' length and say seriously, "You've got to get better so you can go back to being Leo's mommy."

I was very touched by this, especially since I felt I owed her and Rob a huge apology for what they had witnessed. As far as being Leo's mommy...hmmm. I had guessed they were some of the people who thought I wasn't legally fit for that. But that crisis had passed, thank goodness.

Eventually my friends Andy and Anita, two people I had noticed not hearing from, each called and wanted to visit me at my dad's. While Andy and I were setting up a time, I was floored to realize that he didn't know I had done this to myself. His abrupt, "Wait a minute, what?" in the middle of our conversation made me take a deep breath and then, haltingly, explain. The silence that followed made me writhe inside. I learned that telling people what had happened over the phone was the worst. They don't get any clues from your eyes or expression as to where you're going with the story. It's a dreadful feeling holding that silent telephone, waiting for them to say something, anything, in response.

The first time I had had to do this was when my dear old friend Douglas tracked me down at Dad and Kaye's. We've known each other since before I was married, and seen each other through a total of two weddings, three divorces, the acquisition (as it were) of three children, and countless moves and job changes. Although Douglas is a rolling stone, constantly changing contact information without letting me know so I can keep up with him, he always manages to track me down and call me up out of the blue after months or even a year of silence. He has visited me in multiple homes in three states, including just after my separation, with his girlfriend.

He and I chatted for quite a while, as I put off explaining why I was staying at my dad's. He told me the heart-wrenching tale of one of our former co-workers who had died of cancer, leaving a husband and three young children behind. That didn't make it any easier to tell him what I'd done. The first thing he said after the inevitable stunned silence, was, "That just made me sick, when you said that."

There was judgment there, for which I could not blame him, after he had watched our coworker fight so hard for her own life. I still regarded my suicide attempt as my Great Shame, the one I had so presciently dreamed of years before. Ever since my breakdown in Oregon, I had considered myself fairly enlightened on the subject of mental health, but my understanding was still limited enough for me to be unspeakably embarrassed about the severity of my illness, and the horrific crisis that had been its ultimate manifestation.

Andy, on the other hand, took the news more calmly. Either he thought he wasn't supposed to know and was being diplomatic, or he had suspected this all along.

We hung up quickly after that, the admission of a suicide attempt being a real conversation-stopper. He had accepted, on behalf of himself and our other Southwest-trip friend Cutler, my invitation to come to tea, and I was excited about seeing them and about having a small project to undertake. I had already made minor efforts to help with food preparation at Dad's, so I thought I could pull it off.

But my recovery continued its decidedly non-linear progression, and on the appointed day, I began to have difficulty breathing. Or possibly, to imagine it, since my lungs had not yet fully recovered from the repeated infections, not to mention the initial violation, and I hadn't breathed at my normal capacity since December second. I may have been excited to have a social engagement and tried to breathe more deeply or quickly, as well. But I was scared enough by the struggle to call Dr. Timothy, the M.D. who practiced with Ginny, for the first time since my attempt.

He had time to process my news between our phone conversation and my arrival at the office. Still, he couldn't hide his shock as he questioned me in the examining room.

"How long were you hospitalized?"

"Seven weeks."

"ICU?"

"ICU for 3 weeks, Acute Care for one, the psychiatric ward for three and a half."

"Were you on a ventilator"

"Yes."

"Wow."

He betrayed no horror, however, when he examined my wounds and removed some sutures for me. I was relieved to have the initial examination overwith—after all, my health care was in his hands from here on, and I was convinced that none of my many medical problems were mental in nature now. He listened to my lungs carefully, one side at a time.

"Your left lung is working at about 75 percent capacity," he told me. "It may be partially collapsed. This happens sometimes with pneumonia.

"I want a chest x-ray," he continued. "You'll have to go over to the Imaging Center."

Unfortunately, he never mentioned that such conditions usually remedy themselves, and if not, can be corrected by a pulmonary specialist with a fairly simple procedure. I learned this by talking to Lisa, who is a doctor, and I was greatly relieved. What do people do who don't have doctor-friends? God knows self-diagnosis by Internet is virtually guaranteed to provoke anxiety!

Several days later, I was able to keep my tea date with Cutler and Andy. Dad and Kaye left, perhaps by design, so I would have to do all the hostessing myself. I was inspired, and prepared little sandwiches as well as a pot of tea and plate of store-bought cookies. I had told the boys to wear their best clothes and be prepared to drink out of china cups with their pinkies held aloft, so Cutty showed up in overalls with a tie-dyed shirt, and Andy wore jeans and a hoodie, and hadn't shaved for days.

But I was touched that they were willing to put themselves into such an awkward situation to see me. And their gruff male kindness and concern, together with their enveloping hugs on arrival and departure, left me feeling optimistic enough about the future to start thinking about going home.

Chapter 24
The Shift

I continued to humor Dad and Kaye and the folks at the Clinic by going through the motions of counseling and psychiatry. I wasn't in a constant state of near-panic, and I slept at night (and any other chance I got), so I was no longer suffering from Anxiety. Depression? Well, maybe, now. I mean, who wouldn't be? Look at the road back I was facing! Look at—well, how I looked! Look at all the relationships I had to mend, all the people I had to face for the first time since I did something crazy—something that the folks at the psyche ward had told me was rarely seen at all, in terms of its violence, and even less often in women. I was even a freak among freaks!

But depression, at least at the level I had it, was sustainable in my view; anxiety had not been. In The Center classes about anxiety, other patients talked about "When I get anxious", or "When I feel anxiety". It seemed I was the only one who had felt it, relentlessly, 24 hours a day, seven days a week, for three months, until it was insupportable. The psychiatrists at the hospital had all talked about my depression, and I got tired of arguing with them. But in my experience, anxiety and depression are two entirely different animals, with one like a shooting pain, and the other a heavy, dull ache.

I suppose it's possible that I'm the first and only psychiatric patient to have had this experience, but I'm doubtful. I believe the medical community is too quick to lump together two conditions that are distinct disorders. In my experience, anxiety is a very high-energy state, a stomach-churning, shaky, tingly, short-of-breath condition; while depression is low-energy, heavy, and inert. I don't deny some common symptoms: hopelessness, loss of interest, in some cases insomnia; but I believe the common diagnosis of depression-and-anxiety is misleading and inaccurate. A depressed person sits and stares, while an anxious person paces the room.

The fact that many anti-depressants work on both conditions further confuses the issue. But I was constantly frustrated during my treatment by what seemed to me to be a lack of understanding of the distinction. I argued with my counselor about it until it became a standing joke between us, and we agreed to disagree. She has the education, of course, and has read many case studies. But I lived it.

***

One afternoon Dad and Kaye sat me down for a talk (not that I'd been standing up). Dad feared for my job, and didn't think I was recovering fast enough.

"You're just not yourself," he said. I certainly couldn't argue with that.

"The old Laura Anne had so much gumption! You don't take the initiative in anything, you're paranoid about your health, and you don't seem remotely interested in going back to work. That's the most important thing: you've GOT to get back to work."

"I know…." I didn't have enough gumption to defend myself.

"Going back to work has to come before moving back to your house, or getting Leo back. You've got to make that your first priority. Your leave is going to run out, and if you lose your job, you've lost your insurance."

"My first priority is taking care of Leo. My second priority is getting my stomach problems solved. If I can't gain weight, I'm never going to get stronger. What if I was at work and I threw up?"

My dad was exasperated. "People throw up at work all the time!" he declared.

"Yeah, and then they go home sick."

"You need a plan, a schedule for going back. You need to call Greg and talk about coming back part-time at first, and working your way up."

"I guess I *could* do that."

"Sure you can! Call Greg now and tell him you want to! See if you can work it out!"

The harder my dad pushed me about going back to work, the more I talked about moving home. He and Kaye were adamant that I should return to my job from their house, so that after work I could come "home" to a good dinner, rather than to my own household chores. Also, who could blame them for wanting to keep an eye on me a while longer? I wasn't to be trusted yet. But Dad's house was becoming close quarters for the three of us. It was a good sign that I was getting restless there.

I had no idea if I could cope on my own, but I could at least visit my old place and putter around. Dad and Kaye were so opposed to me moving back yet that they declined to help me clean and make my house habitable again. So once I had gotten over the hump of driving again (and believe me, Blue River drivers all had guardian angels for a few weeks there!) I loaded up some of my things and went over by myself.

During even a week's vacation, a house can develop that empty smell and feeling. My home was a ghost of its former self, silent and cold, with the cabinet doors standing open and the water rusty in the toilets. The kitchen faucet dripped slowly. Mousetraps—empty, thank goodness—were everywhere.

The pantry doors were ajar, and every item that wasn't canned had been put in a sealed container by Dad and Kaye. There were several tools and a roll of paper towels by the sink, and the things I always kept on the counter were out of place. I automatically started putting them back.

I caught my breath when I saw the tiny lemon tree I had started from seed four months earlier, sitting on the kitchen windowsill. It looked exactly as it had when I left it: about an inch tall, with only the two seed leaves to its credit.

("Plant some seeds," my colleague Gwen had advised. "That will make you feel better.")

The soil in the pot was completely dry, and the temperature by that windowsill had doubtless dipped well into the 40's. The baby tree had essentially been refrigerated for ten weeks. I looked at it and saw a symbol of myself: all growth suspended, simply staying alive through the dark winter months.

But spring was coming. As I marveled at the tiny life, so durable and yet so fragile, I made a promise. "I'm going to make you grow again," I said as I carefully watered it. "I'll feed you and water you and put you out in the sun, and you will grow and thrive." Maybe if *it* could….

The large eat-in kitchen was the heart of the house, and the place where I was first drawn, but there were other things to see. Taking a deep breath, I walked back toward the bathroom where I had attacked myself. In the laundry room, a new outside door stood where John and Rob had battered down the old one, with the new-construction smell still clinging to it. The bathroom door was still splintered, the lock compromised. My mother-in-law had cleaned the floor and walls—a task I couldn't begin to imagine for her—and the stained rugs were gone. I took another breath and raised my eyes to the mirror, where I had last seen my reflection positioning the knife to stab my throat a second time, to finally get it right.

There, that was overwith. I was emaciated, but my wounds were healing and there was no blood this time. Eventually I would put on makeup in this mirror again—in theory, at least. I would wipe away the shower steam to comb out my hair. I would toss my dirty clothes on the washer on my way out of the bathroom, pulling the tie snug on my robe as I went.

It was too much to hope for that I would feel good, that I would go into the kitchen and make coffee, pick up the paper and read the headlines before waking up Leo for school. I remembered that life as if it were someone else's—someone so lucky, who had no idea how lucky she was. How fortunate to be able to pour a bowl of cereal and eat it without even thinking, to pick out an outfit and be happy with her appearance, to make plans for her day without hopelessness and fear. That wouldn't happen, of course. But I could at least live independently again, taking care of my son and my job, fulfilling my responsibilities. And I could always *remember* what it was like to feel joy.

Next, I went into my bedroom. There was the flowered quilt on the queen-sized bed that barely fit, with the dresser and bureau, within the white concrete walls. The side window that allowed a slant of midday sun across the center of the bed. The closet door that always stood open to show my poster of Captain Jack Sparrow, my "friendly face to wake up to".

I lay down carefully, folding my hands over my chest. This was repose, right here, this was my haven. My thoughts ran over the day I had sat up and taken the overdose here, and then went mercifully blank. After a few moments I made myself get up—it was cold, and Dad and Kaye were probably freaked, and there was one more thing I wanted to do.

The sky was pale and the treetops were bare through the big picture window in my living room, just as they had been when I left. The gas logs were cold, the television dark. I stretched out on the sofa and faced the window. It had been such a good life. How had I lost it? How much of it could I possibly get back?

***

On February 6th, I began writing in the new journal my dear friend Chris had given me while I was hospitalized. It didn't seem right to pick up where I'd left off in my old volume. That had been another life, one I'd ended, effectively. I was starting anew. From February to May of 2008, I used the new book to write down lists of things I'd accomplished, like the first time I drove. I wrote lists of things I wanted to do, like play the piano or bake a cake, as well as what I saw as the problems I had to overcome in order to recover. I also searched, constantly, for a mantra that would inspire me all the way back to health if I just kept repeating it to myself. I test-drove many:

I will do what it takes to get better.
I have the resources I need to get better, and I am not afraid.

The tone of my entries is determined but often discouraged, as I encountered setbacks. After detailing several on Feb. 7th, I concluded, "But as I always tell myself, it's all my own dang fault."

Now that I was in counseling, I was getting pressured from all sides but one to find a counselor for Leo. John maintained that Leo was "doing fine". I personally was quite skeptical about counseling, given all my experiences; and I was very protective of my 10-year-old being put into a situation that might make him uncomfortable, after all he'd been through. I didn't want Leo to think something was wrong with *him*, and I wanted to be darn sure I trusted any adult I left my child alone with, particularly when it came to discussing emotionally charged issues. At the same time, I knew I owed him the opportunity to open up about his feelings to someone he could say anything to, unlike a family member. So I talked to Audrey about it, and I made some calls to the counseling center at the university. I kept coming up against roadblocks, so the situation remained unresolved for a long time.

I was seeing Dr. Timothy constantly, as he no doubt made his way through the inch-thick stack of my hospital records and got a clearer picture of what precisely had gone down. I continued to complain of shortness of breath and pain upon breathing, and at one appointment he said he wanted to rule out a pulmonary embolism.

I didn't know what one was, exactly, but I knew it was bad.

"Would that just be…the end of me?" I asked fearfully.

"Not necessarily," he replied matter-of-factly.

"Jesus Christ," I breathed. "Not necessarily? You mean I could die?"

"Well, when someone has a clot in their lung, they're hospitalized and put on an IV of coumadin until they reach therapeutic levels," he said. "You're small, so I think you would be therapeutic pretty quickly. You would have to be hospitalized for the treatment, though.

"I don't *think* it's what's going on, but I just want to rule it out. A blood test can tell us that's *not* what's going on, but on the other hand a different result doesn't necessarily mean you do have a clot. If that were the case I would want a CT scan of your lungs".

"At the Imaging Center?"

"No, that would be at the hospital."

I digested this.

"What causes pulmonary embolisms?" I asked.

"Mostly being sedentary."

My heart sank. I guess Dad and Kaye had been right to try to keep me vertical!

I trotted obediently to the lab, where my blood sample was drawn, and the doctor said he would call me at home that night as soon as he'd heard the results.

I never enjoyed the nightly TV-watching at Dad's, but that night was the worst yet. We kept a cordless phone with us on the sofa, so when it rang we wouldn't miss it.

"I'm not completely satisfied with your results," the doctor told me. "They're not the results we'd expect, exactly, if you *had* an embolism, but they're not normal enough to rule it out, either."

"So I have to have the scan?" I asked dispiritedly.

"Yes. I'm going to call the hospital with the orders," he said. "You'll need to call there tomorrow morning to find out what time they want you to come in."

I excused myself and went upstairs at the next commercial. As I lay in bed, I thought of Sara's reaction when I told her about my doctor's visit. When I said how frightened I'd been at the possibility of dying, she laughed. "*That's* ironic," she said without apology. It took several minutes for my clouded brain to compare my current, normal, fear of death with the frenzied violence with which I had sought it only two months before. That had to be progress, right? And *wouldn't* it be ironic if I didn't make it now?

Mother Nature truly had it in for me that winter, for the next morning we had eight inches of fresh snow, and the road had not been plowed. Dad didn't want to risk it, but sensing my distress, he eventually dug out the car he had left at the bottom of his driveway, and got me across town. There I learned that I was supposed to have fasted for 12 hours, and was told to come back that afternoon. There was also confusion over my doctor's orders, and he could not be reached since his office was closed on Fridays. But someone somewhere pulled some strings as I sat hopelessly at Outpatient Admissions, and somehow, much later, I had the CT scan.

Meanwhile, I looked at everyone in the hospital searchingly. How sick were they? How much, if any, of it was emotional? How much was caused by unhealthy habits, how much genetics, what was just the luck of the draw? Would the young man with his face in his hands, trembling, get the help he needed and recover? What was the prognosis for the elderly man sitting beside me, holding his wife's hand? And what about the people who worked there? Did they appreciate their health? Was it depressing working in a hospital? Did they have their own medical fears, from being surrounded by pain and pathology all the time?

The CT scan was another bizarre procedure to chalk up to life experiences, but not really distressing in and of itself. Afterwards, the technicians told me to sit out in the hall for 30 minutes, to be sure I wasn't going to have a reaction to the strange serum I had been given prior to the procedure. I was thinking about how no one would find Dr. Timothy on a Friday, so I wouldn't be able to get my results until Monday, when a nurse came around the corner with a phone in her hand.

"Dr. Timothy," she said, holding it out to me.

Fortunately, I didn't have time to think about the significance of this, before the familiar brusque voice was saying, "Well, you don't have a clot."

Relief poured over me as I listened to his thoughts on why I still struggled to breathe, and what would happen if the collapsed part of my lung didn't re-inflate on its own. None of it sounded scary.

I was grinning like an idiot when I hung up and turned to my dad.

"Can we get a milkshake on the way home?" I asked.

***

I returned to work on Valentine's Day 2008. I took the elevator to the fourth floor and walked carefully and self-consciously down the hall, hoping not to recognize any students. My office was abloom with red and pink: roses, a welcome-back banner, and plates of Valentine's cookies and brownies. My boss, Greg; several other professors; and Andy, bearing a plastic daffodil, were all there.

I had sent ahead the rather ungracious word that I didn't want to be hugged on return, because of my fear of flu contagion! So everyone stood around awkwardly, offering tentative words of greeting on yet another occasion for which no etiquette tracts are written.

"Have a brownie," urged Greg, no doubt alarmed by my waiflike appearance.

"Um, I just ate," I demurred, knowing the treats were not within my realm of digestive possibility. "You all eat, please," I said, and handed the plates around.

Everyone laughed as I took a bottle of Clorox wipes out of my bag and began cleaning my telephone and keyboard, but it was not a joke to me. The student who had been working in my stead had left a cheerful note on the desk, saying she had been diagnosed with pneumonia! (my worst nightmare) and would be out for a few days

After several minutes in which little was said and even less was eaten, I seized upon an item of work on my desk. "I'm going to send a fax," I announced, and rose to dismiss everyone. In relief they headed back to their offices, and I turned to the copy room and resumed my life as a member of the work force.

My first day was only four hours long, but it exhausted me. Worse, it shone a light upon just how compromised my brain function was. I suppose everyone else was terrified that my mental condition was permanent, but I just muddled on without really considering the long-term. It took all my strength of mind to focus on remembering what the lady in HR had told me five minutes ago when I called her, or what in heck Greg was talking about right now.

I stuck to my goals of answering the phone, getting the mail, and going through my email, and no one asked me to do a single thing. Their kid gloves were on—for all I know, some of them were at their computers googling how to deal with someone who has attempted suicide, so as not to set them off again! I felt sorry for my colleagues, but I had to concentrate on myself, and not their discomfort.

And now that I had finally satisfied my dad's demand of returning to work, I felt the light had turned green for moving back to my house. My second day at work was a Friday, and that weekend, I went home. My gumption level had increased.

***

The next time Audrey visited me, she sat in my glider and I curled into the corner of my own sofa, facing my big picture window with its painting of still-bare trees and white sky. I was proud to welcome her to my own neat, modest house, knowing that she visited many clients in trailers and depressing apartments—it was proof to her that I might be crazy, but I had been independent and at least reasonably successful in my "previous" life! I knew that many of her clients couldn't work, and lived on disability, and I still felt different from the rest of them, like I needed to show her that there had been a huge mistake!

I still struggled with vertigo at this point, although I had quit the walking cane for good. I did what I could to increase my lung power, blowing into the spyrometer I had been given at the hospital, repeatedly every day. My voice was getting stronger, and sometimes, for lack of anything better to do towards my recovery, I sat up in bed with my mom's old Baptist hymn book and sang, finding myself out of breath at the end of each line.

But the great luxury of being home was finally being able to lie on the sofa in front of my gas fire, sometimes far into the night. I felt cozy, secure and peaceful there, and my mind could wander where it would. No one muttered in her sleep from beyond a curtain, no one woke me to take my vital signs, no one ordered me to get up, go to breakfast, get dressed, *do* something! I had dreamed of this indulgence for so long that I went so far as to move my alarm clock to the living room in case I slept through the night there. Which I did sometimes, waking up in a sauna, but happy!

I came up against a major issue when I was ready to have Leo back with me at home. Whereas he hadn't shown any reluctance to be with me, he was very afraid to be in the house where everything had happened. His last memories of it, Kaye told me, were of an ambulance, fire truck, and three police cars parked in the driveway, their lights flashing. I tried in vain to point out to him that none of it was the house's fault, but such feelings do not respond to logic. Finally I asked John if we could borrow his dog, Lacy, for Leo's first weekend with me, and John agreed. I had to further concede the living room sofa to Leo and the dog, and allow them to sleep out there with the light on. This setup left Leo and me sleeping on either side of the same wall, and it was at this time that we began our now long-standing tradition of tapping out good-night messages to each other.

Once these negotiations were settled, oh the heaven of that first weekend! Saturday morning I propped myself up with pillows in bed, and drank a cup of tea looking out my side window, as Leo and Lacy watched cartoons snuggled up on the couch together. Thus began another tradition I maintain to this day of having my first "cuppa" in bed, not only on weekends, but every day of the week. This involves setting the alarm clock earlier, but it's such a lovely, gentle way to ease into a day, that I highly recommend it. After all, if I'm not going to be good to myself, who is?

***

We were working back up to Leo being with me under our usual arrangement: every night but Wednesday, and every other weekend. I tried very hard to walk a line between celebrating being home together, and getting back to normal. I didn't fuss over him as I had at my dad's, but I planned food he would like and suggested we do things together like watch Jeopardy or play Nerf basketball (with me propped up on my bed). Afterward I would casually ask him to bring his dirty clothes to the laundry room, or take out the trash. When I explained my balancing act to Audrey in one of our sessions, she remarked that it sounded like I was "doing everything right".

As she left that day, for the first time, I began to think there might be something TO this counseling business, after all! I even wrote in my journal that night, "Audrey has more insights than you would expect", without seeing the irony. I had seen my share of counselors, and never "clicked" with any of them, but then, I had never really given any of them a chance. I had not been in the mindset to change my attitude with Audrey, either, especially when I first met her.

She looked very young, that first day at my father's house, and all I could think was, "What could she possibly know about life?"

A year later, she confessed to me that "The first time I met you, I didn't think this was going to work."

"Well, I thought you looked about 15!" I cried in my defense.

"I get that a lot," she responded.

But I began to warm to her, and over time to realize that she was encouraging me in practical and realistic ways. The result of this was that I began to let down my guard and cry in most of our sessions, as I admitted how uncertain I felt about my ability to meet all the challenges ahead.

The psychiatrist was quite another matter. With a little bit of my old spirit, I labeled Dr. Marshall "Gloomy Gus" for his unsmiling visage and confident predictions that I must accept the "new normal" and stop wanting to get my old life back. "I'm just so freakin' determined," I sobbed to him at one appointment.

Dr. Marshall focused on medications, as has become the single purview of psychiatrists today, and he continued to suggest more. When I complained about the inconsistency of my stomach, he doubled my anti-depressant. At our next meeting he suggested adding something else. I was wary of anything other than my tried-and-true 20 mg of my old standby, but I tried what he suggested, eventually quitting the second med but continuing with the higher dose of the SSRI.

At one appointment, when I was being gloomy myself, Dr. Marshall surprised me by opining that my recovery had been "actually amazing".

"You basically gutted yourself," he intoned bluntly. "And yet you're sitting here now, you're working, you're caring for your son."

That was a remark to put in the vault! I would repeat it to everybody. But meanwhile, my stomach problems continued, and the shrink's various potions did not solve them. Although I was slowly gaining weight (around 100 pounds now), I was still far from what Dr. Timothy called my "fighting weight" of 115. Frustrated and frightened that these issues were permanent, I talked to Dr.Timothy and was referred down the mountain, to the very hospital where I had been confined, for an upper endoscopy to check for ulcers.

(journal entry)
Feb. 24—Throw-ups, endoscopy, whatever, dammit, I am going to get better. Every day is the first day of the rest of my life. Every day is the worst my scars will ever look, because they will only fade from here until I die. And I'm not even sure I'm afraid of death now, when it comes. After what I've been through.

Of course Dad and Kaye drove me to the appointment, and I felt like their little girl again. I actually hoped I did have an ulcer, since they are very treatable now, and it would be a solid, physical reason for my gastrointestinal distress. But it wasn't the case.

The procedure itself was fascinating. I believe many people are put under for endoscopies, but I was only given something lovely in an IV that made my vision swim in a matter of minutes, and me not care about much! The only part I remember is a voice saying, "Swallow the camera! Swallow the camera!" and then the rather unpleasant feeling of something poking around in my stomach. The next thing I knew, I was sitting up in the recovery room and a nurse was asking if I wanted a Pepsi.

The doctor show me the pictures—in full color, no less!—of my digestive tract, and I must say, it was a thing of beauty. Pink, well-formed, and squeaky-clean (thanks to my fast!), it had no blemishes or faulty construction.

This was great, but it still left me still unable to eat normally, and now with no explanation, no treatment plan.

I was tired and discouraged when I got home that day, and I did not need what happened next. My mail contained a letter from an archdiocese, of all things, addressed by hand to me—not junk mail. My only connection with the Catholic Church had been in the form of passing on jokes about it, mostly told to me by my ostensibly Catholic husband. So I opened the letter in bewilderment.

> "Dear Ms. Nicholson,
> The Records show that on May 6, 1989, John Nicholson attempted marriage with Laura Anne Buchman; however, the marriage was not in the presence of a Catholic priest or deacon. Said marriage is therefore now rendered null and void.... "

My first reaction was of disgust, that John was jumping through hoops to satisfy the Catholic Church. Why couldn't he and Carrie just hire an officiant and get married wherever they wanted to? Was he really pretending to be Catholic—or spiritual at all—for some priest?

Then I felt the slap in the face of the very wording, "attempted marriage with". They might as well have said, "at the hand of an inferior being, not blessed by our Pope". I couldn't believe John hadn't given me a heads-up that this was in the works, so that at least I would have seen it coming. And to have this on top of everything else!

I won't repeat the phone conversation that subsequently took place between me and my former spouse, but its tone was not one of mutual respect. I tore up and threw out the letter, and after that first day, I mostly viewed the whole subject with contempt. I told John that henceforth I would introduce him as my "baby daddy", since we had never been married, and asked if Leo, now a bastard, would be allowed to be part of or even attend his and Carrie's holy marriage. (Best friend Joni later explained to me that even though Catholics declare marriages null and void, they do NOT consider the progeny of them to be illegitimate! The Church waves its magic wand again!)

I have since learned, to my amusement, that the archdiocese legally had to contact me at the *beginning* of the annulment process, not just at its conclusion; and that therefore, in a rich ironic twist, John's *annulment* is now null and void!

To his credit, my baby daddy told our son that the whole annulment stunt was "B.S."

***

I felt, for months, that if I could only start eating normally again, I could enjoy watching the weight come back on, and I could begin to really recover. As things stood, I was never sure how my stomach would react to any but the blandest foods, and I had a chronic problem with excessive salivation. I frequently took anti-nausea meds, in addition to calcium tablets with every meal. I was given an anti-nausea diet, but found it boring and not conducive to weight gain. In frustration, I wrote in my journal that, "I don't WANT to be a person who has to eat an anti-nausea diet! So damn the torpedoes, I'm eating what I want! If I throw up, I throw up!" But life was not good with the weakness of being underweight, in addition to my mental confusion. I was still having some balance problems and now my hair was starting to fall out! I could make steps forward, but always the food issue slapped me back, countering any progress. One night, after going early to bed, I called my sister's minister for some encouragement. I felt I just couldn't burden my sister again, and I tried hard not to alarm my father.

"I'm really not just saying this because I'm a minister," Shelly said, "but you might find it helps to come to church. There are a lot of people there who care about you and would support you in your recovery."

"Oh I know, they've been wonderful," I assured her. "It's just that Sunday is one of two days where I can do what I need to do the most—sleep!"

A few minutes after we hung up, the phone rang again. It was Shelly.

"You're not—I mean, you're not going to…"

"Oh, no!" I interrupted. "No! I'm not going to do anything crazy."

"Okay," she said. "Call me any time you need to."

The following Saturday morning, I lay in bed late and called Lisa. I always felt guilty for calling her when I needed medical advice, but on the other hand, who among my doctors cared about me like she did? And I certainly wanted to talk to her as a friend, too.

"I notice that when I take an anxiety pill, I can eat," I mentioned during the conversation.

"Uh-huh." Pause. "So, take it!"

"But I'm so afraid of becoming addicted! I mean, I can't take it forever. And eventually they'll stop prescribing it for me…."

Lisa had her doctor's voice on now. "L.A., I would *not hesitate* to take it if it helps you eat—at least until you gain the weight back."

"Well…okay."

If I have never made it clear to Lisa what those words did for me, I need to tell her now. For six months, I had not been able to eat normally. But now, with her professional and personal blessing, I began to take a small amount of the anxiety medication daily…. and I began to eat.

I was tentative at first, but gained confidence with each day. Milkshakes were one of my mainstays; for some reason, I never had any problem with them. I began getting braver: trying fast food and eventually even finding out I could take Excedrin for my bad headaches again. The queasiness, middle-of-the-night throwups and dry heaves dissipated; it was wonderful! My strength began to slowly return and my spirits to lift, and at the same time, spring was coming to the mountains! It was a happy convergence of conditions conducive to healing.

One evening, snuggled up on the sofa with Leo, I noticed the distressing scars on my wrist in full view, and quickly hid them. But then I realized he had seen them, that time and maybe many others, and he hadn't said a thing. He had accepted me, scars and all, still his mother. We sat on the couch that night and "studied" for his science test—and, in a deplorable act of parenting, I giggled at everything he didn't know. The more questions he couldn't answer, the harder we laughed, until he was saying he didn't know just to keep the hilarity going. It was that first tiny flickering of "normal" that I'd been looking for with him. Not "new normal"—*normal* normal!

The next time I had to change my computer password at work, I made it "Stillmom1".

***

On my To Do list now, I had "Crossword puzzles", "Eat lunch at school with Leo", and "Reach out to others".

The puzzles were intended to sharpen my mental acuity, which, in its current state, was really impairing my ability to be an effective secretary. I bemoaned this fact to a coworker.

"I used to multitask with the best of them—I was a champion multi-tasker! Now I can barely uni-task!" I lamented.

"It'll come with practice," she said matter-of-factly, and I felt a glimmer of hope.

If I'm brain-damaged, they just have to love me, anyway!

I asked Leo if he'd like me to join him for lunch at school one day, almost as a test: it involved me, but not the house, and I really wanted to know if, deep down, he *was* uncomfortable with his crazy mother. When he answered without hesitation that he would "love it!" I was thrilled. Of course then I had to go there, and face that teacher who knew the awful thing I had done to him, those kids who might or might not know.

To make matters even less comfortable, on the agreed-upon day, I learned that the fourth-graders were eating lunch in their classroom, rather than the bustling cafeteria. I sat at a table with a group of boys, pulling the sleeves of my sweater over my wrists under the table. "This is our posse," said one unsmiling child, nodding at the assembled group.

"I see," I answered brightly, and from there the conversation dwindled. But Leo's teacher was very kind, saying she would love to have a cup of coffee if I ever wanted to talk. And that night I was able to cross another item off my list!

The "reaching out" part went back to the point I had argued in The Center, that "We cannot always feel happiness, but we can always give it". I was fully ready to sacrifice myself upon the altar of making up to everyone the horror I had put them through, hoping that as a side benefit it might lift me up some. I was still quite uncertain about how completely I could recover. But I was determined to give Leo a good life, and win back his trust, and I still had that seed my dad had planted at the back of my mind about stopping someone else who was suicidal. I wasn't sure where one found suicidal people, but if one showed up in front of me, I was determined to do all I could!

Make your life better.

So I began smiling at strangers, giving people compliments whenever I legitimately could, offering encouraging words or help to people who seemed to be struggling. It might sound cheesy, but in fact I was being very selfish: whenever I clearly brightened someone's day, it would make *me* feel good. I could still do it!

It will get better.

I also began to reach out to my own friends, both those who had called or visited me and those I had not heard from. I was too tired every night to do anything extra, but I tried to make myself call people, knowing that the more support I had, the better. I had to get over the hump of talking to people for the first time, even some who didn't know what had happened. I sent some long, handwritten letters of explanation.

Most of my life has been good, and it will be good again. So many people are behind me!

Regarding those close to me, I figured everyone had a right to yell once. This happened in the natural course of things with most of my family. I was still apologizing to people, and I was certainly a long way from forgiving myself. On February 28th, in a despairing journal entry, I wrote of my "desperate, selfish, cowardly act. How am I sup-posed to handle the rest of my life?"

Toward the end of March, John approached me about having Leo spend an extra night a week with him. I was stunned. "Why would you do this to me now?" I asked.

We were standing in my driveway after he had brought Leo home.

"Go inside," I told Leo. "You can watch TV."

"*You* need to read the separation agreement," John said. "That's the schedule we agreed to—we should've been doing it all along."

"So why haven't we?"

"Because I'm a nice guy!"

His voice was beginning to rise as I objected. "You know, it was just Leo and me for three months," he said, "We became very close!"

"Well I'm glad, that's the silver lining of all this," I stammered.

"I've been letting you have him the extra night, but he hates be-ing here, and I don't blame him. I have to *convince* him to come over here!"

I was getting rattled now, and I was offended by his tone. "I'll get the separation agreement right now!" I said angrily, turning for the house.

When I came out, I paged furiously through the document on the trunk of my car, eventually finding the custody arrangement. I was shocked.

"You're right," I said, beginning to cry. "You're right." How could I not have known this?

"Please don't do this," I begged, "don't do this now. I need my family; he's all I have left."

My appeal for pity made John even angrier. His turn, I guess.

"You're not okay!" he yelled. "Your emotions are all over the place! Your family stuck you back out here after the first suicide at-tempt, and you did it again! I didn't even know about it until Sara let it slip! I'm not going to put Leo in the position of being here with you when anything could happen!"

I was sobbing now. "I'm doing well, my psychiatrist says so," I de-fended weakly. "I'm driving, I'm working at my job…."

John was getting in his car. "I'm leaving before I say something I'll regret" he fumed, and slammed the door shut, jamming the car into reverse. As he backed down the driveway I turned for the shelter of the house, gasping, and made my way in. I didn't understand completely what had happened, but I was outraged and scared at the same time. I grabbed a beer from the refrigerator, cracked it open and headed straight to my room, where I drank it in long, shuddering gulps.

Leo appeared at the door. "What did Dad say? What's going on?" he asked uncomfortably.

"I'm very upset," I leveled with him. "Your dad wants you an extra night a week, and that's what it says in the separation agreement, so I have to agree. I'm upset because I'm losing another night a week with you."

Leo was quiet for a long time, then turned and went back to his television.

By the time I had finished the beer, I was calmer.

Several days later, I wrote my former husband a scathing email about our scene in the driveway. It sits in my "Drafts" folder to this day. What I did send to him was one short paragraph: "As for trying to make me feel guilty, you can stop. I wallowed in guilt for two months, and it wasn't productive. I'm not going to do it anymore."

No one could be more determined than I to get better.

***

On my first birthday since my hospitalization, I turned 45. "A watershed day," I wrote in my journal on March 25, 2008. The only professor I ever talked to about my condition sat on the sofa in my office that day as I mulled over its significance.

"I just improve in one area and slip in another," I sighed. "What if all my hair falls out? I mean it's really freaking me out! You should see the floor of my bathroom after I comb it—or the shower after I shampoo. It's really all coming out! Do you know what I'm gonna look like? All these scars and now bald?"

Gwen couldn't help laughing.

"Laura Anne, you have more important stuff to deal with than your hair! People lose their hair all the time, because of chemotherapy.

People lose their hair in India because they get these fungal diseases. This is not something you should worry about."

"I guess there are wigs…"

"You don't have to wear a wig; look at that student who has alopecia. She wears scarves and big earrings every day—she looks fantastic!"

"That's true," I admitted, mulling it over. "I guess it could grow back, too, if I get healthy again."

"Of course it could—it probably will!"

"You know," I realized, "I could live *another* 45 years. I *would* like to enjoy it."

"Well, yeah," Gwen said, stating the obvious. "Might as well!"

It's not courage if you're not afraid!

***

Easter Sunday, 2008. Leo was out of town with John's side of the family for Easter egg hunts with his little cousins, gobs of candy, church services and celebratory feasts. I decided I was ready to host a holiday of my own.

Everyone thought it was premature, but I assured them I could handle it. I farmed out four dishes to Sara and Kaye, leaving me with only the ham (easy), the dessert (make ahead) and the bread (buy from a bakery!) so there was little I had to do. Before he left with his dad, Leo had cut out crayon drawings of flowers and taped them up on our glass front door, replacing his snowflake cutouts. They were my decorations.

So what if I'm brain-damaged?

I invited not only Dad and Kaye, Sara, and Drew and Mason, who were in town, but also my friend Anita, who had been wonderfully supportive. In spite of the fact that Easter was early that year, we lucked into a pretty day, and the lawn in front of my house was green. The first pictures taken of me since the previous Thanksgiving were made that day, and when I look at them, I don't appear completely skeletal!

We sat at my outdoor table after the meal, and watched the boys pitch plastic baseballs to each other and bat them ridiculous distances off the property. After everyone else had left, I had to admit to my sister that I was totally beat.

"Of course you are!" she cried. "This was…monumental!"

I still used a film camera then, and when I went to pick up my developed photos from the drugstore a few days later, I was in for a surprise. After I gave my name, the clerk handed me two envelopes.

"Oh, I only had one," I told her.

"Nicholson? L.A.?"

"Yes."

"These are both for you."

I looked down at the handwriting on the second packet; it was mine. The date: Sept. 10, 2007.

I stepped back from the counter.

I've always been the sort of geek that picks her photos up the day they are ready—and has them in an album, or mailed to others, that night. These had been left by me for months, even before my suicide attempts. I had evidently forgotten about them. I opened the package slowly.

There I was, in all my pre-anxiety glory: tan, healthy, my arm around a family friend who had brought her son for a weekend visit over Labor Day. We were taking a hike with our boys and John's dog, who was wearing a yellow string bag Leo had fitted her with. I remembered. We had been partway to the trailhead, in the car, when I asked Leo what was in the bag, and he answered casually, "a toad." We had set it free on top of the mountain, after it rode up on Lacy's back.

And there was Molson, who couldn't go on the hike, in the last stages of his illness, every vertebra visible on his back. I had had him put to sleep that Tuesday, to *make it stop* for him.

I'm not one to get my "mind blown" easily, but this did it. It took me a few moments to collect myself before I drove home and called my sister.

From the other set of prints, a shot of the boys' batting practice from Easter became my computer wallpaper at work the following week, and it gave me hope every time I saw it. Especially during the spring snows, howling winds, and freezing temperatures that winter still had left for us.

Chapter 25
Tipping the Scales

Now that I was eating well and gaining strength, my thoughts began to turn to other things. I was behind on just about everything in terms of personal business. With Dad's help, I made an appointment with an accountant to get my taxes done. I went to the dentist (wearing a turtleneck) and afterwards, started bleaching my teeth again. I got Fotini, the student with the great scarves, to trim my hair in her apartment just a couple of miles from my house. I put everything on a wall calendar my father had bought for me, and kept a pocket notebook in my purse, at Dr. Marshall's suggestion, to write down anything I might forget.

I was wearing, day in and day out, the clothes Kaye had bought me while I was in the hospital: long-sleeved sweaters, corduroy pants and skirts in size zero, but I needed warm-weather clothes that wouldn't swallow me like everything currently in my closet. Shopping is exhausting to me at the best of times, so I broke it down into sessions I could handle.

Anita went with me when I decided to buy a pair of jeans. I was so thrilled when I found some I liked, because the size ones were too small! Triumphantly I bought the size twos. Then we looked for high-necked, short-sleeved tops.

"I like that one the salesgirl is wearing," I whispered to Anita.

"Excuse me, that is the cutest top, where did you get that?" my friend piped up to the cashier.

"Oh, thanks! I got it at Banana Republic right here in the mall, but it was a while ago."

After paying for my jeans, we headed straight over there, where we scoured the racks unsuccessfully.

I was getting tired and a little lightheaded by the time Anita popped up from behind a rack holding the very top we'd been hunting!

It was too small, and hugged where I would have had curves, had I had curves, but Anita beamed at me, and assured me it was "hot!" What could I do? I bought it.

On another excursion, I bought a pretty, sage-green bath set to replace the red rugs that had obviously been unusable after my "accident", as Leo's school counselor called it. This gave the pale gray bathroom an entirely new look and symbolized a fresh start to me. Next, I scored new tennis shoes, which are pretty much what I live in.

Realizing that high-necked, cool, sleeveless tops are hard to find, I turned to the Internet for those, using free time at work to hunt them down. When I found a cotton mock-turtle that I loved, I ordered it in four colors, and then painstakingly hand-sewed darts into each collar, since they gaped on my skinny neck and showed my scars anyway.

At home, I divided my clothes into "Now", "Someday", and "Never Again", according to their necklines. I didn't even want to see the spaghetti-strap summer tops and the sweetheart-neckline sweaters I had been able to wear before, so I hid them in a spare closet.

I told myself there was nothing wrong with my legs and my face, so I should concentrate on shorts, skirts, and makeup as the summer arrived.

Speaking of makeup, I tried it on my scars. It was a big improvement, but you still couldn't miss what had happened. Jewelry never seemed to hit just right to cover the place I had stabbed myself in the throat—NOT something you want to explain to people. I still remember the first day I wore a blouse, with only one button unbuttoned and a heavy layer of foundation on the scar. I looked at myself in the mirror, and brightened my lipstick. "I'll just have to smile a lot," I told myself. "Then people will have to look up!"

When I went back to my regular hairdresser, who knew what had happened thanks to Sara clearing the way for me, I complained bitterly about my hair loss. Every time I had a trim, my hair just got shorter, no matter how little I had taken off.

"But there's new hair coming in under here," Jennifer said. "It's about an inch and a half long, and really fine and curly." Woo-hoo!

It took months, in the end, for my hair to really grow back, and in the meantime I had what are known as "chemo curls"—the baby-fine tendrils that are your body's best efforts after trauma. But I was not going to be bald, and it turned out there was a simple explanation for what had happened. I had lost so much weight that my body had shut down all non-vital systems: my skin had dried and peeled, my nails looked dreadful, and any nutrients available were directed to more important functions than growing hair.

Had anyone explained this to me, I could've saved a lot of worry and a lot of time researching wigs and headscarves on the internet! But it wasn't important, next to lung function and gastrointestinal health, and I had never asked. When I finally did, Dr. Marshall put my mind to rest about it.

I love Leo so much, and I loved the life we had here. I am going to get it back. I will be here for him no matter what until natural causes take me away.

***

By early April, I was beginning to feel, occasionally, like I might be doing a little better at keeping up with things at work. One thing I couldn't seem to get a grasp on was how I had managed to keep being paid the whole time I was gone. There was no way I had had that much sick time.

I had forgotten about the university's Voluntary Shared Leave program. When someone needed more medical leave than they had sick time, Personnel invited other employees to donate their vacation, in increments of half-days, so that the sick person could keep getting paid. I had been given over 140 hours.

It was the first time I had ever understood why people say they feel humbled when they are recognized by others. I was utterly humbled by so many people giving their vacation time to me—I had never given anyone an hour! The whole system is anonymous, so I didn't know who to thank. But I knew professors don't have vacation, per se, so it had to all have been staff people, and I didn't even know that many other staff! I so wished I could thank my benefactors, but couldn't think of any way to learn their identities.

Eventually I found out that a friend of Kaye's whom I don't know well at all, had given me an entire week. When I called to thank her, I found myself stumbling over the words. "I"ll tell you what," I said at last. "When I'm better, when I'm through all of this, I'm going to give vacation every time anyone asks!"

I said the same to John the next time we spoke. "When all this is over, I'm going to be a better person, I really am."

The smart aleck in me reared her sharp tongue. "*You* could stand to be a better person, too!" I said, and giggled. "But that's a conversation I should have with Carrie!"

I was really tickled now. "I'm sorry," I said, "Couldn't resist."

"That's okay," said John affably. "I've got a thick skin."

"Yeah, that's kind of a shame, too!" I said. "A little pain might behoove you!"

Oh, I cracked myself up.

***

I hadn't talked with my landlady—had avoided it entirely. But the mice were back, and I didn't see how she could say no to me having a cat now. I needed one for practical reasons as well as for Pet Therapy. No cat could replace Molson, but a warm, furry body would be nice to have around on the nights I was alone. I mentioned a cat to Sherry's husband when he came around setting traps (and caught two mice the first night).

"Not my call, she'll have to okay it," he replied.

Is THAT all you got?

Finally I approached Sherry by email, using all my best PR skills. And she capitulated.

Which is how Bingo Bon Jovi became a part of our lives. Leo named him before we even looked at any cats, and as it turned out, the moniker suited him perfectly. Bingo was a large, neutered male who could pass for a Maine coon cat, and the lady at the pet adoption confided to me, "This is the one, right here" before she even got him out of his crate. He was about a year old, with gorgeous green eyes and a sumptuous coat. "He's a lover boy!" she told me, as I filled out the papers and Bingo viewed the proceedings from his cage noncommittally. Another woman was looking at him before I even wrote out the check. "Stay away from my cat!" I thought, but said nothing.

Leo and I were both delighted that Bingo did in fact love to be with people, ideally on them, whether they were seated or supine. Leo no longer needed Lacy sharing his sofa, as Bingo became the first cat I had ever seen who was content to sleep under a blanket, with only his head above it, just like a person. I still came home at lunch sometimes to rest, and once I fell asleep with Bingo's front paws on my shoulder, and woke with his chin there. Somehow, he sacrificed no dignity by being a cuddle kitty.

And the mice's glory days in my house were over! My dad took one look at my new pet and remarked, "I can hear the mice trembling in fear!"

Be cheerful and brave, love Leo, and lift others up.

***

Although I was sharpening up, I was still misplacing and forgetting things far more than I used to. I ordered a book about changing how your brain works and read that one of my favorite pastimes, ping-pong, is excellent brain exercise. So I started working on my dad to get a table for his garage.

Dad and I have a long history of great ping-pong matches, beginning at home when I was in high school and continuing during the time I accompanied him to Cambridge, England for a sabbatical, and the time in Athens when John and I had our own table. It wasn't hard to convince him that he needed to make this investment for the sake of his daughter's recovery.

At first only Dad and I played, but eventually my nephews began coming around, sometimes with girlfriends, on their way back to college or on their school breaks. Sara soon joined in, as well as the "little boys", 10-year-old Leo and 12-year-old Mason. Dad and Drew and I annoyed everyone with our cutthroat matches and shrieks of victory or defeat, but nonetheless the tournaments became regular Sunday afternoon events, culminating in large English teas prepared by Kaye. If this was really helping my brain recover, it was a win-win situation.

I was into making amends now, atoning for the hurt I had caused. Everyone in the family had gotten their chance to yell at me, and I had apologized profoundly to everyone except my ex-husband and my former in-laws. The ones who had discovered me, bashed a door in to reach me, comforted Leo as I was taken away, and mopped up pools of my blood. I was too shy to say anything to their faces, but I sat down in April of 2008 and penned a long letter to Rob and Agnes, saying how sorry I was that I had put them through that, and how well my recovery seemed to be going. The next time I spoke to Agnes she brought the letter up, thanked me, and said how nice it was. I felt forgiven, and I still have a good relationship with my mother-in-law.

I did not write John.

Chapter 26
What Are You, Crazy?

Sometimes, now, I even wanted to stay up past 8:30, when Leo turned in. Of course the only way I could do that was by reading in bed. Leo was only a few feet away in the living room, where the TV, stereo and fireplace were; I had to go through there to get to the kitchen. If I tried to talk on the phone he would wake and complain about the noise. The only solution was going to be a different house.

I had been renting now, counting the time with John at Forest Hills, for nearly four years. After a decade of home ownership, I had never expected to go back, unless very briefly, to renting a place. My lawyer had urged me to buy *something*, and start building up equity, as soon as I got divorced, and I knew there were huge tax advantages to home ownership, as well. I was on my own now for the future, for Leo's college and my own retirement—for, after all, who would date someone scarred like Frankenstein, and by her own hand?

And as much as ever, I longed for a dog, maybe two! Leo and I had actually picked one out at the Humane Society several weeks after Molson's death, but when we did the paperwork, our landlady's permission was required, and Sherry had said no.

These three motivations led me to begin trolling the internet for real estate listings. I mentioned this to Audrey.

"Don't you think that's a little much to take on right now?" she asked, in a rare display of doubt of my abilities.

"It's the only thing I can get excited about," I explained.

And it was. I had known for a long time how important the place I live is to me, and as much as I adored the little river house, it was not mine, and it was never going to work for Leo. I was still not 100%, either physically or emotionally, but I was strongly motivated.

Believe in myself. Believe in Leo. Believe in others. Just believe.

I began to do the math. My income was modest, and qualified me for a loan which, together with what I could put down, might score me a hovel beside a crack house. I didn't want to touch my retirement savings or my "car fund", which was there for the day my 16-year-old Honda Accord finally gave up the ghost.

I approached Henry, knowing there was money my mom had left me held in trust by him. He thought a downpayment on a house was a great use for it, God bless him forever. My father also chipped in with a stated amount of "early inheritance". It wasn't an impossible dream! If I could handle the upkeep, I could swing the finances. My gumption was increasing exponentially.

I had never owned a house without a husband, of course. John had been the go-to guy for lawn mowing, gutter-cleaning, and venturing into scary crawl spaces when the need arose. But I had become a lot handier since living without him—even killing my own cave crickets (I always told John that was the reason I married him.) Leo was old enough to be a lot of help now, too, and I had "big lug" nephews on call—for a buck, anyway!

I polled my coworkers for good real estate agents. Several people mentioned that I had told them John was in real estate now, would I use him?

I ended up with a seasoned veteran of not only hundreds of sales, but three divorces! And within days of beginning to work with me, Dana told me John had been hired as a new agent at her firm!

Blue River is a tough market to buy in. It's a resort area with a large university, and prices are high. Many neighborhoods once genteel have become pocked with student rentals featuring poor upkeep, loud music, and recycle bins overflowing with beer and wine bottles. Any neighborhood intown is subject to this sort of reverse gentrification, and outside the town limits, protective zoning is limited.

The hilly terrain, small population, and eclectic nature of its inhabitants (students, farmers, artists, intellectuals) have not lent themselves to the development of subdivisions, so many homes are simply beside a two-lane highway or off in a "holler" by themselves. I wouldn't have minded being isolated but I knew Leo wanted neighbor kids, which he hadn't had at all at our current place.

All my life I've been apprehensive about new neighbors, always dreading the garage band, the howling dogs, the loud domestic disputes. What transpired in Oregon did nothing to help me get over this. Frankly, I always thought the fewer neighbors, the better, which was why the private river house was such a haven for me.

But I didn't feel that way now. I wanted Leo to be happy, and felt I owed him that. I was also gradually becoming more confident, as I recognized that I was essentially coming back from the dead, with impressive results! I was beginning to recognize that the only thing I had to fear, was fear itself—and I wasn't afraid.

I printed out information about a dozen houses before I met with my agent, but her list was completely different from mine! When I asked her about the ones I had pulled, she always knew something: "That place is sold/under contract/nasty/impossible to get to/in a bad area," she would say. Yet she managed to find all kinds of interesting possibilities that I hadn't even seen. (This is why you get an agent, I thought.)

And so we went out. Leo always rode with us, as I wanted him to feel very much a part of this process. I realized his priorities wouldn't mesh with mine ("Mom! A treehouse!" "Yes, dear, and no heat except a woodstove!") but I still wanted him to weigh in.

At first it was discouraging. It occurred to me that all the doubters might be right—maybe I couldn't handle this. In fact, the house hunt reminded me of my favorite quote about job hunting: "The story of a job search is this: No no no no no no no no no no no no yes!" I began to wonder if I could ever afford a house I would actually want to live in. But my agent, Dana, didn't seem discouraged, so we soldiered on.

On one outing, the three of us took a break for lunch at Wendy's. I had learned to use expensive specialty makeup, cuff bracelets and flesh-colored adhesive pads to disguise my wrist scars, but Dana still might have noticed them. Whether she had or not, Leo blew the whistle on me that day when the subject of my recent hospitalization came up. "That was when you cut yourself," he said, rather pointedly.

It was the first and only time Leo exposed me like that, and I dropped my eyes to my food and murmured something like, "I went through a very bad time". Dana was kind and diplomatic, nodding

sympathetically and letting the subject drop. Of course, later, Leo and
I had a little talk!

As we fine-tuned our search, we began to hit upon houses that
were actual possibilities. After nearly losing heart, I was thrilled. I began chattering to Leo regularly at home about the advantages and
disadvantages of this house or that one, getting his feedback and trying to sort out what mattered most. And then one day we opened the
door of a cottage in a one-road neighborhood on a hill near my sister's
home, and my heart leapt.

I had already mentally approved the charming older neighborhood, when the front door swung open. The 1970's floorplan and
kitchen were nothing special, but there were glass doors leading to a
back patio, and through them was an inspiring view of a narrow, private garden backed by a stone retaining wall, filled with tulips and
daffodils in bloom.

The interior of the house was decorated in muted greens and
earth tones, and I was both elated by the blooms visible in back and
soothed by the modest, homey interior. I was so thrilled I kept waiting for something awful to appear as we walked through the house,
but all I saw were three decent-sized bedrooms and two baths, in the
same soothing colors, and a one-car attached garage, perfect for our
one car.

On the patio in the backyard, I had visions of cookouts with friends
and family, or hanging around with Leo and the dogs we would adopt,
sipping iced tea in a chaise lounge on a sunny afternoon, or puttering
around the garden in my robe and slippers with my coffee on a Sunday morning. The property was decent-sized, but on a steep slope,
meaning little had to be mowed. The only space for batting practice or
Frisbee was the quiet street, but that was doable, as long as the players
were ready to race down the hill after any errant hits or throws!

Oh it sang to me, all right. I immediately put in a call to my dad
and my uncle, who had been a realtor for a few years before retiring, to
come and see my find. I emailed the computer listing to my sister and
several friends. I started mentally preparing offers.

Dana kept me practical, talking about inspections and repair
cost-limits, but I was elated. When my dad came to see the place, he

walked through with little to say, his brow furrowed. "He wants to find stuff wrong with it, but he can't!" I chirped to the realtor. My father was concerned about maintenance (me being a girl, and all) and had been pushing me to buy a newly constructed house that he had found, that had warranties on everything but how many species of birds would sing on the windowsills. But he really couldn't find anything major to worry him, and after my uncle's okay, he agreed to front the early inheritance he had promised me if I wanted to make an offer.

After the tedium of putting together a contract with Dana, we sent it off and I held my breath. Of course the sellers countered, but I came back with an offer they agreed to. My house was Under Contract! *My* house!

That night, April 20, 2008, I made the entry in my journal I'd been waiting to make for months:

"I'm BACK, baby!"

***

My Facebook status bar was very active during this time. "L.A. is excited!" "L.A. is holding her breath…" "L.A. is not putting all her eggs in one basket!"

But I was, of course. All the other houses I had seen dropped right off my radar as soon as I had a contract on this one. And I really wasn't worried—John and I had bought and sold three houses, and we'd never had a contract fall through. No one foresaw any difficulties, and once I had qualified for my loan, I considered the deal done.

But the day I met the inspector at the house, everything changed. The gentleman Dana had recommended was a jolly sort, but he did not look happy when I pulled up in the driveway. He had a little pile of sawdust by his car, and he started by telling me he was seeing those all through the crawlspace—signs of wood-boring insects.

Then he began talking about the moisture in the basement. How long it had been collecting. The damage it had done. He began speaking of pump systems and wood replacement. In the front of the house, he pointed at the narrow space between the bottom of the wood siding that covered the exterior and the ground—saying really, the whole house should be lifted up another six inches. By the time he rapped his knuckles on the paneling inside the garage to show me that it simply gave way to his hand, I was both utterly defeated and thankful that I had learned all of this in time.

The sellers let me out of the contract without argument, apparently embarrassed by the condition of their house.

And Leo and I were back at everyone's least favorite Square.

***

The lease on our rental house expired July 15. I couldn't remember how much notice I was required to give the landlady, but it was early May now and I was starting over in my search for a new home. I felt a bit under the gun.

I wrote Sherry an email telling her of the failed contract, and that I was still looking. After the personal catastrophe I had lived through in her house, I hoped for and expected a little flexibility. She was after all, technically, a friend of the family.

Sherry's email back read:

I am so sorry about your house contract falling through. You and Leo need to find a place where you can really put down roots. Meanwhile, please sign the enclosed renewal lease at $25 more per month, or give me notice by May 10.

Angrily, I pulled my copy of the lease out of my file, scanning through it to confirm this ridiculous notice deadline—more than two months! And I was vindicated: I was only required to give 45 days' notice to move out.

Whew! I wrote Sherry back a very sweet message, saying that she was actually mistaken, and that I would certainly let her know our decision by May 30. Then I wrote in my journal that no matter when *I* knew what was happening, I'd be damned if I'd let her know a thing one day before that.

My Facebook status changed to "L.A. is glad she still has her longbow finger!"

And Dana and Leo and I went back out.

Chapter 27
L.A. Nicholson Has Prevailed

Mother's Day, 2008. Every year since his adoption, I have had a picture taken of Leo and me on Mother's Day. This one would be the exception, because of my vanity. What was left of my hair was dry and frizzy. I was still very thin. But Leo's fourth grade class was having a "Mother's Day Tea", and I would not have missed it for the world.

I dressed in one of my high-necked sleeveless tops and white Capri pants, and tied a blue bandana over my head. I put on makeup and dangling earrings, hoping he wouldn't be ashamed of me beside all the pretty, young mommies. In spite of the warm day, I pulled a lightweight white blouse I had bought to cover my arms over the whole sad ensemble, and drove to the school.

Before the tea, there was a short play, a scene from <u>Charlotte's Web</u>. Leo had a plum part—Farmer Zuckerman, and I had supplied him with a frayed straw hat and a red kerchief as well as red suspenders for his jeans. He looked perfect.

When I entered the small theater, I saw John and Carrie immediately. I chose a seat in the same row, further down, and got their attention to wave and smile. Then, since I felt I had to prove I was okay, I proceeded to "work the crowd", talking animatedly and laughing with every parent I knew. They were all just as nice as pie. No one referred to my long absence or compromised appearance. I'd learned this was procedure, and it made it easier for me, on the surface at least, even if it wasn't great for real human connection and support.

Although Leo was adorable in the play, he was traumatized afterwards by some forgotten lines and needed a hug from his mom. Several, as it turned out. John and Carrie hung back.

"Well, we're off to tea—sorry, it's just for moms!" I said somewhat cattily, and headed down the hall with my arm around my son.

Although I squirmed in my child-size seat beside all those healthy mommies, I will never forget that tea. Mrs. Klutz had gone all out, and so had the children. Each of us was served on a personalized placemat featuring poems about us by our kids. As we enjoyed our cookies and juice, each mom was brought to the "rocking chair of honor" in front of the room and introduced by her son or daughter. The child then told the class three things about his mother, and read his poem aloud.

Leo had no stage fright here. I had no idea what three things he would choose to announce, and waited to hear them somewhat nervously. They turned out to be total surprises and not 100 percent accurate, but I'll never forget them.

"This is my mom, Laura Anne Nicholson," Leo said. "She loves to garden, she has lived in England, Maryland, and Canada (*two out of three—not bad*), and she has a button collection!"

***

As much as that first house sang to me initially, the next one Dana showed me did not. All I could think was "Brady Bunch house" when we pulled into the drive. In fact I almost told her I didn't need to go in it, but then decided that since we were there, I'd be polite. It was certainly a terrific location, a mile out of town but still in Leo's school district, just uphill from a scenic horse farm, in an established neighborhood of much more expensive houses on very large lots.

This one, though, was modular. It had pinky-red shutters. A stoop, rather than a front porch. A one-third acre lot. The front yard had a silly little fake wishing well in a tiered flower bed, and no trees. Perfect for batting practice, but boring as hell.

The front door, when it opened, nearly hit the wall of the stairwell that divided the home's two levels (oh yeah, it was a modular *split-level* Brady Bunch house!) We went up, to the main part of the house. My eyes widened with each step.

The living room had huge windows, great light (seeing as how there were no TREES!) and beautiful, honey-colored hickory floors. It led into an enormous kitchen with more large windows, a tiled floor, and cherry cabinets. All I could think was, why did someone spend this much money on the interior of a modular house? We continued down the hall to three bedrooms: large, medium and small, all with the gorgeous floors; and two full baths. But there was more.

Downstairs was paneled and carpeted, and looked like the basements of all my high school friends, growing up. The kind of place where you play darts or have slumber parties. It was cool down there (the house, like most in Blue River, had no A/C), and there was a closet with washer-dryer hookups. Right in the middle was the best feature of all—a woodstove! Insurance against running out of fuel oil, or ice-storm power outages! Not to mention how I love a wood fire!

There was also a one-car garage, and a rope swing, and a place for our basketball goal. A rather humble deck in the back looked over a modest circle of a lawn that sloped down to woods that stretched pretty much as far as the eye could see. In fact, the property was surrounded by woods, although on one side they gave way quickly to the only close neighbor.

I looked around in wonder at the surrounding houses: two across the street and far up a hill, and the one next door, all worth probably twice the value of this house. My feelings had done a 180.

***

I had a lot on my mind now. Hopes and fears about the new house, concern about Leo, financial issues, work, my health. Audrey suggested scheduled "worry time", and one evening I made a set of notes under that heading. The first worry category was "House Overload!", with subheadings such as "Inspection", "Mortgage", and "Moving". Then there were work items ("Budget!"—my nemesis, with my brain still not up to speed), "Scars", "Leo", "Exercise", and "Muddleheaded". Below each item I had made notes with ideas and plans to handle it.

The last item of my Worry List was "Jury Duty". I had been called for the second week of June, and I was pretty nervous about it. I had never served on a jury, though I'd been called many times in Atlanta. The crime scene wasn't nearly as frightening here in Blue River, and under normal circumstances I might have been rather intrigued by the idea, and the change from my routine. But now I had all kinds of things to think about—how would I cover my scars in summer, what if they saw them and asked me about it, what if they found out I'd been Locked Up in the Psyche Ward? I'd be thrown off any jury in humiliation in front of my fellow townspeople! (probably *not* with torches and pitchforks, but that would be how it would feel!)

On the other hand, being summoned indicated that I was not on some sort of civic duty blacklist, that I had never been charged with a crime even though I'd technically committed one, and that my temporary loss of freedom was not public knowledge. I rather enjoyed telling John I had jury duty, since I was sure that he saw me as a card-carrying member of the lunatic fringe now. But the county government saw me as a law-abiding citizen who could potentially be trusted to decide a fellow citizen's fate!

Meanwhile, classes at the university had ended, and my Southwest student friend Taylor needed a place to live that summer, the three days a week she wasn't out of town in our department's field school. We hadn't had a housemate since Teresa, and I delightedly offered her our spare room, which she took, by email! (Or, as I told Sara, "Leo unseen!") I was excited about having the company, and Leo always loved guests in the "Laura Anne Inn". Taylor was cheerful, kind, and athletic, and she had a younger brother around Leo's age. I pictured wiffle ball games and tag football on the lawn—the sorts of things that I always had on my journal Do-To-Feel-Better lists.

I told Taylor that we might well be in a different house by the time she joined us, but I was sure we would have a place for her. As it turned out, the offer I eventually made on the Brady Bunch house was accepted and the contract negotiations completed by mid-May. I held my breath when I met the same inspector at this house, and he tortured me with minor repair issues for a while, but in fact this inspection was *not* a disaster, and the house was going to be mine. I had been under the gun to find a house, and somehow avoided getting shot!

I began beaming a lot, including at work. One of my colleagues, a quiet intellectual, remarked one day that, "Just in the last few weeks, you seem so much better. So much more like yourself." I had evidently made the right decision about buying a house. Having plans to move to a better place, and this time to own it, was having that magical effect on me again.

I was over 100 pounds now. I was eating a *lot*. Dr. Marshall had urged me to eat pasta, oils and fats, the "shitty white bread", even, and I was taking full advantage. Along with milkshakes I was enjoying pizza, chocolate and Cheetos, and establishing some very bad habits! But it certainly was fun. It never ceased to thrill me, being able to eat without fear.

Taylor moved in with us for the last month before our move. Leo made a door sign for her room, and we did everything we could to make her welcome and comfortable. She could not have been a sunnier presence, and we only wished she was around more! Some evenings she played the guitar on the front porch, and sometimes she tossed various balls with Leo or joined him on this summer's toad hunts. How good it was to see it all coming back! Fireflies, flowers, the does with their fawns in the meadow of the river bottom, the great blue herons that almost couldn't be bothered to move when you approached them! I could hardly believe that I was there and enjoying another summer. If someone had told me it would happen while I was in the hospital, I would have shaken my head sadly, utterly certain of their mistake.

Although Leo was still sleeping on the sofa, he seemed, otherwise, fine. I had bought him two gerbils to replace the one that had died while I was ill, and those poor rodents had entirely too much excitement. He took them up in the treehouse and let them loose, along with the toads, when he had friends over. He put them in an old tire and slowly rolled it, for a giant exercise wheel. He let them meet the neighborhood dogs, nose to tiny nose, while he held them tightly for their own protection.

One day we spotted a fat groundhog waddling across the middle of our front yard. Soon after, a fox began making regular appearances. The rabbit population was having its spring explosion, and Bingo was on safari day and night. Whenever he brought us a baby rabbit, still alive, I would free the poor creature and keep the cat in the house for awhile. But he obviously knew where the dens were, and my rescues were probably futile. The helpless bunnies reminded me of me just a few months before—badly hurt, and without defense. Now I was the healthy one, doing what I could to save them. I was like the social workers and therapists that had visited us in the psyche ward: pulled together, cheery, competent. I had looked at them at the time with such a disconnect, such despair. I had thought to myself, "I was like you once. You would never believe it, but I was just like you." I smiled at the thought of them seeing me now.

The rabbit slayage really bothered Taylor, who was so kind-hearted she took the creature-saving to a whole new level. At work one afternoon, I got a call from her, at the house.

"Bingo was chasing a rabbit, an adolescent rabbit, and I caught it," she said.

"What do you mean, you caught it?"

"It was running away from him and I got in front of it and caught it in my hands! It's hurt, but I've given it food and water, and put some Neosporin on its wounds. I'm just keeping Bingo outside."

"Are you telling me there's a teenage rabbit in my house?" I asked, in mock alarm.

"Well, it's in a box!"

"Oh honey," I laughed. "That thing is not gonna make it in a box. It'll be too scared to eat or drink. But I guess putting it back outside would be pretty much fatal."

"Well, yeah! I called the Wildlife Rescue people and they wouldn't take it, because it's a rabbit!" she said indignantly. "What's it gotta be, a bald eagle?!"

In spite of the fact that this was a life-and-death drama, from one point of view, I was quite tickled by the whole episode. I wondered how many rabbits had had Neosporin put on their wounds! Fortunately the dilemma of what to do with the patient was solved when Taylor left the next day to go home for the weekend. She took Bunny with her and put it out in the woods near her hometown.

The fishermen were back at the river now, and Leo really wanted to join them. I decided he was old enough, at ten and a half, to go down there without Molson, as long as he stayed out of the water and didn't give anyone more information than his first name and that he lived, "around here". On his own, he quickly cadged spare fishing equipment and soon had a jerry-rigged pole with a line, hook, and floater. He never did catch a fish (mushrooms and other random food scraps probably not being their favorite bait), but he once scored a reject from another sportsman, and came home with it proudly.

The last frost date passed, and I put my plants outside. My tiny lemon tree had its first real leaves now, and I gave it the place of honor on our porch rail. It, like me, was waking up from a long sleep.

The week of my jury duty came and went without a hitch. I wore my light, long sleeves and high necks, and no one suspected a thing. I was eventually chosen as the alternate on a jury for a methamphetamine case, even though I had worked with the defense attorney's wife at the university, and the prosecutor was my pediatrician's husband. It seemed about half the chosen jury had closed on a house with the defense attorney at some time! The testimony was depressing and the defendant had little hope of acquittal, when I was excused from the case. All the jurors had been present every day, so I was not needed in the deliberations. I was glad to leave, and also glad that I didn't live in a trailer with a mean dog, and cook meth for a living.

In fact, I was about to become a homeowner! The closing was set for June 26th, and I had scheduled movers. The morning of the closing I had Leo take a picture of me holding up the check and lit up like a jack o'lantern! Although you can see, if you look closely, the makeup I used to cover my scars, and my poor hair is very short, I am clearly both thrilled and proud.

After we signed the papers, I drove straight to *my* house. I had brought a folding chair with me which I set up in the sun on my deck. I called several friends on my new cell phone with the jubilant news, identified the trees surrounding my backyard, and met a neighborhood dog who came visiting. I imagined my furniture on the patio, and Leo and me eating dinner there, our pets-to-be milling around our feet. I closed my eyes and turned my face up to the sun, taking it all in.

And the next day I changed my Facebook status, ostensibly to reflect the successful purchase of a house. But it really referred to my entire physical and emotional recovery, my repaired relationships, my redeemed sense of self. L.A. Nicholson had prevailed.

Epilogue

While I was fortunate enough to be on the island of Oahu in December 2009, visiting Liz (who was off on another adventure), I went to the beach alone one day. There were not many people around and the weather was perfect. I was gazing at the water from the shade of my own personal palm tree, when I suddenly thought of The Center. I thought of the people sitting in that dayroom, in front of that inane television, right at that moment. It was startling; two of my worlds collided. My heart ached for those people, and I wished there was some way to reach them with my story of hope. Hence, this book.

It was my father who planted the seed for this book in my mind while I was hospitalized. At first it was the idea of somehow absolving myself of what I considered to be my terrible crime. It was an apology, community service, penance.

But as my recovery progressed, I felt less and less connected to the woman who had raised her hand against herself. When I pictured her lying on that bathroom floor, I felt sorry for her. I was learning to separate my character from my illness.

Through reading, talking with my counselor and psychiatrist, and meeting others dealing with mental illness, I have grown to understand what happened to me much better than I did at the time. True understanding goes beyond a doctor's visit and a diagnosis. It goes beyond medication, counseling and even recovery.

Consider the human anatomy. Kidney disease can lead to renal failure. Acid reflux leads to heartburn. Disorders of the brain, whether they are caused by chemical imbalances or physical trauma, can lead to mental illnesses. Just as acid blockers reduce heartburn, and the esophagus can begin to heal; the right medicine at the right dose can correct a serotonin or dopamine imbalance brought on by stress, allowing a person to begin recovering from a state of depression or anxiety. The difference that has drawn such a huge dividing line between mental and "physical" illness in our society, is that the brain controls thoughts, speech and action. When *it* is the organ altered, the patient's personality can change. This is seen more clearly in some patients with brain tumors, bleeding on the brain, or traumatic brain injury.

In short, there is *not* "mental illness" and "physical illness", but rather a continuum that is our total health, and one cannot and should not be separated from the other. Accident victims who are paralyzed often become depressed; and depressed people often lose or gain weight, or become ill. *The body functions as a whole.* As a society, we will not ever "forgive" the mental patient until we accept and embrace this fact.

Even as scientists make great strides in understanding mental illness, society continues to lag behind, clinging to notions of morality, weakness and blame. I was fascinated to read recently, for the first time, the 1962 book One Flew over the Cuckoo's Nest, and then to watch the film. Mental health care has certainly improved since those days, which were themselves a great improvement over the previous decade. But the thing that was most striking to me was not the differences between today's psychiatric wards and those of the sixties, but the eerie similarities.

I look forward to the day when the brain, in all its glorious complexity, is mapped and understood to the point that physicians can begin to prescribe medications for brain disorders with a higher degree of confidence and a higher rate of success. I may not live to see this day, but I feel sure it will come. Neurological research and discoveries will bring a new day to the sad places that are today's psychiatric wards. So many sufferers and their families will be freed from guilt and despair.

I feel a certain degree of confidence when I say that not many people have been at a lower place than I have. Wherever you are, and however you feel, you are not at this moment, and most likely never have been, lying on a bathroom floor with self-inflicted slash and stab wounds, fighting off the medics trying to save your life by saying, "I want to die! I want to die!" I was.

It's been three years now since that day. My son and I live in the "Brady Bunch house" with our two dogs, two cats, and two gerbils. I am now the mom of a teenager! whom my ex and I share amicably. I still work in the university anthropology department, and I have copy-edited my first book for a professor. I dig in my garden, walk my dogs, hike in these mountains. I travel, visit friends, and entertain. My hair has grown back. I have grown back into, and then out of, my old clothes!

A year after I started counseling, Audrey told me that The Clinic really couldn't justify my slot in its Team program any more, considering how well I was doing. I had known this day was coming. Our "sessions" had become walking around my garden sipping tea, or talking about the latest movies—although Audrey always dutifully asked about any symptoms I might be experiencing.

I was both elated and sad. If you're going to get kicked out of something, a counseling program for the most severely compromised patients is a good thing to get kicked out of! But I would miss Audrey, and our talks. A tiny part of me was a little scared, too, but Audrey had the answer for that.

We made up a diagram, that started with how great I felt now and branched off into the events or circumstances I could foresee that could upset me (Leo getting into trouble as a teenager, serious illness, financial setbacks etc.) With each of those circumstances I made myself two possible paths: a positive one and a negative. The positives were easy: call Audrey, go to my doctor, call a family member, walk a dog. And because I am a smart aleck, the negatives were things like "Curl up into a ball and drink a lot" leading to "end up in The Center again". I did it initially to humor Audrey, but when I was done with my "flow chart", as I called it, I was actually rather pleased. The simple, straightforward choices appealed to my analytical personality. If A, then B. If you choose C, you may end up at F!

I put the diagram in my bedside table, and it is still there. I hugged Audrey good-bye, and on my last visit to Dr. Marshal, shook his hand. I felt certain he thought I would be back, but I haven't seen him since, except around town!

Now I stay on my anti-depressant, take care of myself and live an active and wonderfully complex life, and if I need that little anxiety pill every month or so, I don't hesitate to take it. Dr. Timothy handles my prescriptions, and after seeing me through such horror, I think he's pretty pleased with the result.

I have actually gotten the diagram out twice, pretending I was just double-checking a recipe for a direction I was pretty sure I knew. It's such a sensible, appealing coping mechanism. I felt better after looking at it both times.

In May of 2010, I was asked to train as an "In Our Own Voice" presenter for the National Alliance on Mental Illness. In "IOOV", two people share their stories of mental illness and recovery in an effort to reduce stigma. I have found it wonderfully rewarding, and never more so than when I presented for the local medics that October. I solicited that presentation, because I wanted to explain to those who respond to suicide calls how it is that people get to that point. I assumed that the turnover rate in such a stressful job would be too high for the men who responded to my call to still be there, three years later.

But when I walked into the station, a young man introduced himself and said quietly, "I was your medic". At a loss for words, I simply threw my arms around him and was finally able to whisper, "Thank you." It was the most meaning I have ever put into those common words.

That gentleman, Corey, introduced me to the other medics who were involved that day: the first group in a chain of medical heroes who saved my life. We have become friends who support each other in our respective efforts: mine of advocacy, theirs of saving lives. I can't imagine a nobler calling than these young men have.

I know I am not immune to future problems; this propensity to develop anxiety disorder under severe stress is in my genes. I can get a little blasé about it because I have never become ill when taking my medication, and I never plan to go off it again. But medicines can become less effective over time, or problematic side effects can develop with age; some drugs even go off the market. So I will always have a risk of another illness. What I won't have is another suicide attempt. That lesson, I have learned.

What will I do if anxiety strikes again? First, I'll pull out my flow chart, which is the voice of the healthy me. I'll read it, make the right choice, and follow my own advice. I'll get outside, exercise, and spend time with people, animals and plants that I love. I won't isolate myself. I won't hide my symptoms and my thoughts about them from my family. I'll get enough sleep, and take as-needed medicine. If the symptoms aren't resolved quickly, I'll call my doctor and counselor, and move right into treatment. I will research other medications and share what I find and how I think it might apply to me with my health care providers. If I have a crisis, I will drive straight to the hospital and check myself in—without hesitation or shame.

I was so determined, during my recovery, to get my life back. What I got back was better. Having almost lost everything, I now appreciate everything I have. An unexpected aspect of what I consider My Life, Part Two, is that I have become fascinated with world events, news, and even politics, something I couldn't abide in my previous life. I think my overall awareness is heightened; I'm interested in almost everything!

I notice references to suicide everywhere. In books or movies, in the newspaper, on the covers of the tabloids at the grocery store checkout line. Once you start talking about it, almost everyone knows someone who has tried, or who "succeeded", and many people have had one or more such events within their families. For a while there it made me feel better when Leo heard about a suicide or an attempt—in history, of course—because I hoped it made him realize that he was not alone in having had this phenomenon touch his life.

It is still a taboo subject and even I, loudmouth advocate that I am, don't mention it lightly to anyone. To tell someone my story, I have to have the time to do it justice and a reason to share it with them. So I occasionally give honest but intentionally limited answers to probing questions, such as "Why were you in the hospital?" "I had pneumonia," I will say, or even, "I was under a large amount of stress and ended up getting very sick".

But on a broader scale, suicide *has* to come out of the closet. It has to stop being a subject of shame. When it reaches the light of day as the manifestation of legitimate illnesses that it usually is; *then* we can educate ourselves; we can deal with it directly, and we can admit that it can happen to anyone. Then and only then will we begin to reduce suicide rates.

I know there are people out there who feel like I did in the fall of 2007. My message to them is this: there is help for everything. It may be hard to find. You may have to beat the bushes to get it. You may suffer through bad counselors, bad diagnoses, and bad medicine. But you have to persist, and you must be your own advocate. Help is there.

If you begin to see death as the only answer, don't hide it and plot your suicide like I did. Tell someone. Call a helpline. Walk into an emergency room. Say, I am desperate, I am on the verge. I need help.

No matter how bad you are feeling, you *can* feel better. Believe that and don't let it go.

***

Almost a year after my attempts, Sara and Leo and I were having dinner in a restaurant when Leo excused himself and my sister said abruptly to me, "I owe you an apology".

My mind ran over what the perceived offense might have been, but came up blank.

A local teenager had recently committed suicide, and his obituary, with his high school senior portrait, had been in our paper. Sara knew the family.

"When I saw that," she began, "my heart just broke, for his family—but also for him. Because he was so unhappy that this seemed to him like the best thing to do—like the only thing he could do. And I realized how insidious depression and anxiety are, what terrible illnesses. And I realized that in your case, I never looked at it that way. I just thought, how could you do this to us?"

I blinked. "Oh, well…that's okay!" I smiled. This revelation had been totally unexpected—I was speechless (something my sister would be the first to tell you, rarely happens!)

But it was a moment of understanding for her, apparently triggered by something I had said once, when thinking out loud about those days: "It didn't *feel* like a choice."

What I wish for others who love someone who has attempted or committed suicide is that they reach this same place, where they no longer blame the victim or themselves for the results of medical illness. So much pain could be alleviated. But as long as the subject of suicide stays underground, suicide survivors, and suicide attempt survivors, may never even have these conversations.

The life I have now is all-engaging, but I still stop to reflect, as I did that day on the deck of my new house, on where I was, where I am now, and the long journey it took to bridge that distance. Then my thoughts turn to The Center, and the people there now.

And I've come to the realization that at any given moment, there are people sitting under personal palm trees on the beach in Hawaii, and people languishing in psychiatric wards, without hope. I have been both.

Acknowledgments

With love and thanks to my family; Corey, Brian, and Paul; Liz, Holly, Julie, Dr. "Timothy", Ginger, Greg, Errol, Derek, Dr. Edward Hallowell, Jennifer Rothman, NAMI, and all the folks at the best little ER in the world.

About the Author

L.A. Nicholson was born in Georgia and raised in North Carolina, where she graduated from UNC-Chapel Hill with a degree in biology. She has written numerous articles for gardening and general interest magazines as well as horticultural journals. Her professional experience ranges from plant tissue culture to public relations.

After recovering from severe Generalized Anxiety Disorder, Nicholson wrote her story to reach out to other sufferers. She is a certified presenter for the "In Our Own Voice" program of the National Alliance on Mental Illness. Nicholson lives in North Carolina with her son and many pets. This is her first book.

Made in the USA
Charleston, SC
15 January 2012